Microsoft®
Office 2016
At Work

FOR

DUMMIES®

A Wiley Brand

Microsoft® Office 2016 At Work

FOR DUMMIES®

A Wiley Brand

by Faithe Wempen

Microsoft® Office 2016 At Work For Dummies®

Published by: **John Wiley & Sons, Inc.**, 111 River Street, Hoboken, NJ 07030-5774,
www.wiley.com

For general information on our other products and services, please contact our Customer Care Department within the U.S. at 877-762-2974, outside the U.S. at 317-572-3993, or fax 317-572-4002. For technical support, please visit www.wiley.com/techsupport.

Wiley publishes in a variety of print and electronic formats and by print-on-demand. Some material included with standard print versions of this book may not be included in e-books or in print-on-demand. If this book refers to media such as a CD or DVD that is not included in the version you purchased, you may download this material at http://booksupport.wiley.com. For more information about Wiley products, visit www.wiley.com.

Library of Congress Control Number: 2015952187

ISBN 978-1-119-14460-1 (pbk); ISBN 978-1-119-14465-6 (epdf); 978-1-119-14464-9 (epub)

Manufactured in the United States of America

10 9 8 7 6 5 4 3 2 1

CONTENTS AT A GLANCE

TABLE OF CONTENTS

INTRODUCTION

Microsoft Office 2016 is by far the most popular suite of productivity applications in the world, and with good reason. Its applications are powerful enough for business and professional use, and yet easy enough that a beginner can catch on to the basics with just a few simple lessons.

If you're new to Office 2016, this book can help you separate the essential features you need from the obscure and more sophisticated ones that you don't. For the four major Office applications I cover in this book — Word, Excel, Outlook, and PowerPoint — I walk you through the most important and common features, showing you how to put them to work to make it easier to do your job.

I designed this book for time-pressed Office users who simply want to figure out the task at hand without spending a lot of time looking for answers. This full-color book presents the most common Office tasks in illustrated, step-by-step instructions and organizes them so that they're easy to find, read, and apply. It covers classic Office tasks such as typing and formatting text, calculating with spreadsheets, organizing email and to-do lists, and creating PowerPoint presentations.

About This Book

This book is organized into chapters, each split into a series of common tasks. It begins by familiarizing you with Office 2016 and showing you how to perform basic tasks such as starting and exiting each application, entering text, moving around, and saving your work. Then it covers each of the four main applications:

Word (Chapters 2–6): A word processing application, suitable for creating reports, newsletters, manuscripts, memos, and mail merges.

Excel (Chapters 7–11): A spreadsheet application, great for storing data lists, calculating columns of numbers, and creating graphical charts that summarize numeric data.

Outlook (Chapters 12–13): An email and personal information management application you can use to send and receive mail, manage an address book, and track your daily to-do list.

PowerPoint (Chapters 14–17): A presentation graphics application for building and delivering attractive presentations that include graphics, animations, and even sound and video.

You can read the chapters in any order, at any time. Although each task is explained step by step, if you have trouble with a particular task, I recommend reading the entire chapter for that task — it's just possible that you'll find a different, better approach to accomplishing the task.

Foolish Assumptions

This book assumes that you can start your computer and use the keyboard and mouse (or whatever device moves the pointer onscreen).

Office 2016 runs on Windows 10 (the newest version of Windows), Windows 8, and Windows 7 computer operating systems, so I assume you're using one of these. The examples in this book show Office 2016 running in Windows 10, but Office works mostly the same on all operating systems. If you are using Office applications on some other platform, like Linux, Mac, or a tablet or smart phone, things may not look or work exactly the same as described in this book.

Icons Used in This Book

The following icons highlight important or useful information in this book.

Tips can save you time or make it easier to do something.

This icon emphasizes useful information to keep in mind when using Office.

Watch out! This icon alerts you about something that can hurt or wipe out important data. Read this information before making a mistake that you may not be able to recover from.

Beyond the Book

www.dummies.com has a heaping handful of additional Office information:

- You can find a cheat sheet with shortcuts for working in Office 2016 at www.dummies.com/cheatsheet/office2016atwork.

- Visit www.dummies.com/go/dummiesvideo to access the *Office 2016 For Dummies* online video course, featuring 150 how-to videos on Office 2016.

To gain access to the online video, all you have to do is register. Just follow these simple steps:

1 **Find your PIN code.**

- **Print book:** If you purchased a hard copy of this book, turn to the inside back cover of this book to find your PIN.

- **E-book:** If you purchased this book as an e-book, you can get your PIN by registering your e-book. Go to www.dummies.com/go/dummiesvideo and follow the instructions. You'll be asked to fill in some registration information and answer a security question to verify your purchase. Once you handle those steps, you'll receive an e-mail with your PIN.

2 Go to www.dummies.com/go/dummiesvideo.

3 **Follow the onscreen instructions to create an account, enter your PIN, and establish your own login information.**

Now you're ready to start watching your videos! Your PIN gives you access to watch as often as you want for 12 months after you register. Once you create your registration, simply return to the video site and log on with the username and password you created. No need to enter your PIN a second time.

If you have trouble with your PIN or can't find it, contact Wiley Product Technical Support at 877-762-2974 or go to http://support.wiley.com.

Where to Go from Here

This is your book; use it how you want. You can start at the beginning and read it straight through, or you can hop to whatever chapter or topic you want. For those of you who are pretty new to computers, you might want to start at the beginning. If you're new to Office, the beginning part will give you a good foundation on what features work similarly in all the programs.

If you're new to Office 2016, I recommend that you start by reading Chapter 1, which introduces Office 2016 concepts you may not be familiar with, and explains what all (or most) of the Office apps have in common.

CHAPTER ONE
Getting to Know Office

Microsoft Office is a suite of applications. A *suite* is a group of applications designed to work together and that have similar user interfaces in order to cut down on the learning curve for each one. Office 2016 includes a word processor (Word), a spreadsheet program (Excel), a presentation graphics program (PowerPoint), and an e-mail program (Outlook). Depending on the version of Office, it may also include other programs. Sweet, eh? Er . . . *suite*.

Because all the Office apps have similar interfaces, many of the skills you pick up while working with one program also translate to the others. In this lesson, I introduce you to the Office interface and show you some things the programs have in common. For the examples in this lesson, I mostly use Word and Excel, because they are the most popular of the applications. Keep in mind, though, that the skills you learn here apply to the other applications, too.

Throughout the book, the examples all show Windows 10 as the operating system. Where Windows 7 or 8 are substantially different, I let you know what to expect.

In This Chapter

- ➡ Starting and exiting an Office application
- ➡ Using the Ribbon
- ➡ Using the File menu
- ➡ Creating a new document
- ➡ Changing the view
- ➡ Saving your work
- ➡ Closing a file
- ➡ Opening a saved file

Start and exit an Office application

There are several ways to start Office applications. For example, you can select it from the Start menu's All Apps list. (Hint: It's in a folder called Microsoft Office 2016, so look in the "M" section.) You can also use the Search feature: with the Start menu open, begin typing the application's name and then click its name when it appears. Depending on how your PC is set up, you might also have shortcuts to one or more of the Office apps on your desktop or taskbar, or pinned to the top level of the Start menu.

You can also double-click a data file that's associated with one of the Office applications to start that application.

The following steps explain how to start an Office application in Windows 10; if you are using earlier versions of Windows, check out the Tips throughout this book that point out differences:

1 On the taskbar, click the Start button.

   If the application you want to run appears at the top of the Start menu, click it and you're done with these steps.

Figure 1-1: Click Start and then click All Apps.

2 Click All Apps.

If you have Windows 8.1, the All Apps button is a down-pointing arrow at the bottom of the Start screen. If you have Windows 7, click All Programs instead of All Apps.

3 Scroll down to the section for the first letter of the application name. For example, to run Word, scroll down to the W section.

In step 3, if you have Windows 8.1, the applications won't be in the lettered sections because the alphabetical list is only for modern apps, not desktop apps; scroll to the right to find the Microsoft Office 2016 section. If you have Windows 7, all the folders and shortcuts are arranged in a single alphabetical list, so it should be fairly easy to find Microsoft Office 2016.

4 Click the desired application.

Figure 1-2: Scroll to the W section and click the desired application.

5. Press the Esc key to bypass the Start screen that appears.

In Word, Excel, and PowerPoint, a Start screen appears when you run the application from which you can select a template for a new document or open an existing document.

6 Click the Close (X) button in the application window's upper-right corner to close the application.

If you have any unsaved changes, you are prompted to save them here. See "Save your work" later in this chapter for more information about saving.

Figure 1-3: The Close button shuts down an application.

Now let's try opening and closing again, this time using a different method for both.

7 Click in the Search box on the taskbar.

Figure 1-4: Click in the Search box.

8 Begin typing the name of the application to open (for example, type *Excel*).

9 In the search results that appear, find the name of the application you're typing, then click that name. The application opens.

Figure 1-5: Search for the application's name and then click it in the search results.

10. Press Alt+F4 close the application.

Now that you know how to start and exit Office applications, let's take a look at the interface of a typical Office application.

Work with the Ribbon

All Office applications have a common system of navigation called the *Ribbon,* which is a tabbed bar across the top of the application window. Each tab is like a page of buttons. You click different tabs to access different sets of buttons and features. To explore the Ribbon, follow these steps:

1. Open an Office application, as discussed in the previous section, and if needed press Esc to bypass the Start screen.

2 On the Ribbon, click the desired tab.

3. Click the desired command.

Figure 1-6: Click a tab, and then click the desired command.

Here are some key facts to know about Ribbon commands:

A Not all commands are available all the time. For example, you can't paste content until you first cut or copy it. Commands that appear gray (dimmed) are currently unavailable.

B Buttons are organized into groups. The group names appear at the bottom.

C Some groups have dialog box launchers; these open a dialog box or task pane relating to the commands in that group. The one in the Font group, for example, opens the Font dialog box.

D Some buttons, such as Bold or Italic, are on/off toggles. Each time you click the button, it switches its state from one to the other.

E Some groups contain drop-down lists from which to choose settings such as fonts or sizes.

F Some buttons work as a group from which only one button can be selected at a time. One example is the four buttons in the Paragraph group that control horizontal alignment of paragraph text.

G Some buttons have a small arrow on them. In some cases, if you click the button face (not the arrow), the current setting is applied. If you click the arrow, on the other hand, a menu opens for changing the current setting. In other cases, clicking the arrow or the button face has the same effect: opening a menu.

H Some groups, such as the Styles group, contain galleries from which you can choose settings by graphical example.

I You can hide the Ribbon to save space by clicking the Collapse the Ribbon arrow or pressing Ctrl+F1. When you do so, the tab names remain onscreen; click a tab name to reopen the Ribbon. Then click the Pin the Ribbon icon (the tiny pushpin) at the far right end of the Ribbon to re-pin it open.

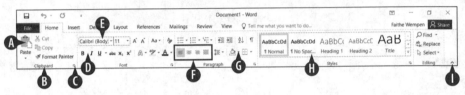

Figure 1-7: Ribbon controls.

J Depending on the width of the application window, some groups may appear collapsed. When a group is collapsed, it appears as a single button with the group's name. When you click the button, a palette appears containing all the group's individual commands.

Figure 1-8: When the application window is not wide enough to display all the Ribbon content, some groups appear collapsed.

Use the File menu

In each Office application, clicking the File tab opens the File menu, also known as *Backstage view*. Backstage view provides access to commands that have to do with the data file you're working with — commands such as saving, opening, printing, mailing, and checking the file's properties. The File tab is a different color in each application. In Excel, for example, it's green. To explore Backstage view, follow these steps:

1. Click the File tab. Backstage view opens.

2 Click the desired page from the navigation pane at the left.

The pages are the same between applications. Table 1-1 summarizes them.

3 If applicable, click a section. Not all pages have sections.

4A Click the desired command.

OR

4B Click the back arrow or press Esc to leave Backstage view without making a selection.

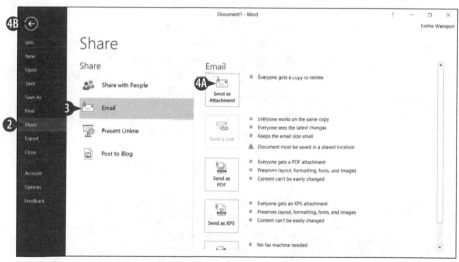

Figure 1-9: After clicking File, click a page and choose the command to issue.

Table 1-1   Pages on the File Menu in Word, Excel, and PowerPoint

Page	What You Can Do
Info	See and edit file properties
	Password-protect the file and restrict editing
	Inspect the file for privacy, accessibility, and compatibility
	Recover unsaved versions
New	Start a new file using a template
Open	Open an existing file
Save	Save the active file for the first time, or save changes to an existing file using the same settings
Save As	Save changes to an existing file using different settings
Print	Print the active file
Share	Invite others to view or edit the file online
	Send the file via email to others
	Present online (Word and PowerPoint only)
	Publish slides (PowerPoint only)
	Post to blog (Word only)
Export	Create a PDF or XPS version
	Change the file type
	Create a video (PowerPoint only)
	Package a presentation for CD (PowerPoint only)
	Create handouts (PowerPoint only)
Account	View and change the active Microsoft account
	Change the background and theme for the application window
	Connect to online services (OneDrive, YouTube, Facebook)
	Manage updates and subscriptions
Options	Control application settings
Close	Close the active document

Create a new document

When you start an application, a Start screen appears. From there, you can choose a template on which to base a new document. (I'm using *document* generically here to refer to a Word document, Excel workbook, or PowerPoint presentation file.) If you just want a blank file with default settings, press Esc to start one without having to choose a template. (Choosing the Blank template is the same as pressing Esc.)

You can also create additional new files without exiting and restarting the application. If you want an additional blank file with default settings, the easiest way is to press Ctrl+N. If you want a new file based on a template, follow these steps:

1 Click the File tab, and click New. A gallery of templates appears.

2A Type a keyword in the Search for online templates box and press Enter.

OR

2B Click any template you want, then skip to step 4.

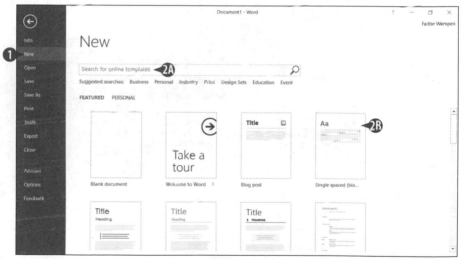

Figure 1-10: Select a template thumbnail, or type a keyword to search for templates.

③ In the search results, click the desired template to see details about it.

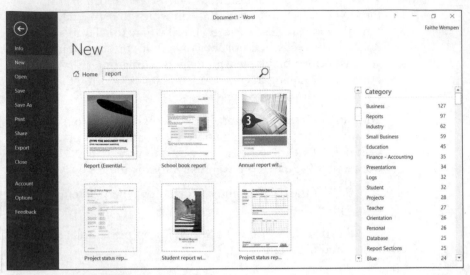

Figure 1-11: Choose a template from the search results.

④ Click Create to download the template and start a new file based on it.

Figure 1-12: Choose a template from the search results.

Depending on the template you choose, the document might not behave exactly like a blank document would. There might be pre-entered content, special formatting, or text placeholders. You are not locked into any of the content or formatting that comes with a template. You can delete any content that you don't want, and make any changes as desired.

Enter text

Because of the layout differences among Excel, Word, and PowerPoint, the process of entering text in each program differs.

Word

Word places text directly on the document page (unless you happen to be using a template that employs text boxes, which is common for complicated layouts like newsletters). To type text in a Word document, just start typing. The *insertion point* (a flashing vertical line) shows where the text you type will appear. (See Figure 1-13.)

Press Enter to start a new paragraph. (You don't have to press Enter at the end of each line, because Word wraps text to the next line automatically as needed.)

To edit text, press Backspace to erase the character to the left of the insertion point or Delete to erase the character to its right. You can also select text (see "Select text" in Chapter 2) and then press either of those keys to delete the selection or type new text to replace the selection.

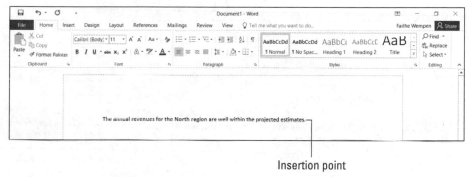

Insertion point

Figure 1-13: Type text directly onto the document page in Word.

Excel

Excel stores text in *cells*, which are boxes at the intersections of rows and columns. To type text in an Excel cell, click the desired cell to make that cell active, and then type.

TIP

It's okay if the text is so long that it doesn't fit in the cell. The text can spill over into cells to the right if they are empty. In Chapter 7 you will learn how to format an Excel worksheet to correct cell width problems.

When you are finished typing in that cell, click a different cell, or press an arrow key on the keyboard to move one cell in the direction of the arrow, or press Enter to move to the cell below the active one.

If you need to edit the text in a cell, double-click the cell to move the insertion point into it, or click the cell to select it and then make your edits in the formula bar, which lies between the Ribbon and the column headings. (See Figure 1-14.)

Formula bar

Insertion point

Figure 1-14: Type text and numbers into cells in Excel.

PowerPoint

PowerPoint places text in movable, resizable boxes on slides. Different slide layouts come with different placeholder boxes, and you can change layouts if you want a slide to have different placeholders. You can create your own text boxes, but you can't type text directly onto the slide. Everything has to be in some sort of box or frame. To place text in a placeholder, click inside it and start typing. At that point, text editing is the same as in Word. (See Figure 1-15.)

Text placeholder with text

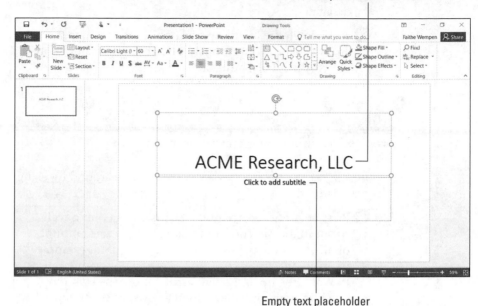

Empty text placeholder

Figure 1-15: Type text into placeholders on a slide in PowerPoint.

Move around in an application

As you work in one of the Office applications, you may add so much content that you can't see it all onscreen at once. You might need to scroll through the document to view different parts of it. The simplest way to scroll through a document is by using the *scroll bars* with your mouse.

Scrolling through a document with the scroll bars doesn't move the insertion point, so what you type or insert doesn't necessarily appear in the location that shows onscreen.

You can also get around by moving the insertion point. When you do so, the document view scrolls automatically so you can see the newly selected location. You can move the insertion point either by clicking where you want it or by using keyboard shortcuts.

Figure 1-16 provides how to move around in a file using the scroll bar:

Ⓐ Click a scroll arrow to scroll a small amount in that direction. In Excel, that's one row or column; in other applications, the exact amount varies per click.

Ⓑ Click to one side or another of the scroll box (or above or below it on a vertical scroll bar) to scroll one full screen in that direction if the file is large enough that there's undisplayed content in that direction.

Ⓒ Drag the scroll box to scroll quickly in the direction you're dragging.

Ⓓ Hold down the left mouse button as you point to a scroll arrow to scroll continuously in that direction until you release the mouse button.

Figure 1-16: You can use a scroll bar to move through a file.

Figure 1-17 summarizes the ways you can move around by using the keyboard:

Ⓐ Press an arrow key to move the insertion point or cell cursor in the direction of the arrow. The exact amount of movement depends on the application; for example, in Excel, one arrow click moves the cursor by one cell. In Word, the up and down arrows move the cursor by one line, and the right and left arrows move it by one character.

Ⓑ Press Page Up or Page Down to scroll one full screen in that direction.

Ⓒ Press Home to move to the left side of the current row or line.

Ⓓ Press End to move to the right side of the current row or line.

Ⓔ Hold down Ctrl and press Home to move to the upper-left corner of the document.

Ⓕ Hold down Ctrl and press End to move to the lower-right corner of the document.

Figure 1-17: You can use keyboard controls to move through a file.

Change the view

All Office applications have zoom commands that make the data appear larger or smaller onscreen. Zoom is measured in percentage, with 100 percent being the baseline. A lower number makes everything appear smaller and farther away; a higher number zooms in for a closer look at a smaller portion of the file.

Figure 1-18 shows how the zoom controls work.

Ⓐ Click Zoom Out to decrease the zoom.

Ⓑ Drag the slider to change the zoom quickly.

Ⓒ Click Zoom In to increase the zoom.

Ⓓ Click the current percentage to open a Zoom dialog box.

Ⓔ Use the Zoom dialog box to select a preset zoom amount.

Ⓕ Use the Zoom dialog box to select an exact numeric zoom value.

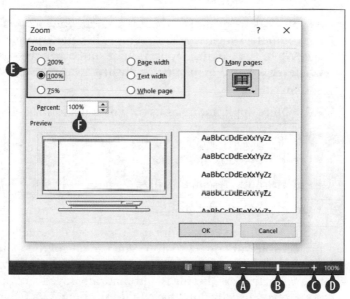

Figure 1-18: Each application enables you to zoom in and out on your data.

In addition, depending on what you're doing to the data in a particular application, you may find that changing the view is useful. Some applications have multiple viewing modes you can switch among; for example, PowerPoint's Normal view is suitable for slide editing, and its Slide Sorter view is suitable for rearranging the slides.

To change the view, use the buttons on the View tab, in the Views group. The views are different for each application. Figure 1-19 shows them for Word.

(A) The Views group contains buttons for the available views.

(B) Turn optional screen elements on/off with the check boxes in the Show group.

(C) The Zoom group provides an alternative method of controlling zoom.

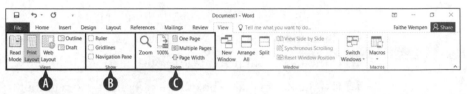

Figure 1-19: Choose a view from the View tab.

Save your work

As you work in an application, the content you create is stored in the computer's memory. This memory is only temporary storage. When you exit the application or shut down the computer, whatever is stored in memory is flushed away forever — unless you save it.

Each Office application has its own data file format. For example:

- **Word:** Document files, `.docx`
- **Excel:** Workbook files, `.xlsx`
- **PowerPoint:** Presentation files, `.pptx`
- **Outlook:** Outlook data files, `.pst`

Word, Excel, and PowerPoint use a separate data file for each project you work on. Every time you use one of these programs, you open and save data files. Outlook uses just one data file for all your activities. This file is automatically saved and opened for you, so you usually don't have to think about data file management in Outlook.

Each application has three important file types:

- **Default:** The default format in each application supports most Office 2007 and higher features except macros. The file extension ends in the letter *X* for each one: Word is `.docx`; Excel is `.xlsx`; PowerPoint is `.pptx`.

- **Macro-enabled:** This format supports most Office 2007 and higher features, including macros. The file extension ends in the letter *M* for each one: `.docm`, `.xlsm`, and `.pptm`.

Macros are recorded bits of code that can automate certain activities in a program, but they can also carry viruses. The default formats don't support macros for that reason. If you need to create a file that includes macros, you can save in a macro-enabled format.

- **97–2003:** Each application includes a file format for backward compatibility with earlier versions of the application (Office versions 97 through 2003). Some minor functionality may be lost when you save in this format. The file extensions are `.doc`, `.xls`, and `.ppt`.

The first time you save a file, the application prompts you to enter a name for it. You can also choose a different save location and/or file type. When you resave a previously saved file, the Save As dialog box doesn't reappear; the file saves with the most recent settings. If you want to change the settings (such as the location or file type) or save under a different name, choose File ⇨ Save As.

Follow these steps to save a file for the first time:

❶ Click the File tab, and click either Save or Save As.

Because you have not previously saved this file, the Save As page displays regardless of which you choose.

❷ Click the general location in which to save:

- *This PC:* Saves to your own computer
- *OneDrive:* Saves to your online OneDrive storage, which is a free Microsoft-provided online storage space associated with your Microsoft account

③A Click one of the recently used folders on the right side of the screen. These are all specific folders within the general location you chose in step 2.

OR

③B Click Browse to open the location you chose in step 2 to its default folder.

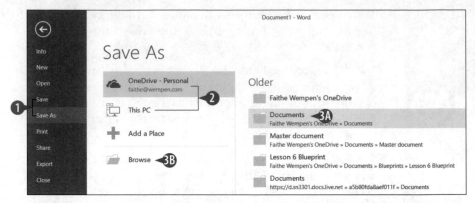

Figure 1-20: Choose File ⇨ Save As, and then select a general location in which to save.

4 Type the desired file name in the File name box, replacing the generic name there.

5 (Optional) Change the file type by choosing from the Save as type drop-down list.

6 (Optional) Change the save location if desired. See "Change locations when saving or opening files" later in this chapter for details.

7 Click Save.

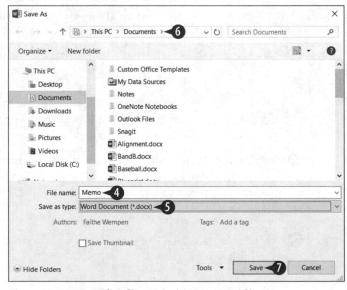

Figure 1-21: Specify a file name, location, and file type.

When you save your work on an already-saved file, you can use File ⇨ Save or the Ctrl+S keyboard shortcut if you want to save using the same name, location, and file type. If you want to change any of those things, you must use File ⇨ Save As so that the Save As dialog box reopens.

If you want the Save As dialog box to appear immediately when you choose File ⇨ Save As, rather than showing the general locations first on the Save As page, choose File ⇨ Options. Then in the Options dialog box, click Save on the left and then mark the Don't Show the Backstage When Opening or Saving Files check box.

Close a file

When you exit an application, you automatically close any open files in it. Closing each file is not necessary before opening another file because each application can have many data files open at once. However, you might want to close files anyway to free up your computer's memory, which may make it run a little better.

To close a file without exiting the application, click the File tab and click Close. If you are prompted to save your changes, click Save or click Don't Save, as appropriate.

Open a saved file

When you open a file, you copy it from your hard drive (or other storage location) into the computer's working memory, so the application can access it in order to view and modify it. To open a saved file, follow these steps:

1 Click the File tab, and click Open.

2. Click the general location from which to browse files to open:

- *Recent (selected by default):* Shows a list of recently used files.

- *This PC:* Shows files from your own computer.

- *OneDrive:* Shows files from your online OneDrive storage.

3A If you chose Recent in step 2, click one of the files on the list. Skip the rest of the steps.

OR

3B If you chose This PC or OneDrive in step 2, click one of the location shortcuts that appear, or click Browse.

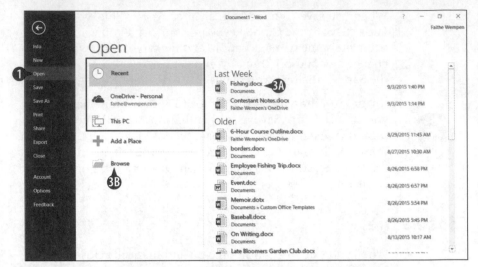

Figure 1-22: Select a location from which to browse available files to open.

4️⃣ If needed, browse to a different folder. See "Change locations when saving or opening files" later in this chapter.

5️⃣ Click the desired file name in the Open dialog box.

6️⃣ Click Open.

Figure 1-23: Choose the file to open and then click Open.

Change locations when saving or opening files

Office 2016 uses the current Windows user's OneDrive as the default storage location. OneDrive is a secure online storage area hosted by Microsoft. Anyone who registers for the service, or who logs into Windows 8 or later with a Microsoft ID, is given a certain amount of free storage space, and can purchase more.

You can also save your files locally, where the default location is your Documents personal folder. In Windows, each user has his or her own separate Documents folder (based on who is logged in to Windows at the moment).

To understand how to change save locations, you should first understand the concept of a file path. Files are organized into folders, and you can have folders *inside* folders. For example, you might have

- A folder called *Work*
- Within that folder, another folder called *Job Search*
- Within that folder, a Word file called `Resume.docx`

The path for such a file would be

```
C:\Work\Job Search\Resume.docx
```

When you change the save location, you're changing to a different path for the file. You do that by navigating through the file system via the Save As dialog box. The Save As dialog box provides several ways of navigating, so you can pick the one you like best.

Figure 1-24 points out some ways of changing the location in the Save As or Open dialog box.

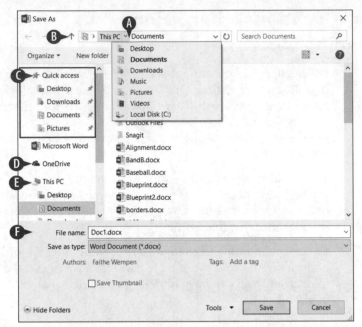

Figure 1-24: Use the controls in the Save As or Open dialog box to change locations.

Ⓐ Click one of the right arrows in the address bar to open a menu of locations.

Ⓑ Click the Up One Level arrow to go up one level in the folder hierarchy.

Ⓒ The Quick access list holds shortcuts to commonly used locations; you can place your own favorite locations here too by dragging them here.

Ⓓ To browse your OneDrive from the top level, click OneDrive.

Ⓔ To browse the local PC from the top level, click This PC.

Ⓕ Click a location in the navigation pane to jump to that location.

CHAPTERTWO
Creating a Word Document

Microsoft Word is the most popular of the Office applications because nearly everyone needs to create text documents of one type or another. With Word, you can create everything from fax cover sheets to school research papers to family holiday letters.

In this chapter, I explain how to create, edit, format, and share simple documents. By the end of this chapter, you'll have a good grasp of the entire process of document creation, from start to finish, including how to share your work with others via print or email. Later chapters build on this knowledge, adding in the fancier aspects such as using styles, graphics, and multiple sections.

The type of formatting covered in this chapter is commonly known as *character formatting* (formatting that can be applied to individual characters). Character formatting includes fonts, font sizes, text attributes (such as italics), character spacing (spacing between letters), and text color. You can apply each type of character formatting individually, or you can use style sets or themes to apply multiple types of formatting at once.

In This Chapter

- Starting a new Word document
- Selecting and formatting text
- Applying themes and style sets
- Checking spelling and grammar
- Emailing a document to others
- Sharing a document in other formats
- Printing your work

Start a new document as Word starts

When you start Word, a Start screen appears, as in Figure 2-1. From here you can:

A Click one of the shortcuts to recently used documents to reopen one.

B Click Blank Document to create a new blank document. You can also press Esc to do this.

C Click one of the template thumbnails to start a new document with that template.

D Click in the Search for online templates box, type a keyword, and press Enter to look for more templates, as you learned to do in Chapter 1.

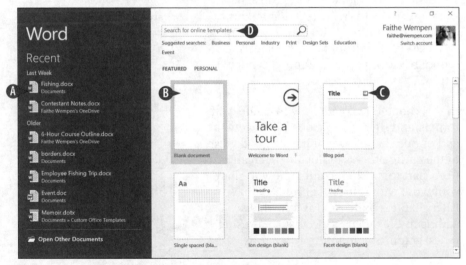

Figure 2-1: From Word's Start screen, click Blank Document.

The Start screen shown in Figure 2-1 appears only when Word starts up; you can't get back to it without exiting Word and restarting. However, you can access all its features in other locations in Word at any time. You can choose File ⇨ New to start a new document (covered in Chapter 1), or press Ctrl+N to start a new blank document based on the default settings. Or, to access the list of recently used documents, choose File ⇨ Open.

Even when you start a blank document, you're still (technically) using a template — a template called Normal. The Normal template specifies certain default settings for a new blank document, such as the default fonts (Calibri for body text and Cambria for headings), default font sizes (11 point for body text), and margins (1 inch on all sides).

If you stick with the default values for the Normal template's definition, the Normal template doesn't exist as a separate file. It's built into Word itself. You won't find it if you search your hard drive for it. However, if you make a change to one or more of the Normal template's settings, Word saves them to a file called Normal.dotm. If Word at any point can't find Normal. dotm, it reverts to its internally stored copy and goes back to the default values. That's useful to know because if you ever accidentally redefine the Normal template so that it produces documents with unwanted settings, or if it ever gets corrupted, all you have to do is find and delete Normal.dotm from your hard drive, and you go back to a fresh-from-the-factory version of the default settings for new, blank documents. The template is stored in C:\Users*user*\AppData\Roaming\Microsoft\Templates, where *user* is the signed-in username.

Select text

When you apply formatting, it affects whatever is selected. Selecting blocks of text before you issue an editing or formatting command allows you to act on the entire block at once. For example, you can select multiple paragraphs before choosing a certain text font, size, or color.

Here are some mouse methods of selecting text:

Ⓐ Drag across the text with the mouse (with the left mouse button pressed) to select any amount of text.

Figure 2-2: Select text by dragging across it.

B Double-click a word to select it or triple-click within a paragraph to select the entire paragraph.

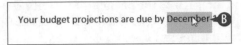

Figure 2-3: Double-click a word to select it.

C Click to the left of a line to select that line; drag upward or downward from there to select additional lines.

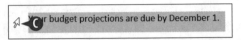

Figure 2-4: Click to the left of a line to select it.

Here are some keyboard methods of selecting text:

- Press Ctrl+A to select the entire document.

- Move the insertion point to the beginning of the text and then hold down the Shift key while you press the arrow keys to extend the selection.

- Press the F8 key to turn on Extend mode, and then use the arrow keys to extend the selection.

Choose between manual and style-based text formatting

In the next several sections, you will learn various ways of applying manual formatting to text, such as changing the font, size, color, and effects. But are you sure that's what you really want to do? Give me a moment of your time to convince you that style-based formatting should be the norm, and manual formatting should be done only on an occasional basis.

Word works best when you allow it to use its Styles feature to consistently format text based on the style applied to it. Chapter 3 covers styles in detail, but here's a quick preview. A *style* is a named collection of formatting settings. The default style is called Normal, and in new blank documents it uses a font called Calibri. If you wanted to change the font used in your document, you could do it in one of these ways:

- Select all the text and then manually apply a different font choice.

- Redefine Normal style to use a different font, which you can do in any of these ways:

- Choose a different style set.

- Change the definition of the Normal style to use a different font.

- Apply a different theme that defines Normal style differently.

- Apply a different set of theme fonts that define Normal style differently.

It might seem like you get the same result any way you go. However, as you start using some other Word features that work using styles, you will realize that they aren't really the same at all.

Manual formatting overrides any formatting that comes from the style, so if you apply a font manually to a paragraph, that formatting will not change when you redefine the paragraph's style in a way that would otherwise change it. Therefore, if you try to do style-based formatting later with a document that you've manually formatted, you may find that your style-based formatting is not working as planned, perhaps in unexpected and frustrating ways.

Does that mean you should never use manual formatting? No. Manual formatting can be very useful sometimes. For example, you might want to emphasize a particular word or phrase by making it bold, italic, or a different color. And, if you are creating a very short memo or letter and you're in a hurry, you might find that manual formatting is right for the situation.

However, if you are creating a multipage document that is going to hang around for a while, take a look at what style-based formatting has to offer. Style-based formatting features are covered in the following places in this book:

- How to apply a different theme (Chapter 2)

- How to change the style set (Chapter 2)

- How to apply styles (Chapter 3)

- How to modify styles (Chapter 3)

- How to create new styles (Chapter 3)

Remove manually applied formatting

If you apply manual formatting to some text and then later decide that you would rather allow the formatting to be determined by the style, you can easily remove it. Just follow these steps:

1. Select the text to affect.

2. Choose Home ⇨ Clear All Formatting. You can also press Ctrl+spacebar.

Figure 2-5: Remove manually applied formatting.

Change the text font

The text in the document appears using a certain style of letter-ing, also called a *font* or a *typeface*. Office comes with dozens of typefaces, so you're sure to find one that meets the needs of whatever project you create. To change a font, follow these steps:

1 Select the text to affect. See the previous section to learn some ways of selecting text.

2 On the Home tab, click the down arrow to the right of the Font box. The Font list opens.

You can point at a font to see the selected text previewed in it before clicking to make your selection in step 3.

3 Click the desired font.

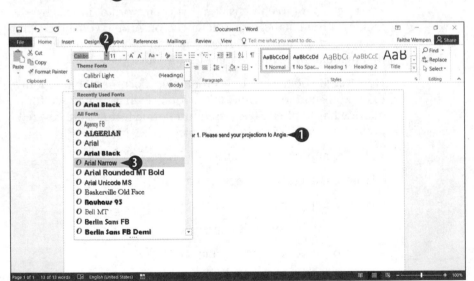

Figure 2-6: Choose a font from the Fonts list on the Home tab.

Notice the Theme Fonts section in Figure 2-6 contains a (Headings) font and a (Body) font. These are the fonts that the document currently defines as the default heading and body fonts, respectively, based on the theme or style set in use. If you apply fonts from the Theme Fonts section, you aren't really applying the listed fonts manually; you are applying the place-holder. If the style definitions change, any text you have for-matted using the choices in the Theme Fonts section will also change.

Change the text size

Each font is available in a wide variety of sizes. The sizes are measured in *points*, with each point being $1/72$ of an inch on a printout. (The size it appears onscreen depends on the display zoom. You learned about zoom in Chapter 1.) Text sizes vary from very small (6 points) to very large (100 points or more). An average document uses body text that's between 10 and 12 points and headings between 12 and 18 points. To change the text size, follow these steps:

1. Select the text to affect.

2. On the Home tab, click the down arrow to the right of the Size box. The Size list opens.

3. Click the desired size.

Here are a few points to remember about changing text size:

A. Instead of steps 2 and 3, you can alternatively click in the Size box and type a number directly. This is useful if you want a size that's not on the list. Word accepts decimal points in font sizes, so you can have 10.5 point text, for example.

B. Clicking Increase Font Size increases the font size by one setting from the Size list. Depending on the size, that might be more than 1 point. For example, notice that the list jumps from 36 straight to 48.

C. Clicking Decrease Font Size button decreases the font size by one setting from the Size list.

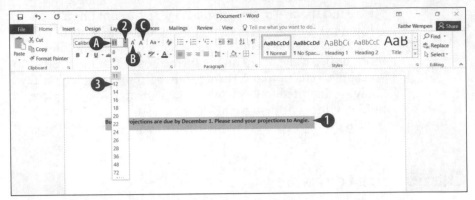

Figure 2-7: Choose a font size from the Size list.

Select colors from a palette

When selecting a color in Word or any other Office application (for text, borders, shapes, and so on), it's important that you understand how Office applications handle color. Take a moment to review this information, as you'll need it many times in the rest of this book.

Every document, workbook, or presentation has a theme. Even plain blank ones have a theme (the default theme). One of the theme's duties is to define a set of color placeholders.

When you are choosing the color for an object, if you choose a color from one of these placeholders, that color choice is dependent upon the theme. If a different theme is applied that defines the colors differently, the object changes color.

As an alternative, Word also offers a set of colors it calls Standard colors, which are fixed choices no matter what theme is applied.

When you make a color choice, you work with a palette like the one shown in Figure 2-8. Here are a few things to note about selecting colors:

A Click Automatic to return the selection to the default. On a white or light-colored background, Automatic is black; on a dark background, it is white.

B Click one of the theme colors, or a variant of one, to select a color that may change if the theme changes.

C Click a color from Standard Colors to choose a fixed color that will not change.

D Click More Colors to choose from a wider variety of standard colors.

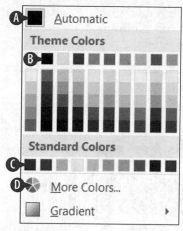

Figure 2-8: Select an appropriate color from the palette

If you choose More Colors, the Colors dialog box opens. This dialog box has two tabs: Standard and Custom.

Ⓔ The Standard tab contains swatches of common colors. Click the one you want.

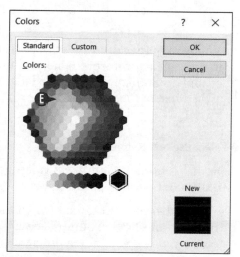

Figure 2-9: The Standard tab of the Color dialog box.

Ⓕ The Custom tab contains a color grid. Click anywhere on the grid to select a color.

Ⓖ The chosen color appears here.

Ⓗ Drag this slider up or down to change the color's lightness.

I If you want a specific color that has a numeric value in a particular color model, select the color model here, and then enter the numeric values.

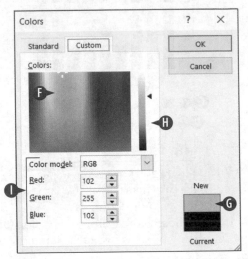

Figure 2-10: The Custom tab of the Color dialog box.

Change text color

You can choose a specific color for selected text to draw attention to it, or to dress up a document to make it more attractive. You can either apply color manually (covered here), or redefine the style to use a different font color (covered in Chapter 3).

To manually change the text color, follow these steps.

1 Select the text to affect.

2 On the Home tab, click the down arrow to the right of the Font Color button. A palette appears.

To apply the color already shown on the face of the Font Color button, click the button face. Opening the palette is necessary only if you want a different color.

3 Click the desired color. See "Select colors from a palette" earlier in this chapter for guidance.

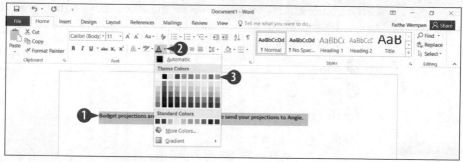

Figure 2-11: Choose a font color.

Apply text effects

Word supports two kinds of text effects. The basic ones, such as bold, italic, and underline, are supported by just about any word processing program you might work with. Stick to these if you are going to be sharing the document with others who might not have a recent version of Word. The more advanced set, such as glow and outline, work only in Word 2007 and later. Figures 2 12 and 2-13 show the effects available of each kind.

Bold	~~Double Strikethrough~~
Italic	Superscript[1]
Underline	Subscript[2]
Double Underline	SMALL CAPS
~~Strikethrough~~	ALL CAPS

Figure 2-12: Basic effects, which work in almost any document format.

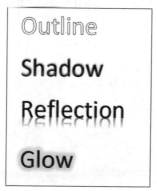

Figure 2-13: Advanced effects, which may not translate well into other document formats.

Certain basic effects are available on the Home tab, in the Font group. To apply one of these, select the text and click its button. Figure 2-14 points out the available effects:

Ⓐ Bold

Ⓑ Italic

Ⓒ Underline

Ⓓ Strikethrough

Ⓔ Subscript

Ⓕ Superscript

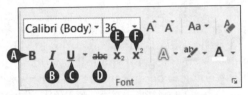

Figure 2-14: Some basic effects can be applied from the Home tab on the Ribbon.

Other basic effects are available only in the Font dialog box. To open it, click the dialog box launcher in the Font group, or press Ctrl+D. Figure 2-15 shows the Font dialog box:

Ⓖ More underline styles are available from the drop-down list.

Ⓗ You can use a different color for the underline than for the text.

Ⓘ Double-strikethrough runs two horizontal lines through the text.

Ⓙ Small caps make all letters capital style but retain their uppercase/lowercase statuses by the size of the letters.

Ⓚ All caps makes all letters uppercase and the same height.

Ⓛ The Preview area shows a preview of your chosen options. In this case, it shows small caps and italic with a dotted underline.

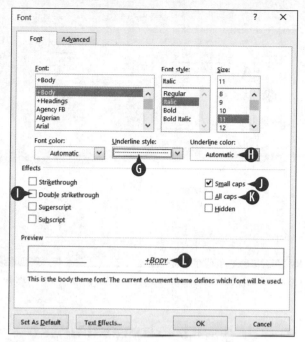

Figure 2-15: The Font dialog box provides a complete set of basic effect options.

Ⓜ To apply the effects shown in Figure 2-13, you must use the Effects button's menu, as shown in Figure 2-16. Point to an option on the menu to open its submenu, and then make your selection.

Ⓝ For quick formatting, click one of these preset combinations of the various effects.

Ⓞ Each menu option opens a submenu.

Ⓟ Click the Options command at the bottom of the submenu to open a task pane where you can fine-tune the settings.

The Number Styles, Ligatures, and Stylistic Sets commands in Figure 2-16 affect the typesetting of the text in subtle ways; these options are rarely used except by publishing professionals.

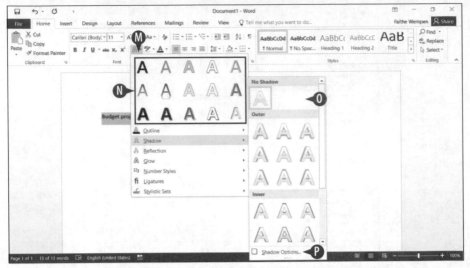

Figure 2-16: Use the Effects button to apply special effects such as the ones shown in Figure 2-13.

Copy formatting with Format Painter

It might take several different operations to get some text exactly the way you want it. Once it's perfect, you can copy its formatting to other text by using Format Painter. This not only saves time, but it ensures consistency. To format text with Format Painter, follow these steps:

1 Select the text that already has the formatting you want to copy.

2 Click Format Painter. The mouse pointer appears as a paintbrush.

3 Drag across the text that should receive the formatting.

After step 3, Format Painter shuts itself off automatically. If you would like it to stay on so you can copy that same formatting to multiple selections, double-click rather than clicking the button in step 2.

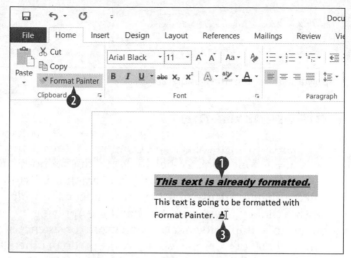

Figure 2-17: Use Format Painter to copy formatting.

Change the style set

In "Choose between manual and style-based text formatting" earlier in this chapter, you learned that each document has default definitions of the formatting. Formatting can be manually applied, or it can be indirectly changed by making a change to the underlying style applied to that text.

One way to change a document's look without manually tampering with individual paragraph settings is to apply a different style set. A *style set* is a collection of definitions for the most commonly used styles in a document, such as Normal, Heading 1, Heading 2, and so on. When you apply a different style set, you redefine these styles without having to manually do so.

1. Start with a document that already has some text typed in it.

   If you just want some dummy text to practice with and don't know what to type, type =RAND(5) and press Enter to generate five sample paragraphs.

2. On the Design tab, roll your mouse over several of the samples in the Style Sets gallery to see the different formatting available.

3. Click the sample that best represents what you want.

   Click More for more choices. (See A in Figure 2-18.)

Figure 2-18: Apply a style set from the Design tab.

Apply a different theme

A *theme* is a named collection of settings for three types of formatting: fonts (one for headings and one for body), colors (one for each of 12 placeholders), and graphic object formatting effects. Themes are useful for ensuring document-wide consistency, but they go even further than that. Applying the same theme to multiple documents can ensure consistency across your entire library of work, including work you do in other Office applications like Excel and PowerPoint.

Each document starts with a default theme applied, which it inherits from the template on which it is based. The Normal template by default uses a theme called Office.

1 On the Design tab, click Themes.

2 Click the desired theme.

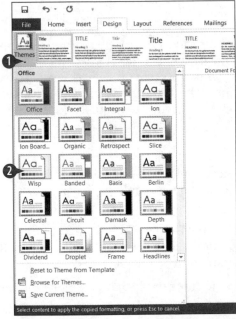

Figure 2-19: Apply a theme to affect the documents colors, fonts, and effects.

You can modify each of the theme's three aspects separately by choosing a color, font, or effect set from the Design tab. These sets do not correspond one-to-one with the themes on the Themes button's list; there are more color, font, and effect sets than there are themes:

(A) Click Colors and choose a different color set.

(B) Click Fonts and choose a different font set.

(C) Click Effects and choose a different effect set.

Figure 2-20: Change one aspect of a theme individually from the Design tab.

Check spelling and grammar

Word automatically checks spelling as you type, comparing each word to its dictionaries. If you type a word that doesn't appear, it places a wavy red (non-printing) underline on it, flagging it for your attention.

You can right-click a red-underlined word to see spelling suggestions, as shown in Figure 2-21:

(A) Click a suggestion to change to it.

(B) Click Ignore All to mark this word as correct in the current document only.

(C) Click Add to Dictionary to mark this word correct in this and all other documents.

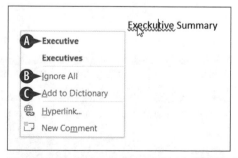

Figure 2-21: Right-click a word with a wavy red underline to see spelling suggestions.

Grammar errors are similar, except they appear with a wavy blue underline. A grammar error might be a usage error such as "is" versus "are" or a punctuation error such as too many spaces between words, as in Figure 2-22:

Ⓓ Click a suggestion to change to it.

Ⓔ Click Ignore Once to ignore this error but not errors similar to it.

Ⓕ Click Grammar to open the Grammar task pane, which is explained next.

Figure 2-22: Right-click a wavy blue underline to correct a grammar error.

In a long document, you may find it easier to use the full Spelling and Grammar tool in Word rather than handle each underlined item individually. Here's how to use it:

❶ On the Review tab, click Spelling & Grammar. A task pane opens. It is either the Spelling task pane or the Grammar task pane, depending on which type of error it encounters first.

Figure 2-23: Choose Spelling & Grammar to start a full check of the document.

In the Spelling task pane, you can do any of the following:

Ⓐ Click Ignore to ignore this instance only but mark other instances in the same document.

Ⓑ Click Ignore All to mark this word as correct in the current document only.

Ⓒ Click Add to mark this word correct in this and all other documents.

Ⓓ Click a suggestion and then click Change to change this one instance to the selected word.

Ⓔ Click Change All to change all instances in the current document to the selected word.

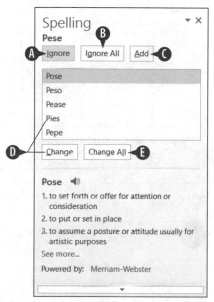

Figure 2-24: Choose what to do with a spelling error.

In the Grammar pane, you can:

Ⓕ Click Ignore to mark this instance as correct.

Ⓖ Click the desired correction and then click Change.

2. Keep working through the spelling and grammar errors Word finds until you see a message that the check is complete.

❸ Click OK.

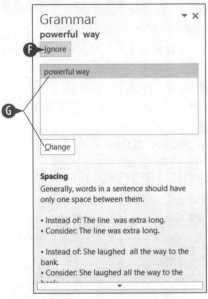

Figure 2-25: Choose what to do with a grammar error.

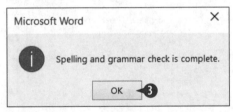

Figure 2-26: Click OK to close the message box.

To customize how the spelling and grammar are checked, choose File ⇨ Options and click the Proofing tab. You can add and remove words from custom dictionaries, ignore certain spelling and grammar errors, and set up automatic corrections for words you frequently mistype.

Email a document to others

Email can be an efficient way of delivering a document to other people. You don't have to leave Word in order to send it, provided you have a compatible email application already configured on your computer, such as Microsoft Outlook. (Word doesn't support web-based email applications such as gmail and Yahoo! Mail for sending documents.) To email a document with Word, follow these steps:

1 Click File, and click Share.

2 Click Email.

3 Click Send as Attachment. A new email opens in your default email application. The file is already attached.

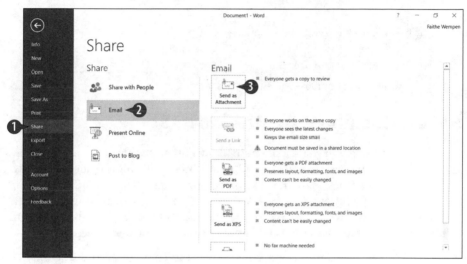

Figure 2-27: Choose to send a file as an attachment.

4 Click in the To box and type the email address of the recipient.

5 Change the subject if desired. The default is the name of the file being attached.

6 Click in the message body and type a message if desired.

7 Click Send.

If the file is saved on a sharable drive, such as OneDrive, the Send a Link button is available, and in step 3 you can choose to send a link rather than the attachment. Linking rather than attaching ensures that the recipient sees the latest version.

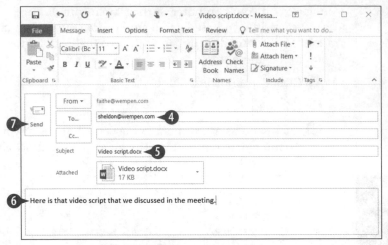

Figure 2-28: Compose the email message.

Save a document in other formats

When you share a document with other people, you are assuming they have Microsoft Word or another application that opens Word files. These days that's actually a pretty safe bet, with all the options available for opening Word files. WordPad, which comes free with Windows, opens Word documents, and the Word Online program at office.live.com is free to anyone with a Microsoft account.

Nevertheless, you might still want to convert a Word document to some other format in some cases. For example, you could save a document in Word 97-2003 format for backward compatibility with early versions of Word, or you could save in Rich Text Format (.rtf) for compatibility with just about any word processing program in the world.

Here's how to save a document in another format:

1 Click File ➪ Export.

2 Click Change File Type.

3 Click the desired file type.

4 Click Save As. The Save As dialog box opens.

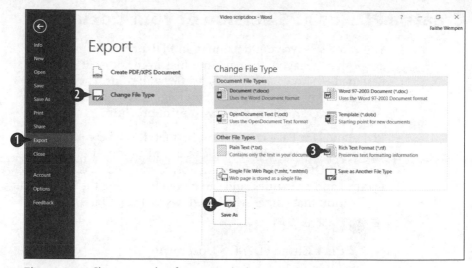

Figure 2-29: Choose another format in which to save the document.

 TIP Instead of steps 1–4, you can choose File ⇨ Save, click Browse, and then change the setting in the File type drop-down list.

5 Navigate to the desired save location.

6 If desired, change the file name. The Save as type setting should match what you chose in step 3.

7 Click Save.

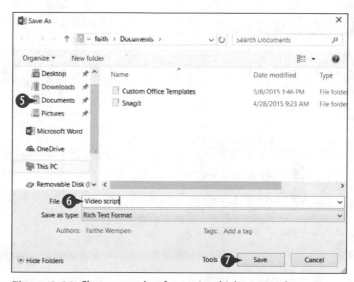

Figure 2-30: Choose another format in which to save the document.

Create a PDF or XPS version of your document

You can also save your document in PDF or XPS format. These are both page layout formats, and files in this format are designed to show pages exactly as they will print. They are not designed to be easily editable. You might save a contract in this format, for example, or a ready-to-print brochure.

PDF stands for Page Description Format. It is a very popular format by Adobe. Anyone with the free application Adobe Reader can read PDF files. XPS is the Microsoft equivalent; is has similar features and properties, and can be opened using the XPS Reader application that comes with Windows Vista and later.

1 Click File ⇨ Export.

2 Click Create PDF/XPS Document.

3 Click Create PDF/XPS. The Publish as PDF or XPS dialog box opens.

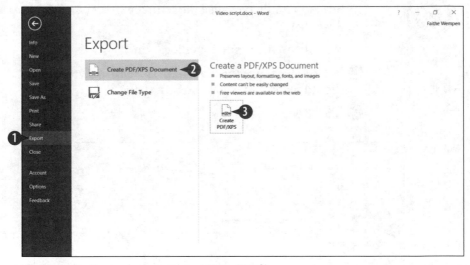

Figure 2-31: Save a document as a PDF or XPS file.

4 Change the file name in the File name box, if desired.

5 Open the Save as Type drop-down list and choose PDF or XPS Document as desired.

⑥ In the Optimize For section, click Standard or Minimum Size.

In step 5, use Standard in most cases. Minimum Size decreases the resolution of the file as it decreases its size. The smaller size may be useful when sending a document via email, provided the document's quality (resolution) is not important.

After step 6 you can click the Options button for a dialog box containing even more options for the resulting PDF or XPS file.

⑦ Mark or clear the Open file after publishing check box as desired. If marked, this option opens the PDF or XPS file in an appropriate reader application, outside of Word, after you save.

⑧ Click Publish.

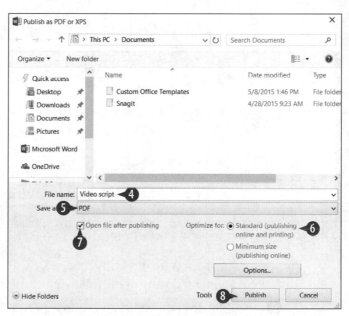

Figure 2-32: Specify saving options for your PDF or XPS file.

Print your work

To print a hard copy of your work, first make sure you have a printer set up in Windows. Follow the instructions that come with a new printer to set it up, or use the Add Printer wizard in Windows to install a driver for an existing printer. (See the Devices and Printers section of the Control Panel.)

After the printer is set up and ready, follow these steps.

1. (Optional) If you only want to print a certain part of the document, select the part you want to print.

2 Click File, and click Print.

3 In the Printer section, make sure the correct printer name appears. If needed, open the drop-down list and choose a different printer.

4 In the Copies box, type the number of copies you want, or use the up or down increment arrows to change the setting.

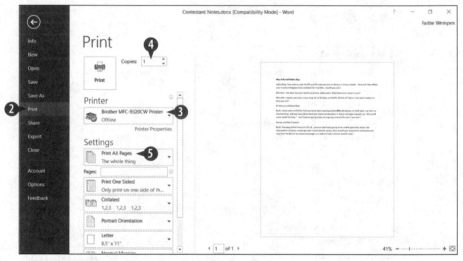

Figure 2-33: Check the printer name and other settings.

5 In the Settings section, if you don't want to print the entire document, do any of the following:

A Open the drop-down list and choose Print Selection. If you didn't select anything in step 1, this option is not available.

B Open the drop-down list and choose Print Current Page.

C Type page numbers in the Pages box. You can specify a contiguous range with a dash like this: 2-15. You can specify individual pages by separating them with commas like this: 2, 4, 5. Specifying a page range automatically sets the drop-down list setting to Custom Print.

Figure 2-34: Set the print range if you don't want to print the entire document.

6. Set any other printing options as desired. For example:

Ⓐ *Print one-sided or two-sided.* When you click this button, you have the option of printing on both sides automatically (if your printer supports that) or manually by flipping the paper over after the first side has been printed.

Ⓑ *Print collated or uncollated.* This is an issue only when printing multiple copies of a multiple-page document. Collated prints the pages in sets (1, 2, 3, 1, 2, 3); uncollated prints all copies of each page together (1, 1, 2, 2, 3, 3).

Ⓒ *Portrait or landscape orientation.* Portrait prints along the narrow edge of the paper; landscape prints along the wide edge.

Ⓓ *Paper size.* Change this setting to correspond to the actual paper size you are using.

Ⓔ *Margins.* Change to a preset such as Wide or Narrow, or choose Custom Margins to enter your own settings.

F *Pages per sheet.* The default is 1, but you can print multiple pages per sheet, shrinking down each page so that they all fit. You probably won't be able to read each page very well, though.

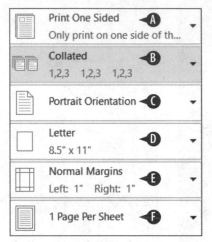

Figure 2-35: Modify any other print settings as desired.

7 When all the settings are the way you want them, click Print.

Figure 2-36: Click Print to print the document with the settings you have specified.

Word has a Quick Print feature that enables you to print with the default settings with a single click. It's not readily available by default, though. To add it to the Quick Access toolbar:

1️⃣ Click the Customize Quick Access Toolbar arrow.

2️⃣ Choose Quick Print.

Figure 2-37: Add Quick Print to the Quick Access toolbar.

CHAPTER**THREE**
Paragraph Formatting

Paragraphs are essential building blocks in a Word document. Each time you press Enter, you start a new paragraph. If you've ever seen a document where the author didn't use paragraph breaks, you know how important paragraphs can be. They break up the content into more easily understandable chunks, which helps the reader both visually and logically.

Paragraph formatting is formatting that affects whole paragraphs and cannot be applied to individual characters. For example, line spacing is a type of paragraph formatting, along with indentation and alignment.

If you apply paragraph formatting when no text is selected, the formatting affects the paragraph in which the insertion point is currently located. If you apply paragraph formatting when text is selected, the formatting affects every paragraph included in that selection, even if only one character of the paragraph is included. Being able to format paragraphs this way is useful because you can select multiple paragraphs at once and then format them as a group.

In this chapter, you learn how to apply various types of formatting to paragraphs and how to simplify and automate paragraph formatting by using text formatting presets called styles.

In This Chapter

➡ Changing a paragraph's horizontal alignment

➡ Indenting a paragraph

➡ Adjusting a paragraph's vertical spacing

➡ Placing a border around a paragraph

➡ Shading a paragraph's background

➡ Creating a bulleted or numbered list

➡ Applying styles

➡ Creating and modifying styles

Change a paragraph's horizontal alignment

The horizontal alignment choices are Align Text Left, Center, Align Text Right, and Justify. Figure 3-1 shows an example of each of the alignment types. Each of these is pretty self-evident except the last one: *Justify* aligns both the left and right sides of the paragraph with the margins, stretching out or compressing the text in each line as needed to make it fit. The final line in the paragraph is exempt and appears left-aligned.

If you apply Justify alignment to a paragraph that contains only one line, it looks like it is left-aligned. However, if you then type more text into the paragraph so it wraps to additional lines, the Justify alignment becomes apparent.

This paragraph is left-aligned. Each line begins at the left margin. This paragraph is left-aligned. Each line begins at the left margin. This paragraph is left-aligned. Each line begins at the left margin. This paragraph is left-aligned. Each line begins at the left margin.

This paragraph is centered. Each line is centered at the midpoint between the margins. This paragraph is centered. Each line is centered at the midpoint between the margins. This paragraph is centered. Each line is centered at the midpoint between the margins.

This paragraph is right-aligned. Each line ends at the right margin, and begins in whatever position is required for that to happen. This paragraph is right-aligned. Each line ends at the right margin, and begins in whatever position is required for that to happen.

This paragraph is justified. Its lines are stretched so that they align with both the left and right margin. This happens for every line except the final one, which is left-aligned. This paragraph is justified. Its lines are stretched so that they align with both the left and right margin. This happens for every line except the final one, which is left-aligned.

Figure 3-1: Example of horizontal alignment.

To affect a single paragraph, click anywhere in the paragraph and then set the alignment. To affect multiple paragraphs, select the paragraphs first.

Use the alignment buttons in the Paragraph group on the Ribbon's Home tab to set an alignment for one or more paragraphs. You can also use the keyboard shortcut for a button:

Ⓐ Left (Ctrl+L)

Ⓑ Center (Ctrl+E)

Ⓒ Right (Ctrl+R)

Ⓓ Justify (Ctrl+J)

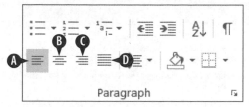

Figure 3-2: Use the alignment buttons on the Home tab.

Indent a paragraph

The indentation of a paragraph refers to the way its left and/or right sides are inset. In addition to a left and right indent value, each paragraph can optionally have a special indent for the first line. If the first line is indented more than the rest of the paragraph, it's known as a *first-line indent*. (Clever name.) If the first line is indented less than the rest of the paragraph, it's called a *hanging indent*. Here are some things to remember about indenting paragraphs:

Ⓐ When a paragraph has no indentation, it's allowed to take up the full range of space between the left and right margins.

Ⓑ When you set indentation for a paragraph, its left and/ or right sides are inset by the amount you specify. Many people like to indent quotations to set them apart from the rest of the text for emphasis, for example.

Ⓒ First-line indents are sometimes used in reports and books to help the reader's eye catch the beginning of a paragraph. In layouts with vertical space between paragraphs, however, first-line indents are less useful because it's easy to see where a new paragraph begins without that help.

Ⓓ Hanging indents are typically used to create listings. In a bulleted or numbered list, the bullet or number hangs off the left edge of the paragraph, in a hanging indent. However, in Word, when you create bulleted or numbered lists (covered later in this lesson), Word adjusts the paragraph's hanging indent automatically, so you don't have to think about it.

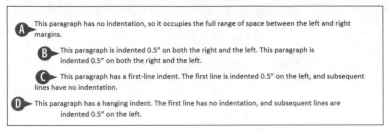

Figure 3-3: Indentation examples.

- To increase or decrease a paragraph's left indent:

  E Click the Decrease Indent button to move the paragraph's left indentation 0.5″ to the left.

  F Click the Increase Indent button to move the paragraph's left indentation 0.5″ to the right.

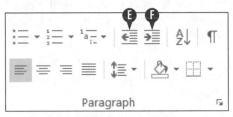

Figure 3-4: Controls for changing indentation on the Ribbon.

You can also change indentation by dragging indent markers on the ruler.

If the ruler doesn't appear, mark the Ruler check box on the View tab.

Select the paragraphs to affect and then drag a marker, as follows:

G The upper triangle on the left is the First Line Indent marker. Drag it to affect only the first line.

H The lower triangle on the left is the Hanging Indent marker. Drag it to affect all except the first line.

I The square on the left is the Left Indent marker. Drag it to affect all lines on the left. If you drag it when the First Line Indent and Hanging Indent markers are set to different values, it moves them both, maintaining the relative distance between them.

J The triangle on the right is the Right Indent marker. Drag it to affect the right indent (all lines).

K The margins for the entire document are indicated by the spot where gray meets white on the ruler. You can drag that spot to change the margins for the while document (not just the selected paragraphs).

Figure 3-5: Drag markers on the ruler to change indents.

 You can also create a first-line indent by positioning the insertion point at the beginning of a paragraph and pressing the Tab key. Normally this would place a 0.5-inch tab at the beginning of the paragraph, but the Word AutoCorrect feature immediately converts it to a real first-line indent for you.

To set left and/or right indents with precise numeric values, use the Left and Right text boxes on the Layout tab, in the Paragraph group. For each of these, enter a number or use the increment buttons:

L Left indent.

M Right indent.

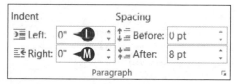

Figure 3-6: You can use the Layout tab's Paragraph group to control left and right indentation.

For the ultimate in indent control, follow these steps to use the Paragraph dialog box:

1 Select the paragraph(s) to affect.

2. Click the dialog box launcher in the Paragraph group on the Home or Layout tab.

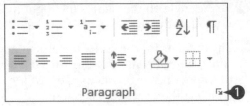

Figure 3-7: Click the dialog box launcher.

3 Set left and right indents in the Left and Right text boxes, respectively.

4 (Optional) Open the Special drop-down list and choose First Line or Hanging.

5 Enter the amount of first-line or hanging indent in the By box.

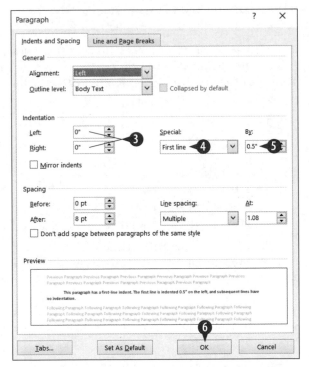

Figure 3-8: Set up indents in the Paragraph dialog box.

6 Click OK.

Adjust a paragraph's vertical spacing

Vertical spacing refers to the amount of space (also known as the leading) between each line. A paragraph has three values you can set for its spacing:

- **Line spacing:** The space between the lines within a multi-line paragraph

- **Before:** Extra spacing added above the first line of the paragraph

- **After:** Extra spacing added below the last line of the paragraph

Adjust line spacing within the paragraph

To change the line spacing, follow these steps:

1. Select all the paragraphs to affect.

2. On the Home tab, in the Paragraph group, click the Line and Paragraph Spacing button to open its menu.

3. Click a number that represents the desired line spacing. 1.0 is single-spaced, 2.0 is double-spaced (one blank line between each line), and so on. The exact amount of space in points depends on the font size used.

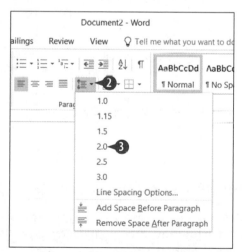

Figure 3-9: Choose a line spacing amount for the selected paragraphs.

Adjust spacing before or after the paragraph

To change the spacing before or after the paragraph(s), follow these steps:

1. Select all the paragraphs to affect.

2. On the Home tab, in the Paragraph group, click the Line and Paragraph Spacing button to open its menu.

3. Click the Add Space or Remove Space command for before or after the paragraph as needed. The default amount of space before a paragraph is 12 points, and the default amount after a paragraph is 8 points, both regardless of font size.

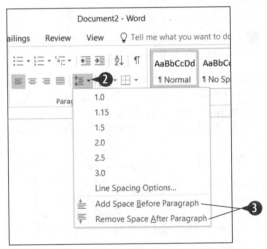

Figure 3-10: Turn the spacing before and/or after the paragraph on or off.

Use custom spacing values

You can use the Paragraph dialog box to control vertical spacing for much more precise control than is possible with the Ribbon method. For example, you can specify a certain amount of space (in points) before and after the paragraph, and you can use custom values for line spacing.

1. Select all the paragraphs to affect.

2. Click the dialog box launcher in the Paragraph group on the Home or Layout tab.

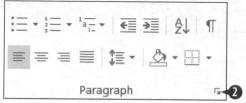

Figure 3-11: Click the dialog box launcher.

③ In the Spacing section, change the values in the Before and After boxes as desired.

④ Open the Line spacing drop-down list and choose a unit of measurement:

- *Single:* No extra space between lines.

- *1.5 lines:* One-half a line of extra space between lines. The actual amount of space depends on the largest font size used in the paragraph.

- *Double:* One line of extra space between lines. The actual amount of space depends on the largest font size used in the paragraph.

- *At least:* Sets the minimum line height to a precise amount for each line of the paragraph. Depending on the largest font size used in the paragraph, the actual amount of space each line occupies may be greater than the setting.

- *Exactly:* Sets a precise line height for each line of the paragraph and does not take font size into consideration.

  If you aren't sure what font sizes you will be using in the final version of your document, don't use Exactly. If you specify a line height that is smaller than needed for the font size you have chosen, some letters may appear cut off at the top or bottom.

- *Multiple:* Like Double except you specify the multiplier. For example, entering 3 results in triple-spacing (two blank lines between each line). You can use decimal places in the number, such as 3.25.

⑤ Enter the measurement in the At box if a measurement is required for the setting you chose in step 4.

⑥ Click OK.

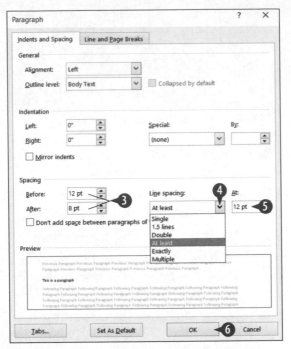

Figure 3-12: Adjust line spacing in the Paragraph dialog box.

Place a border around a paragraph

You can add a border around the outside of a single paragraph to make it stand out from the rest of the document. You can also place a border around multiple paragraphs to visually group those paragraphs together, separate from the rest. Here are some things to remember about placing borders around paragraphs:

Ⓐ If you place the same border around two or more consecutive paragraphs, the border surrounds them as a group, as in Figure 3-13. That way, you can create groups of paragraphs that appear "boxed" together for special emphasis.

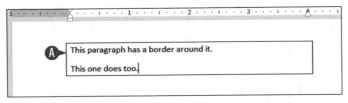

Figure 3-13: A border around two consecutive paragraphs.

B A border need not be on every side of the paragraph. You can place a border only on the bottom side, for example, to make it look like there is a horizontal line under the paragraph.

C You can also put differently formatted lines on different sides. For example, you could have a thick border on the bottom and right sides and a thinner border on the top and left sides, resulting in a border that looks somewhat 3-D.

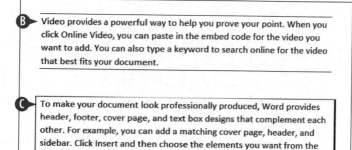

B▸ Video provides a powerful way to help you prove your point. When you click Online Video, you can paste in the embed code for the video you want to add. You can also type a keyword to search online for the video that best fits your document.

C To make your document look professionally produced, Word provides header, footer, cover page, and text box designs that complement each other. For example, you can add a matching cover page, header, and sidebar. Click Insert and then choose the elements you want from the different galleries.

Figure 3-14: Paragraphs with custom borders applied.

- To apply a basic border on one or more sides of a paragraph (or a group of paragraphs), use the Borders button in the Paragraph group of the Home tab.

  D To place a border on just one side of the paragraph, use the Bottom, Top, Left, or Right Border command. Repeat to apply to multiple sides.

  E To remove all borders from the paragraph, choose No Border.

  F To apply borders to all sides, choose All Borders. Note that if multiple paragraphs are selected, borders apply to each side of each paragraph; they don't appear in a single box as in Figure 3-13.

  G To apply borders to all sides of the selected block of paragraphs, choose Outside Borders. In a multi-paragraph selection, this results in a single border around the contiguous group, as in Figure 3-13. In a single-paragraph selection, it is identical to All Borders.

H The Inside border options apply to multi-paragraph selections only, and place borders only between paragraphs, not around the outsides. These same border options are also used for table border formatting, and Inside options are more relevant in tables than for paragraphs.

To create custom borders that include different line thicknesses, patterns (such as dashed or dotted), and colors, use the Borders and Shading dialog box. Follow these steps:

1. Select the paragraphs to affect.

2 On the Home tab, in the Paragraph group, click the down arrow on the Borders button to open its menu, as in Figure 3-15.

3 Click Borders and Shading. The Borders and Shading dialog box opens with the Borders tab displayed.

4 In the Style list, select the desired line style. Some of the styles are dashed or dotted; others consist of multiple lines or different line thicknesses.

5 Open the Color drop-down list and choose a color for the border.

6 Open the Width drop-down list and choose a width if you want a different width than the default for the style you chose in step 4.

7A Click one of the presets under Setting, such as Box, to apply the border to all sides.

OR

7B Click a button in the Preview area for a certain side of the paragraph. Repeat for other sides as needed.

8 Click OK.

If you want different border formatting for different sides, perform steps 1–6 and select certain sides in step 7, and then repeat steps 4–6 and select different sides in step 7.

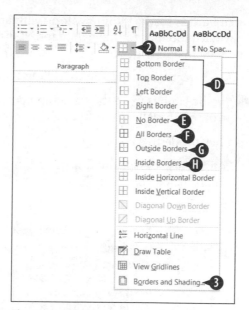

Figure 3-15: Choose borders from the Borders button's menu.

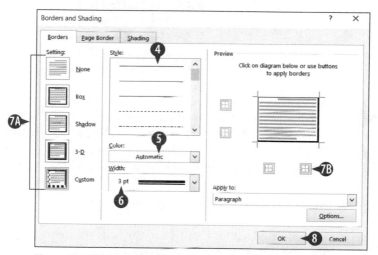

Figure 3-16: Set up custom borders.

Shade a paragraph's background

Shading a paragraph helps it stand out from the rest of the document and adds visual interest to the text. You can use shading with or without a border.

As with a border, shading follows along with any indent settings you may have specified for the paragraph. If the paragraph is indented, the shading is also.

To shade a paragraph's background, follow these steps:

1 On the Home tab, in the Paragraph group, click the down arrow on the Fill button to open its palette.

2 Click the desired color.

You can also click More Colors and then choose from the Colors dialog box. (See **A** in Figure 3-17.)

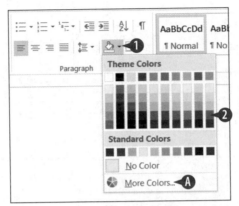

Figure 3-17: Choose a paragraph fill color.

Word applies only solid-color shading to paragraphs. If you want a gradient shading behind a paragraph or you want some other special shading effect such as a pattern, texture, or graphic, place a text box (choose Insert ⇨ Text Box) and then apply the desired shading to the text box as a Fill, like you would with a graphic.

Create a bulleted or numbered list

Use a bulleted list for lists where the order of items isn't significant, and the same "bullet" character (such as • or ⇨) is used in front of each item. You might use a bulleted list for a packing list for a trip, for example, or a to-do list.

Use a numbered list for lists where the order of items is significant and where a sequential step number is used to indicate order. A numbered list might contain the steps for a recipe or a meeting agenda.

Word makes it easy to create bulleted and numbered lists in your documents. You can create a list from existing paragraphs, or you can turn on the list feature and type the list as you go.

Convert text to a list

To convert existing text to a list, follow these steps:

1 Select the paragraphs to convert to a list.

2 On the Home tab, in the Paragraph group, click the Bullets button or the Numbering button.

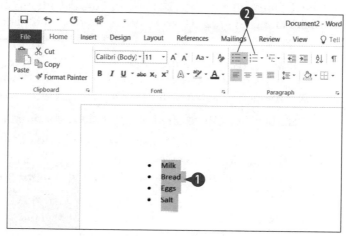

Figure 3-18: Apply bullets or numbering to an existing list.

Type a new list

To enter new text into a list format, follow these steps:

1. Position the insertion point at the desired location.

2 On the Home tab, in the Paragraph group, click the Bullets button or the Numbering button.

3 Type the first list item, and then press Enter.

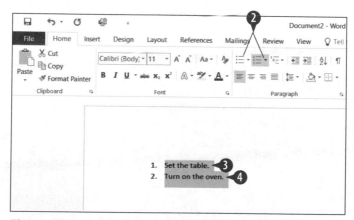

Figure 3-19: Apply bullets or numbering to an existing list.

④ Repeat step 3 until the list is complete.

5. Press Enter twice in a row, or click the Bullets button or Numbering button again, to turn off the list feature.

Change the bullet character or number type

The default bullet is a black circle, and the default number is an Arabic numeral (1, 2, 3). Word offers a variety of other choices, however.

Ⓐ When using the Bullets button or the Numbering button, instead of clicking the button face, click the down arrow to open a list of options.

Ⓑ Then select the desired bullet character or number type.

Ⓒ For even more choices, click Define New Number Format (or Define New Bullet if using bullets rather than numbering). You can then set up a new format in a dialog box.

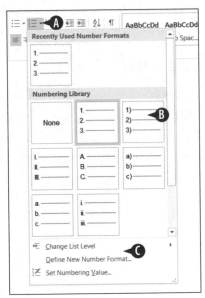

Figure 3-20: Choose a different numbering type.

Apply styles

A style is a named set of formatting specifications. Using a style makes it easy to apply consistent formatting throughout a document. For example, you might apply the Heading 1 style to all headings in the document and the Normal style to all the regular body text. Here are the advantages of this approach:

- **Ease:** Applying a style is easier than manually applying formatting. And changing a style's formatting is a snap. If you want the headings to look different, for example, you can modify the Heading 1 style to change them all at once.

- **Consistency:** You don't have to worry about all the headings being formatted consistently; because they're all using the same style, they're automatically all the same.

By default, each paragraph is assigned a Normal style. The template in use determines the styles available and how they're defined.

In Word 2016, in documents that use the default blank (Normal) template, the Normal style uses Calibri 11-point font and left-aligns the text, with no indentation.

- Ⓐ The Styles gallery on the Home tab contains shortcuts for commonly used styles. The first row appears on the Ribbon itself.

- Ⓑ You can see the rest of it by clicking the More button to open the full gallery.

- Ⓒ To open the Styles pane, click the dialog box launcher on the Styles group.

- Ⓓ Not all styles appear in the Styles gallery — only the ones that are designated to appear there in their definition. The rest of them appear only in the Styles pane.

- Ⓔ To apply a style, select the paragraph(s) that you want to affect or move the insertion point into the paragraph. Then click the style you want to apply, either in the Styles gallery or in the Styles pane.

- Ⓕ If the Show Preview check box is marked, the Styles pane shows each style name using the formatting that style applies.

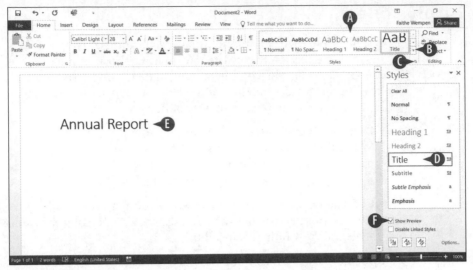

Figure 3-21: Choose a style from the Styles gallery or from the Styles pane.

Modify styles

You can modify a style in two ways: by example or by manually changing the style's definition. The by-example method is much easier, but somewhat less flexible.

Modify a style by example

To modify a style by example, follow these steps.

1. Apply the style to a paragraph.

2. Manually change the paragraph's formatting. For example, you might change the font, font size, color, indentation, and/or line spacing.

3. In the Style gallery or in the Styles pane, right-click the style. A menu appears.

4. Click Update *stylename* to Match Selection, where *stylename* is the style's name.

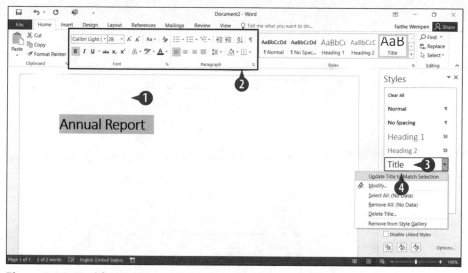

Figure 3-22: Modify a style by updating it to match a paragraph's current formatting.

Modify a style by definition

To modify the definition of a style, follow these steps:

1 In the Style gallery or in the Styles pane, right-click the style. A menu appears.

2 Click Modify.

Figure 3-23: Right-click a style and choose Modify.

3 If desired, type a different name in the Name box.

4 Use the controls under Formatting to redefine the style's character and paragraph formatting.

5 Click the Format button. A menu opens.

Figure 3-24: Redefine the style.

⑥ Click the type of formatting you would like to fine-tune. A dialog box appears for that formatting type. For example, Figure 3-25 shows the dialog box you see if you choose Numbering.

⑦ Select formatting options and then click OK to return to the Modify Style dialog box.

8. Repeat steps 5–7 to further define the style as desired.

⑨ (Optional) Mark or clear the Add to the Styles gallery check box to determine whether or not this style appears in the Styles gallery on the Ribbon.

⑩ (Optional) If you want these changes to be reflected in all new documents based on the current template, click New documents based on this template.

⑪ Click OK.

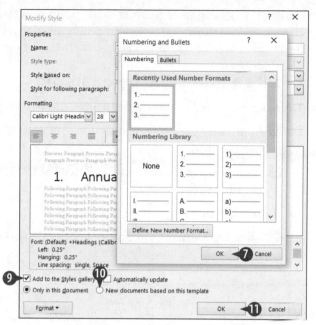

Figure 3-25: Define style settings in one or more of the dialog boxes for individual formatting types.

Create new styles

You can also create your own styles. This is especially useful if you want to build a template that you can give to other people to make sure that everyone formats documents the same way, such as in a group where each person assembles a different section of a report.

When you create your own styles, you can name them anything you like. Most people like to name styles based on their purposes, to make it easier to choose which style to apply. For example, *Figure Caption* would be a good name; *Style13* would not.

Just like when modifying a style, you can create a new style either by example or by manually specifying a style definition.

Each new style is based on an existing style (usually the Normal style) so that if there's a particular formatting aspect you don't specify, it trickles down from the parent style. For example, suppose you create a new style named Important, and you base it on the Normal style. The Important style starts out with identical formatting to the Normal style, which is Calibri 11-point font. You might then modify it to have bold, red text. The definition of Important is Normal+bold+red. That's significant if you later change the definition of Normal to 12-point font. That font size change trickles down to Important automatically, and all text formatted with the Important style becomes 12 points in size.

Create a new style by example

To create a new style by example, follow these steps.

1. Apply a style to some text that is similar to the style you want to create.

2. Change the text's formatting as needed to make it an example of the style you want to create.

3. Select the text.

4. Click the More button on the Styles gallery on the Ribbon to open the Styles gallery and its menu.

Figure 3-26: Set up some text for the new style's formatting and then open the Styles gallery.

5. Click Create a Style.

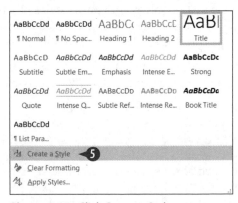

Figure 3-27: Click Create a Style.

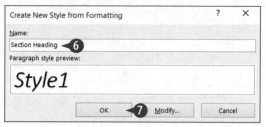

Figure 3-28: Assign a name to the new style and click OK.

⑥ In the Name box, type a name for the new style.

⑦ Click OK.

Create a new style by definition

To create a new style by defining its formatting, follow these steps.

1. Apply a style to some text that is similar to the style you want to create.

2. If the Styles pane does not appear, click the dialog box launcher for the Styles group on the Home tab to make it appear.

3. Click the New Style button.

4. In the Name box, type a name for the new style.

    By default the Style for following paragraph setting is set to the new style itself. This is appropriate if the new style is for body paragraphs. If the new style will be used for headings, and you will usually want the paragraph that follows the heading to be some other style, such as Normal, open the Style for following paragraph drop-down list and choose the desired style. (See Ⓐ in Figure 3-29.)

5. Go to step 4 in the section "Modify a style by definition" earlier in this chapter and complete that procedure to finish defining the style.

Figure 3-29: Create a new style by definition.

CHAPTERFOUR

Formatting Sections, Pages, and Documents

Some types of formatting cannot be applied to individual words or paragraphs, but only to entire pages and sections at once. For example, you can't set the paper size or orientation for individual paragraphs. This chapter looks at a variety of these document-wide settings.

The term "document-wide" is not entirely accurate to describe these types of formatting, however. It's true that normally a document would have only one paper size, for example, or only one number-of-columns setting. However, Word enables you to create section breaks in documents, and have different document-wide settings on either side of the break. A section break enables you to, for example, store an envelope in the same document file as a business letter. This chapter explains how to create and use section breaks to allow for flexibility in your document layouts.

Set margins

Margins are the empty spaces on each side of the page. A normal amount of margin (or at least what Word calls "Normal") is 1" on all sides. You might want to change the margins to accommodate special situations, though. (Helpful hint: if you're a student, don't try to make your research paper seem longer by increasing the margins. Teachers are wise to that trick.)

In This Chapter

➤ Setting the margins

➤ Setting page size and orientation

➤ Creating page headers and footers

➤ Creating page and section breaks

➤ Setting up multicolumn documents

➤ Applying a page border

➤ Applying page background shading

➤ Adding line numbers

Word comes with several margin presets, such as Narrow (0.5″ all around) and Wide (1″ at top and bottom, 2″ on left and right). You can also set custom margins, where you get to specify an exact number for each side of the page individually.

Margins apply to the entire document. If you need part of the document to have different margins from the rest, create a section break, as explained in "Create section breaks" later in this chapter.

① On the Layout tab, click the Margins button.

②A Click one of the presets. You're done.

OR

②B Click Custom Margins to open the Page Setup dialog box to the Margins tab.

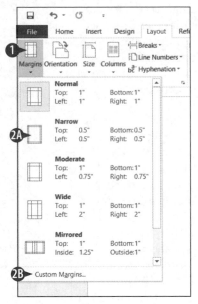

Figure 4-1: Choose a margin preset from the Margins button's drop-down list.

③ Enter the desired value in the Top, Bottom, left, and Right boxes.

The Gutter and Gutter Position settings are for situations where you are printing a double-sided publication that will be bound like a book. The margin closest to the binding should be somewhat larger than the rest to accommodate the binding; depending on whether it's an odd- or even-numbered page, that extra gutter amount should be either on the left or right side of the page. Using the Gutter setting ensures that each page has the gutter on the correct side.

4 Click OK.

Figure 4-2: Set custom margins in the Page Setup dialog box, on the Margins tab.

Set page size and orientation

Page size is the paper size on which you'll be printing your work. You have a page size even if you aren't printing, though; documents that appear onscreen have a page size too, of course. The default page size in Word is Letter, which is 8.5" x 11".

Page orientation is the direction that the text runs on the page. The default is *portrait,* in which the lines of text are parallel to the narrower edge of the paper. The alternative is *landscape,* in which the lines are parallel to the wider edge.

Set page size

You can choose a page size preset from the Size drop-down list on the Layout tab, or you can set a custom page size if none of the ones on the list match the page size you want.

1 On the Layout tab, click the Size button.

2A Click one of the presets. You're done.

OR

2B Click More Paper Sizes to open the Page Setup dialog box to the Paper tab.

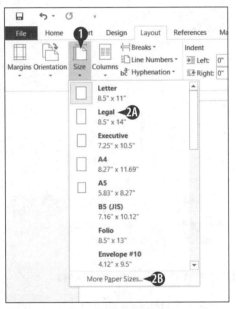

Figure 4-3: Choose a paper size preset from the Size button's drop-down list.

3A Open the Paper size drop-down list and choose a preset. This list of presets is more extensive than the list on the Size button.

OR

3B Enter the paper's measurements in the Width and Height text boxes.

If you don't know what the paper size is called, it may be difficult locating it by name on the list in step 3A. You may find it quicker to enter its measurements in step 3B.

④ Click OK.

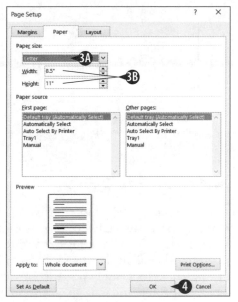

Figure 4-4: Choose a custom paper size in the Page Setup dialog box, on the Paper tab.

When printing a multipage document, you might want the first page to pull paper from a different paper tray in your printer. For example, it is common in multipage business letters for the first page to be on letterhead and subsequent pages to be on plain paper. In the Paper source area of the dialog box (refer to Figure 4-4) you can choose a different paper source for the first page and for other pages.

Set page orientation

Page orientation is pretty simple; there aren't any options for it. Here's how you do it:

❶ On the Layout tab, click Orientation.

❷ Click Portrait or Landscape.

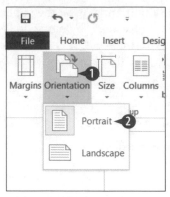

Figure 4-5: Switch between portrait and landscape orientations.

Use page headers and footers

Headers and footers contain content that repeats at the top and bottom of each page, respectively, outside of the top and bottom margins. Every document has a header and footer area, which are both empty by default. The header and footer appear in Print Layout view, Read Mode, and Web Layout view, and also on the printed page. (If you're in Draft view, you might want to switch to Print Layout view to follow along in this section more easily.)

You can place text in the header and footer that repeats on every page, and you can insert a variety of codes in them that display information such as page numbers, dates, and times.

Number the pages

Have you ever dropped a stack of papers that needed to stay in a certain order? If the pages were numbered, putting them back together was fairly simple. If not, what a frustrating, time-consuming task.

Fortunately, Word makes it very easy to number your document pages. And you can choose from a variety of numbering styles and formats. When you number pages in Word, you don't have to manually type the numbers onto each page. Instead, you place a code in the document that numbers the pages automatically. Sweet!

When you use the Page Number feature in Word, it automatically inserts the proper code in either the header or the footer so that each page is numbered consecutively.

TIP Page numbers are visible only in Print Layout view, Read Mode, Print Preview, and on the printouts themselves. You don't see the page numbers if you're working in Draft view or Web Layout view, even though they're there.

To number pages, follow these steps:

1. On the Insert tab, click Page Number. A menu appears.

2. Point to Top of Page or Bottom of Page, depending on where you want the page numbers. A submenu appears.

3. Click one of the presets. The document enters header/footer mode, and the new page number appears in either the header or footer.

TIP The Plain Number 1, 2, and 3 presets are identical except for the placement of the page number, on the left, center, or right, respectively.

Figure 4-6: Choose a page number position.

4. If you want to further edit the header or footer, do so. Otherwise, double-click in the main part of the document to exit from header/footer mode.

TIP In step 4 you can also click Close Header and Footer on the Header & Footer Tools Design tab to return to normal editing.

Here are some additional things you can do with page numbers in Word from the Page Number button's list (Figure 4-6):

- Point to Page Margins for a selection of presets in which the page numbers appear in the right or left margin area.

- Point to Current Position for a selection of presets that enable you to place the page number code in the body of the document rather than in the header or footer.

- Click Format Page Numbers to open a dialog box in which you can select a page number format. *Format* in this context does not mean font, size, or color; instead it means the numbering format, like Arabic numerals (1, 2, 3) versus Roman numerals (I, II, III).

- Click Remove Page Numbers to remove all page numbering codes.

Type text in the header or footer area

In addition to a page number, you can put other content in the header and footer areas of your document. For example, if you're typing the minutes of a club meeting, you might want to put the club's name in the header so that it appears across the top of each page.

Here are two ways of putting content into them: You can use presets to insert codes and formatting, or you can type text and insert codes manually into the headers and footers.

To use a preset, do the following:

1 On the Insert tab, click the Header button, or click the Footer button.

2 Click one of the presets that appears on the list.

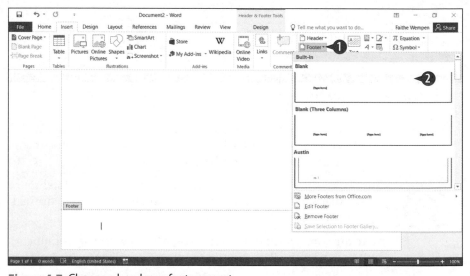

Figure 4-7: Choose a header or footer preset.

To create your own header or footer, follow these steps:

1A. In Page Layout view, double-click the top or bottom margin area of the page.

OR

1B. On the Insert tab, click the Header button or the Footer button and then choose Edit Header or Edit Footer from the menu that appears.

The Header & Footer Tools Design tab appears on the Ribbon.

2. Position the insertion point where you want the header or footer text to appear.

The header and footer have preset tab stops: a center tab stop in the center, and a right-aligned tab stop at the right. So, in step 2, if you want to place something in the center, press Tab once; if you want to place something on the right, press Tab twice.

3. Type the text that you want to appear.

4 (Optional) If you want to switch between the header and footer, click Go to Header or Go to Footer.

5 Click Close Header and Footer.

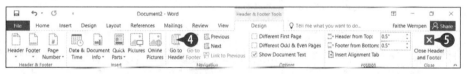

Figure 4-8: Type text into the header or footer area.

In a complex document, you can get very fancy with headers and footers using some of the advanced options on the Header & Footer Tools Design tab, as shown in Figure 4-9. For example:

A You can choose to have a different header and footer on the first page. That might be useful if the first page is a cover sheet or title page.

B You can also have different headers and footers on odd and even pages. That's handy when you're printing a double-sided booklet, for example, so the page numbers can always be on the outside edges.

C You can also create section breaks (covered later in this chapter) and have a different header and footer in each section. When you use multiple headers and footers in a document, you can move between them by clicking the Previous and Next buttons.

D To adjust the header and footer size and positioning, use the settings in the Position group. You can specify a Header from Top and Footer from Bottom position there. For example, if you want a taller header section, increase the Header from Top setting.

Figure 4-9: Use the Header & Footer Tools Design tab to set options for your headers and footers.

Insert a page number code in a header or footer

If you already have the header or footer open for editing (steps 1 and 2 of the previous procedure), you can easily insert a page number code at the insertion point's current position by doing the following:

1 On the Header & Footer Tools Design tab, click Page Number.

2 Click Current Position.

3 Click Plain Number.

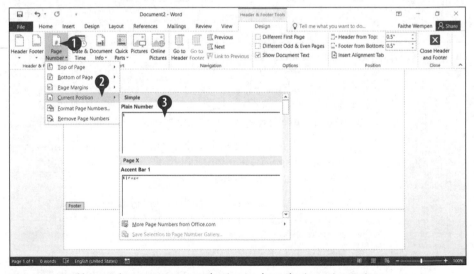

Figure 4-10: You can insert a page numbering code at the insertion point.

Insert a date or time code in a header or footer

If you want to insert a date or time code that automatically updates, do the following:

1 On the Header & Footer Tools Design tab, click Date & Time.

2 Click the desired format.

3 Mark the Update automatically check box.

4 Click OK.

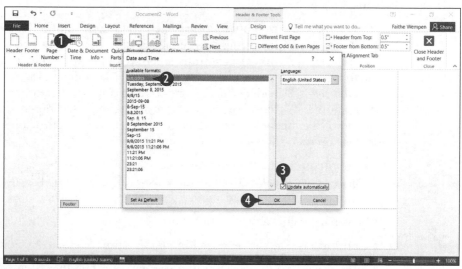

Figure 4-11: Insert an automatically updating date and time code in the header or footer.

Create page breaks

Word automatically creates a page break when you reach the bottom of a page. That's called a *soft page break* because it is variable. If you delete some content on the previous page, the page break point changes. You can also create *hard page breaks*, which are manually created breaks that don't change when the document content changes. For example, you might insert a hard page break to start a new chapter of a story on a new page.

The easiest way to create a hard page break is to press Ctrl+Enter. That way you don't even have to take your hands off the keyboard. You can also choose Layout, Breaks, Page.

To delete a hard page break, move the insertion point to the top of the page that follows the break, and then press Backspace.

If you have a hard time finding the page break to delete it, switch to Draft view.

Create section breaks

Word has a lot of settings that are considered document-wide—in other words, they affect every page of the document. These include vertical page alignment, page size and orientation, line numbering, newspaper-style columns, page watermarks, and headers and footers. These settings are stored in the document's end-of-file marker.

However, there are plenty of times when you might want different document-wide settings in a certain portion of a document, like a different number of columns or a different chapter title in the footer. For those situations, you can create section breaks. A *section break* is a divider that separates one section of a document from another. A section break can store all the same settings as an end-of-file marker, so you can have different document-wide settings on each side of the section break.

It's important to understand that a section break is not the same thing as a page break, although some types of section break also serve as page breaks. There are five types of section breaks:

- **New page:** Starts a new section on a new page.

- **Continuous:** Starts a new section on the same page.

- **Even page**: Starts a new section on a new page, and that page must be even-numbered.

- **Odd page:** Starts a new section on a new page, and that page must be odd-numbered.

- **New column:** Starts the new section in a new column. This is relevant only in a multicolumn layout. (See "Set up a multicolumn document" later in this chapter.)

If you select text before you insert a section break, you actually get two section breaks, one on each side of the selection. This places the selection in its own separate section from the rest of the document. If you do not select text before inserting a section break, you get a single break at the insertion point.

To create a section break, follow these steps:

1A. Select the content that you want to be in its own section.

OR

1B. Position the insertion point where you want the section break to occur.

2 On the Layout tab, click Breaks. A menu opens.

3 Click the desired section break type from the Section Breaks area of the menu.

Figure 4-12: Choose a section break type from the Breaks button's menu.

To delete a section break, position the insertion point just below the section break and then press Backspace. If you have trouble locating the section break, switch to Draft view. Both page and section breaks appear as horizontal lines in Draft view, as shown in Figure 4-13.

Figure 4-13: Section breaks are easily visible in Draft view.

Set up a multicolumn document

There are two kinds of multicolumn layouts you can create in Word: tabular and newspaper-style.

A tabular layout is a table that's used for text positioning. Create a table, as you will learn in Chapter 5, and remove the borders from all cells. The text lines up neatly in the table columns, and your audience is none the wiser that you used a table to make the layout. A tabular layout can coexist in a document with normal text without using section breaks. Tabular layouts are good for aligning the entries in multiple columns with one another, such as a grid of names and addresses.

Newspaper columns, which I cover here, are entirely different. Text snakes down a narrow column from top to bottom, and then starts up again at the top of the next column. In order to use varying numbers of newspaper-style columns in different parts of a document, you have to employ section breaks. Newspaper columns are good for creating newsletters, brochures, and other graphical publications.

Follow these steps to use multiple newspaper-style columns:

1A. To affect only certain paragraphs, select them.

OR

1B. Position the insertion point within the section that you want to affect. If the document has no section breaks, the setting will apply to the entire document.

2 On the Layout tab, click Columns.

3 Click the desired number of columns.

A The Left and Right settings in Figure 4-14 represent two-column layouts where one column is wider than the other.

B If you want more control over the column widths, choose More Columns from the menu, and then specify exact column widths in the Columns dialog box.

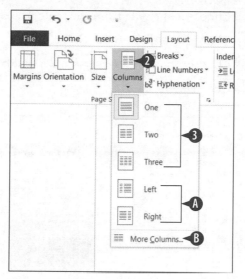

Figure 4-14: Select a number of columns.

If you selected certain paragraphs in step 1A, Word creates two new section breaks in step 3: one at the beginning of the selected text and one at the end of it. The setting you choose in step 3 applies only to the section between those two breaks.

To return a section to using only one column, repeat the steps, selecting One as the number of columns.

Create a page border

A *page border* is a decorative border around the entire page. It is positioned according to the margin settings for that page. So, for example, if you have 1″ margins set up for all sides of the document, the border will appear 1″ from the edge on all sides.

Create a simple page border

You can apply a border to an entire page in much the same way you did with a paragraph in Chapter 3. You can use any combination of line style, weight, and color you like.

To create a page border, follow these steps:

1 On the Design tab, click Page Borders. The Borders and Shading dialog box opens with the Page Border tab displayed.

2 Choose a line style from the Style list.

3 Choose a color from the Color list.

4 Choose a line thickness from the Width list.

5 Click OK.

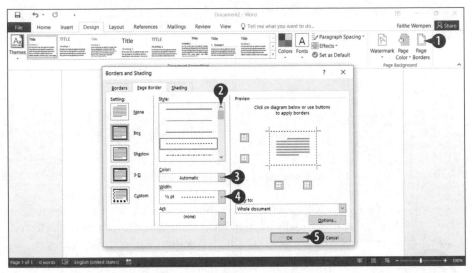

Figure 4-15: Set the options for a page border.

Apply BorderArt

BorderArt uses a repeated graphic image to create a page border. You can select an image and then select a size at which the image should appear. That size determines the border thickness.

To apply BorderArt, follow these steps:

1. On the Design tab, click Page Borders. The Borders and Shading dialog box opens with the Page Border tab displayed.

2 Open the BorderArt list and click the desired image.

3 In the Width box, use the arrow buttons to increase or decrease the size.

④ Check the border in the Preview area to see how it will appear.

⑤ Click OK.

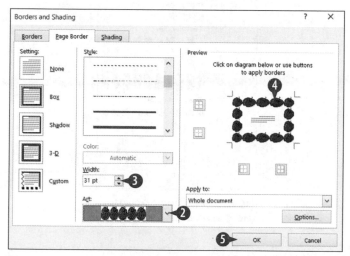

Figure 4-16: Create a graphical border with BorderArt.

To turn off BorderArt, repeat the steps but choose (none) in step 2.

Apply a page background color

Pages have no background by default. That's usually a good thing, because printer ink is expensive, and you'd go broke printing a colored background on every page. Sometimes, though, you might want a background, such as in a document that you plan to distribute online rather than in print.

To color the background, follow these steps:

① On the Design tab, click Page Color.

②A Click the desired color from the Theme Colors or Standard Colors section.

OR

②B Click More Colors, and then select a color from the Colors dialog box and click OK.

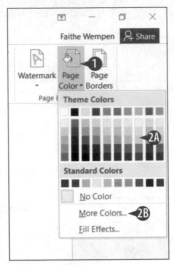

Figure 4-17: Choose a page background color.

Add line numbers

Line numbering can help people refer to specific locations in the document more easily when they are collaborating on drafts. Some legal documents also make use of line numbers.

Line numbering is a document-wide setting (although you can apply it on a section-by-section basis, as with most other document formatting).

You can enable line numbering at a basic level by choosing a setting from the Line Numbers button's drop-down list on the Layout tab, as shown in Figure 4-18. Turn line numbering off by choosing None from this list. (See **A** in Figure 4-18.)

For additional numbering options, do the following:

1 On the Layout tab, click Line Numbers, and then click Line Numbering Options. The Page Setup dialog box opens to the Layout tab.

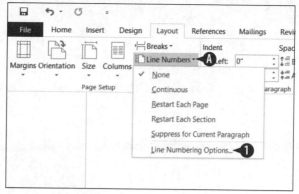

Figure 4-18: Choose a line numbering setting.

2️⃣ Click the Line Numbers button.

3️⃣ Mark the Add line numbering check box.

4️⃣ Set any line numbering options as desired.

5️⃣ Click OK.

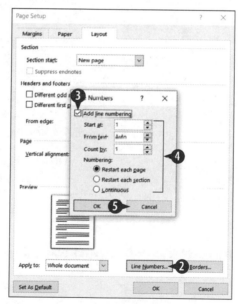

Figure 4-19: Access the Line Numbers button from the Layout tab.

CHAPTER FIVE

Working with Tables and Graphics in Word

Tables help you present rows and columns of data in an orderly way. You can draw tables or create them by using a preset grid.

You can dress up Word documents with a variety of graphics. Graphics can make a document more interesting and can explain visual concepts more easily than text alone. You know the old saying . . . a picture is worth a thousand words. You can import pictures from online sources, use pictures from your collection, or create artwork inside of Word with drawing tools (which is beyond the scope of this chapter).

In this chapter, you learn how to insert and format tables and images and how to position and format pictures in a document. You also learn about the Caption feature in Word, which can caption and number images automatically.

Create tables

A *table* is a grid of rows and columns, somewhat like a spreadsheet. Each of the row-and-column intersections is a *cell*. You can type text into a cell as if it were a text box. Tables are useful for displaying information in multicolumn layouts, such as address lists and schedules. You may be surprised at all the uses you can find for tables in your documents!

In This Chapter

⟹ Creating tables

⟹ Selecting and resizing rows and columns

⟹ Adding and removing rows and columns

⟹ Applying borders and shading to table cells

⟹ Inserting a picture from a file

⟹ Changing a picture's wrap setting

⟹ Moving and resizing a picture

⟹ Captioning and auto-numbering pictures

To create a table in Word, you can either insert a table as a whole or draw one line by line. In most cases, if you want a standard-looking table (that is, one with equally sized rows and columns), your best bet is to insert it. If you want an unusual-looking table, such as with different numbers of columns in some rows, you may be better off drawing the table. You can also convert existing text to a table.

Insert a table

When you insert a table, you have to tell Word to start with a specific number of rows and columns. You can modify the table later to add or remove rows and columns as needed. Creating a table by specifying rows and columns works well when you want a table in which all of the rows and columns are the same width and height (or at least starting out that way).

There are two ways to create a table by specifying the rows and columns you want. Here's the first way, which is quick and simple:

1 On the Insert tab, click the Table button. A menu appears that contains a grid of squares.

2 Drag the mouse across the grid to select the number of cells you want. For example, to create a table with three rows and three columns, drag across three squares across and three squares down, as in Figure 5-1.

3. Release the mouse button. The table is created.

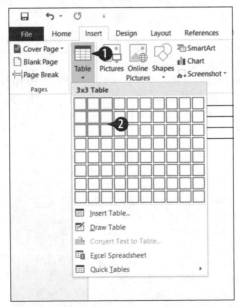

Figure 5-1: Drag across the grid to select the size of the table to create.

And here's the second way, which is a little more work but also enables you to specify some options:

1. On the Insert tab, click the Table button. A menu appears.

2. Click Insert Table. The Insert Table dialog box opens.

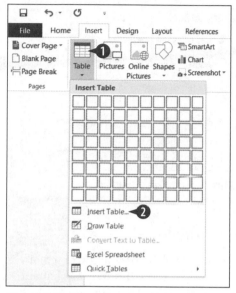

Figure 5-2: Select the Insert Table command from the menu.

3. Enter a number of columns.

4. Enter a number of rows.

5. Choose how you want the table's column width to be determined:

   - Fixed column width makes the table as wide as possible given the document's margin settings, and evenly distributes the available space among the columns.

   - AutoFit to contents allows each table cell to expand as needed as you type text in it.

   - AutoFit to window changes the size of the table as needed so the table is fully visible onscreen. This option is used when creating web pages and is not common in regular documents.

6. Click OK.

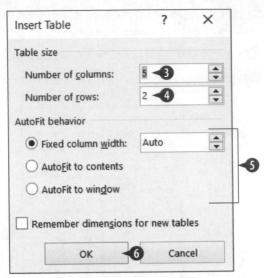

Figure 5-3: Specify the table's number of rows and columns and its AutoFit behavior.

Draw a table

Drawing a table is the best method when you need a table that has unusual row and column arrangement, such as a row that is broken into a different number of columns than other rows or a column that is much wider than the others. When you draw a table, you create each divider individually, so you have ultimate control.

To draw a table, follow these steps:

1 On the Insert tab, click the Table button. A menu appears.

2 Click Draw Table. The mouse pointer changes to a pencil.

3 Drag to draw a box that represents the outside of the table.

4 Drag to draw vertical and horizontal lines inside the box to create the rows and columns.

If you make a mistake in drawing a line, click Eraser and then click the line to erase. You can then click Draw Table to return to drawing mode. (See **A** in Figure 5-7.)

5 On the Table Tools Layout tab, click Draw Table to turn off the feature, or press the Esc key.

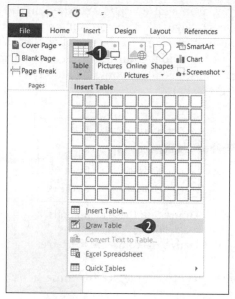

Figure 5-4: Choose the Draw Table command.

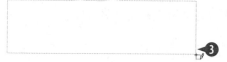

Figure 5-5: Draw the outside of the table.

Figure 5-6: Draw the inner lines of the table.

Figure 5-7: Turn off the Draw Table feature.

Convert existing text to a table

If you already have some text, you can convert it to a table without having to retype it. The catch, though, is that the text must be *delimited* somehow. In other words, there must be some consistent way that one column is to be distinguished from another. For example, you might have some text in multiple tabbed columns, with a paragraph break indicating the end of each row, as in Figure 5-8. (I've turned on the display of hidden characters in Figure 5-8 so you can see where the tab stops and paragraph breaks are.) For best results, there should be the same number of potential columns in each row. The data in Figure 5-8 works because each line contains the same number of delimiter characters (tabs).

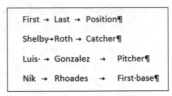

Figure 5-8: These paragraphs are delimited with tab stops, ready to be converted to a table.

To convert text to a table, follow these steps:

1. Select the text to be converted.

2. On the Insert tab, click Table.

3. Click Convert Text to Table.

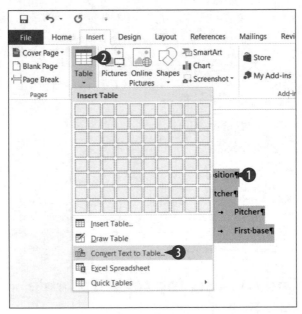

Figure 5-9: Choose Convert Text to Table.

4. Confirm the number of columns. Change the number if needed.

TIP

If the wrong number of columns is reported, you probably have an inconsistent number of delimiters in one or more of the rows. The best thing to do is click Cancel, check your delimiters, and then start over.

⑤ Change the AutoFit setting if desired. See "Insert a table" earlier in this chapter for an explanation of the options.

⑥ Choose the delimiter character if it is not already correctly selected.

⑦ Click OK. The text is converted to a table.

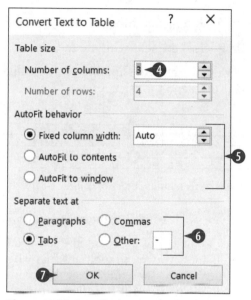

Figure 5-10: Specify the options for the conversion.

Select cells, rows, and columns

Working with a table often involves selecting one or more cells, rows, or columns. Here are some of the many ways to do this:

● To select a single cell, do any of the following:

Ⓐ Triple-click the cell.

Ⓑ Click in the lower left corner of the cell.

Ⓒ Choose Layout, Select, Select Cell.

Ⓓ Click in the cell and then press Ctrl+Shift+Right arrow.

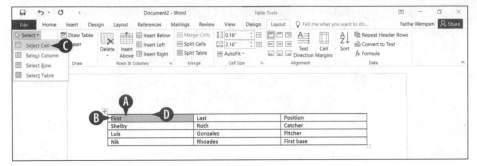

Figure 5-11: Select a single cell.

- To select a rectangular block of cells, do either of the following:

  E Drag across the cells with the mouse.

  F Click in the first cell, and then hold Shift and press arrow keys to extend the selection.

First **E**	Last	Position
Shelby	Roth	Catcher
Luis	Gonzalez **F**	Pitcher
Nik	Rhoades	First base

Figure 5-12: Select a rectangular block of cells

- To select a single row, do either of the following:

  G Click to the left of the row to be selected (outside the table). You'll know you are in the right spot when the mouse pointer becomes a white arrow that points diagonally up and to the right. (This is different from the regular mouse pointer arrow, which points diagonally up and to the left.)

  H On the Layout tab, click Select, and then click Select Row.

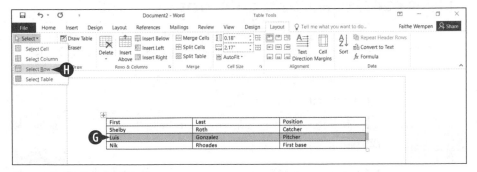

Figure 5-13: Select a single row.

• To select a single column, do either of the following:

Ⓘ Click above the column to be selected (outside the table). You'll know you are in the right spot when the mouse pointer becomes a black down-pointing arrow.

Ⓙ On the Layout tab, click Select, and then click Select Column.

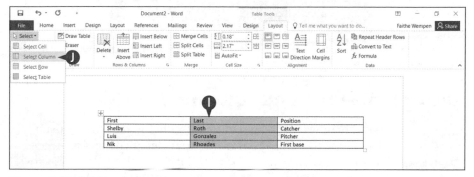

Figure 5-14: Select a single column.

Ⓚ To select multiple rows, click to the left of the first row to be selected (outside the table) and then drag up or down.

First	Last	Position
Shelby	Roth	Catcher
	Gonzalez	Pitcher
Nik	Rhoades	First base

Figure 5-15: Select multiple rows.

Ⓛ To select multiple columns, click above the first column to be selected (outside the table) and then drag right or left.

First	Last	Position
Shelby	Roth	Catcher
Luis	Gonzalez	Pitcher
Nik	Rhoades	First base

Figure 5-16: Select multiple columns.

• To select the entire table, do either of the following:

Ⓜ Click the table selector icon in the upper left corner of the table.

Ⓝ On the Layout tab, click Select, and then click Select Table.

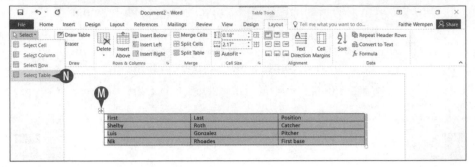

Figure 5-17: Select the entire table.

Resize table rows and columns

Word handles row height automatically for you, so you usually don't have to think about it. The row height changes as needed to accommodate the font size of the text in the cells of that row. Text in a cell wraps automatically to the next line when it runs out of room horizontally, so you can expect your table rows to expand in height as you type more text into them.

If you manually resize a row's height, the ability to auto-resize to fit content is turned off for that row. Therefore, if you add more text to that row later, Word doesn't automatically expand that row's height to accommodate it, and some text may be truncated.

In contrast, in a default-formatted table that uses fixed column widths, column width remains the same until you change it, regardless of the cell's content. If you want the width of a column to change, you must change it yourself.

Change the AutoFit setting

As you learned earlier in this chapter, there are three choices for a table's AutoFit setting. You can switch among these settings with the AutoFit drop-down list on the Table Tools Layout tab, as shown in Figure 5-18. Here are some things to remember about AutoFit:

Ⓐ AutoFit Contents allows each table cell to expand as needed as you type text in it.

Ⓑ AutoFit Window changes the size of the table as needed so the table is fully visible onscreen. This option is used when creating web pages and is not common in regular documents.

Ⓒ Fixed Column Width, the default, makes the table as wide as possible given the document's margin settings and evenly distributes the available space among the columns.

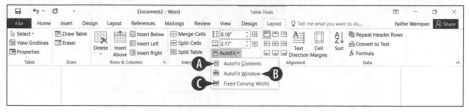

Figure 5-18: Change the table's AutoFit setting.

Resize individual rows and columns

Here are several ways to resize rows and columns.

Ⓐ To resize a row, drag its bottom border up or down.

Ⓑ To resize a column, drag its right border right or left.

Ⓒ To specify an exact height for a row, enter it in the Height box on the Table Tools Layout tab.

Ⓓ To specify an exact width for a column, enter it in the Width box.

Ⓔ To make all rows of equal height, click Distribute Rows.

Ⓕ To make all columns of equal width, click Distribute Columns.

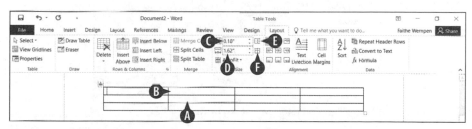

Figure 5-19: Resize rows and columns.

Add and remove rows and columns

To add a row to the bottom of a table, position the insertion point in the bottom right cell and press Tab. Using this method you can keep growing your table as you type.

To add a row or column anywhere else, follow these steps:

1. Select a row or column adjacent to where you want the new one.

If you want to insert multiple rows or columns, select multiple rows or columns.

② On the Table Tools Layout tab, click one of the Insert buttons in the Rows & Columns group.

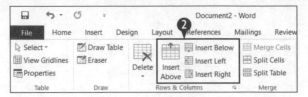

Figure 5-20: Insert rows or columns.

To remove a row or column, follow these steps:

1. Select the row(s) or column(s) to be deleted.

2. On the Table Tools Layout tab, click Delete.

You can also delete rows and columns without selecting entire rows or columns beforehand like this:

1. Click in any cell in the row or column to delete.

2 On the Table Tools Layout tab, click the down arrow on the Delete button, opening a menu.

3 Click Delete Columns or Delete Rows.

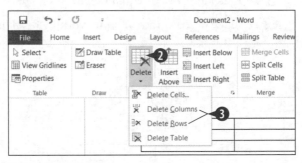

Figure 5-21: Delete rows or columns.

Apply borders to table cells

Gridlines are the dividers that separate a table's rows and columns. Gridlines can be displayed or hidden onscreen (via Table Tools Layout ⇨ View Gridlines). Gridlines do not print, and when displayed onscreen, they appear as thin blue or gray dashed lines.

You probably won't see the gridlines in most tables because they're covered by borders. A *border* is formatting applied to a gridline that makes it appear when printed. By default, table gridlines have a plain black ½ border.

You can change the borders to different colors, styles (such as dotted or dashed), and thicknesses or remove the borders altogether.

TIP When you apply a border to an individual cell, it's pretty straightforward: right, left, top, and bottom. When you apply a border to a group of cells, though, there are additional options, such as inside (applies only to the borders between the selected cells) and outside (applies only to the borders around the edge of the selection block).

Follow these steps to apply a border.

1. Select the cell(s) to affect. See "Select cells, rows, and columns" earlier in this chapter.

2A On the Table Tools Design tab, click the down arrow on the Border Styles button and click the desired border style. The colors of the border styles depend on the theme colors in the document.

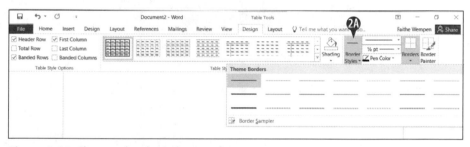

Figure 5-22: Choose a border style to apply.

OR

2B On the Table Tools Design tab, use the Line Style, Line Weight, and Pen Color lists to define the border you want.

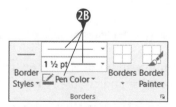

Figure 5-23: Define the border using the tools in the Borders group.

3A Click the down arrow under the Borders button to open its menu, and then click the desired border to apply. Repeat as needed to apply additional borders. For example, you might apply Top Border and then apply Bottom Border.

OR

3B Click the Border Painter button, and then click on each gridline individually in the table to apply the border settings to it. Press Esc or click the Border Painter button again to turn the feature off.

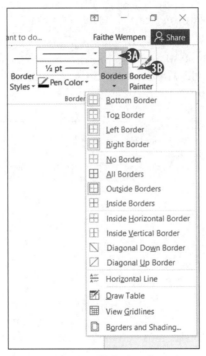

Figure 5-24: Apply the border using either the Borders button's list or the Border Painter feature.

To remove all borders from the table, open the Borders button's list and choose No Border.

You can copy border formatting with the Border Sampler feature, which is somewhat like the Format Painter feature. Open the Border Styles button's list (refer to Figure 5-22) and click Border Sampler. The mouse pointer turns into an eyedropper. Click a border to be copied, and the mouse pointer turns into a pen tool. Then click the border to receive the formatting. Press Esc to turn the feature off when finished.

Apply shading to table cells

Shading, in this context, refers to a background fill in a table cell. Each cell can have a different shading, although that would be uncommon. Shading is typically used to differentiate one row or column from another. For example, you might shade every other line a light green to simulate an old-style paper accounting ledger, or you might shade the top row of your table differently from the other rows to indicate that it holds column headings.

In Excel, you can apply special shading effects to cells, like gradients and textures. You can't do that to Word tables; shading is strictly a solid-color proposition.

To apply shading to one or more cells, follow these steps:

1. Select the cell(s) to affect. See "Select cells, rows, and columns" earlier in this chapter.

② On the Table Tools Design tab, click the down arrow on the Shading button. A palette of colors opens.

3. Click the desired color.

(A) Choose colors from the Theme Colors section of the palette to apply theme colors (which change if you change the document theme).

(B) Choose from the Standard Colors section to apply fixed colors.

(C) To remove shading from the selected cells, choose No Color.

(D) Choose More Colors to open a Color dialog box with more fixed color choices.

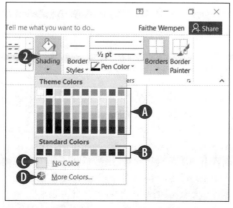

Figure 5-25: Choose a shading color for the selected cells.

Insert a picture from a file

Word accepts pictures in a wide variety of graphic formats, including JPEG, TIF, GIF, BMP, and PNG. You can drag-and-drop pictures from File Explorer directly into a Word document, or you can insert them with the following procedure.

To insert a picture from a file, follow these steps:

1. Position the insertion point where you want the picture to appear.

2 On the Insert tab, click Pictures. The Insert Picture dialog box opens.

3 Select the picture you want to insert. You might need to navigate to a different location.

4 Click Insert.

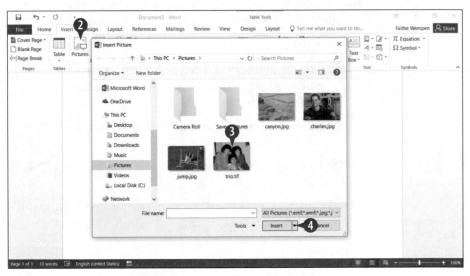

Figure 5-26: Insert a picture from your own files.

Find pictures online

The bad news about online images is: there's no more clip art. Microsoft has discontinued their clip art repository, and clip art is no longer available in Office products. The good news is that you can search the entire Internet for pictures via Bing image search without leaving Word. The search results include only images that are licensed by Creative Commons, meaning you can use them without having to pay a fee.

WARNING!

Not all Creative Commons licensed images are free for every usage. Some are free only for non-commercial use, for example. Check a picture's source and license before you commit to using it in a publication.

To insert an online image, follow these steps:

1. Position the insertion point where you want the picture to appear.

2. On the Insert tab, click Online Pictures. The Insert Pictures dialog box opens.

3. In the Bing Image Search box, type keywords that represent what you want.

4. Click the Search button or press Enter to perform the search.

Figure 5-27: Type your keywords in the Bing Image Search box.

5. Click the Close icon to clear the Creative Commons note from the screen.

6. Click the desired image.

Scroll down to see more images. (See **A** in Figure 5-28.)

7. Click Insert.

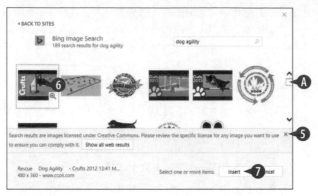

Figure 5-28: Type your keywords in the Bing Image Search box.

Manage picture placement and size

After you insert a graphic in a document, you may decide you want to move it or change how the text around it interacts with it. For example, you might want the text to wrap around the graphic or even run on top of it.

You can size and position a graphic in several ways. You can manually size or move by dragging; you can specify exact values for height, width, or position on the page; or you can use the Word placement commands to place the image in relation to other content.

Change a picture's wrap setting

By default, a picture is inserted as an inline image, which means it's treated like a really large text character. That's not usually the best way for an image to interact with the text, though. More often you want the text to flow around the image so that if the text moves (due to editing), the graphic stays where you put it. You can change a picture's text wrap setting to control this.

The most common wrap settings are:

- **In Line with Text:** The picture flows in with the text and is treated like text.

- **Square**: Text wraps around the picture's rectangular outer frame.

- **Tight:** If the picture is rectangular, same as Square, but if the picture has a transparent background, like with clip art, the text wraps around the picture itself, not its frame.

- **Through:** Text runs right through the picture, as if the picture were not there.

- **Top and bottom:** The picture interrupts the text vertically; text flows above and below it, but not on the sides.

To set a picture's wrap:

1 On the Format tab, click Wrap Text.

2 Click the desired setting.

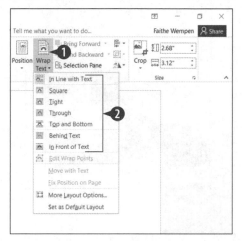

Figure 5-29: Choose a wrap setting.

Here's a shortcut alternative. When a picture is selected, a Layout Options icon floats to its right. You can click this icon for a quick menu from which you can control text wrapping, as shown at Ⓐ in Figure 5-30.

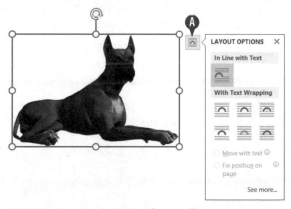

Figure 5-30: Another way of controlling text wrap.

Move a picture

To move a picture, drag it. Position the mouse anywhere over the picture (except not over a selection handle on the border) and drag.

The mouse pointer becomes a four-headed arrow when it's positioned correctly for moving, as shown at (A) in Figure 5-31.

If it won't drag, the picture is probably as In Line with Text as its wrap setting. Change this (for example, to Square), as you learned in the previous section, and it will become draggable.

Figure 5-31: Drag a picture to move it.

Resize a picture

You can resize an inserted picture to any size you like. Here are some things to know about resizing pictures:

(A) To resize a picture, drag one of its selection handles. A selection handle is a circular marker on the outer frame of the picture.

(B) As you drag, a dotted outline shows the new dimensions, and the mouse pointer appears as a crosshair.

(C) When you drag a side selection handle, the picture may become distorted because you are changing its aspect ratio (its height-width ratio).

(D) To keep the picture's aspect ratio constant, drag a corner selection handle instead.

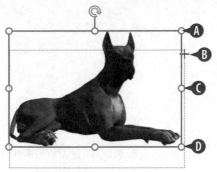

Figure 5-32: Drag a selection handle to resize a picture.

Rotate a picture

To rotate a picture, drag its rotation handle. (See **A** in Figure 5-33.)

Figure 5-33: Rotate a picture by dragging its rotation handle.

If you want more precise control over the rotation, such as rotating to a specific angle, follow these steps:

1. Select the picture.

2 On the Picture Tools Format tab, click Rotate Objects to open a menu.

3 Click More Rotation Options. The Layout dialog box opens to the Size tab.

Figure 5-34: Choose More Rotation Options.

④ In the Rotation box, type a number from 0 to 359.

⑤ Click OK.

Figure 5-35: Enter a precise value in the Rotation box.

Caption and auto-number pictures

In a business or academic document, you might have many pictures or other illustrations, and you might want to refer to them numerically. If you use the Caption feature, Word will keep the figure numbers sequential even if you move content around and add or delete content.

To add a caption to a picture, follow these steps:

1 Right-click the picture and choose Insert Caption.

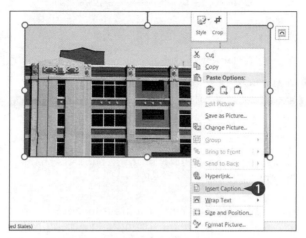

Figure 5-36: Right-click the picture and choose Insert Caption.

Instead of step 1, you can select the picture and then click the Insert Caption button on the References tab.

2 In the Caption box, after the figure number, type the caption that should appear.

3. Set any other options as desired:

A If appropriate, open the Label list and choose Equation or Table. Equations, tables, and figures are all numbered separately.

B You can also click new Label to add another type to the Label list, like Illustration, for example.

C Open the Position list and select a position for the caption if you don't want the default setting.

D If you don't want the word *Figure* (or Equation, or Table) to appear in the caption, mark the Exclude label from caption check box.

E For more control over the numbering, such as number format, click the Numbering button.

F If you want all figures to automatically be captioned, click AutoCaption and then use the AutoCaption dialog box to set up captioning options.

3 Click OK.

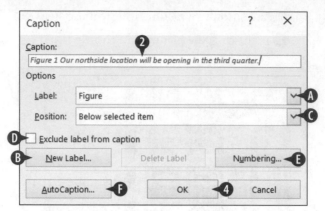

Figure 5-37: Enter the caption to use, and set captioning options.

In a technical document, you might want to have a table of figures. That's like a table of contents except it lists the figures and their captions and tells what page each one is on. To set up a table of figures, use the Insert Table of Figures command on the References tab.

CHAPTER SIX

References and Mail Merges in Word

Need to create a long, complicated document? Maybe one with research citations and a bibliography? Microsoft Word has you covered. Word offers a variety of tools for automating the potentially arduous tasks of creating footnotes, bibliographies, indexes, and tables of contents. In this chapter you learn how to create all of these.

Word is also great for merging, too. A mail merge combines a generic document with a database to create individual, personalized copies of the document for multiple recipients. If you have to send out similar copies of a document to hundreds of people, mail merge can save you hours and days of work. Mail merge also can be used to address envelopes and labels for mailing.

In This Chapter

⯈ Creating a table of contents

⯈ Inserting footnotes or endnotes

⯈ Citing sources and creating a bibliography

⯈ Creating an index

⯈ Creating and printing a mail merge

Create a table of contents

A table of contents (TOC) appears at the beginning of a document, listing each of its headings and its page number. This book has one. A TOC can contain multiple levels of headings, with the minor ones more indented or in a smaller font to distinguish them. Figure 6-1 shows an example.

Contents

Using the Explorer Interface...1
Understanding Windows Explorer...2
Displaying the Menu...3
Displaying the Folders List...3
Moving Between Locations...4
Browsing a Folder...4
Browsing a Different Disk...5
Opening the Folders Window...5
Opening Additional Folder Windows...6
Changing How Folders and Files Appear...6
Managing Files and Folders...7
Selecting Files and Folders...7
Creating a New Folder...8
Renaming a File or Folder...8
Copying or Moving a File or Folder...9
Copying or Moving with the Clipboard...9
Copying or Moving with Drag and Drop...10

Figure 6-1: A multi-level TOC example.

Check heading outline levels

The TOC feature in Word relies on heading styles, so before you create your TOC, you need to make sure that all the headings in the document are assigned an appropriate heading level.

If you use the built-in styles in Word (Heading 1, Heading 2, and so on), you don't have to worry about the outline levels. Just apply the styles to the headings, as you learned in Chapter 3, and you're good to go.

However, if you have created your own heading styles, they might not be configured for the correct outline level. For example, your major heading style in the document might not be assigned Level 1 on the outline.

Here's how to change a style's outline level:

1. On the Home tab, click the dialog box launcher in the Styles group, opening the Styles pane.
2. Point to the style, so an arrow appears to its right, and then click the arrow to open a menu.
3. Click Modify.

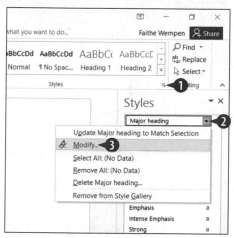

Figure 6-2: Select the Modify command for the heading style.

④ In the Modify Style dialog box, click Format to open a menu.

⑤ Click Paragraph.

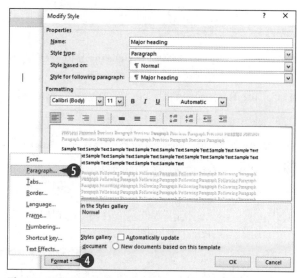

Figure 6-3: Choose to modify the paragraph formatting for the style.

⑥ Open the Outline level drop-down list and select the desired outline level.

⑦ Click OK to close the Paragraph dialog box.

8. Click OK to close the Modify Style dialog box.

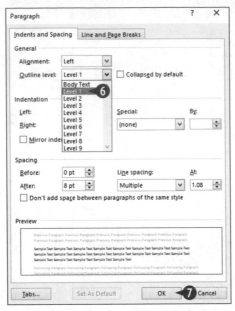

Figure 6-4: Change the style's Outline level setting.

Generate the TOC

When your headings are just the way you want them, go ahead and create the TOC. Here's how:

1. On the References tab, click Table of Contents. A menu opens.

2. Click Automatic Table 1. You're done.

Not enough options for you? Here's a more option-rich method:

1 On the References tab, click Table of Contents.

2 Click Custom Table of Contents.

3. Change any options as desired in the Table of Contents dialog box. For example, you can:

A Choose to include page numbers or not. That might seem like a no-brainer because what good is a TOC without page numbers? However . . .

B If you enable Use hyperlinks instead of page numbers, each TOC entry is a live hyperlink to that section, so if the reader is using the document on a computer, page numbers might not be needed.

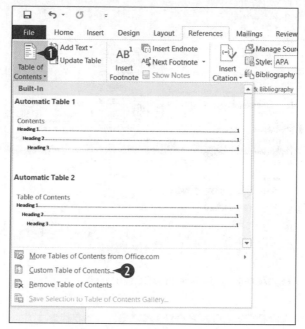

Figure 6-5: Choose to customize your TOC.

The Use hyperlinks instead of page numbers check box is somewhat misleadingly named, because it doesn't automatically disable page numbers. It just turns on the hyperlinks.

C You can choose whether or not to right-align page numbers. If you don't, the page number will appear to the right of the heading.

D If you do use right-alignment, a tab leader (a dotted line) runs between the heading and the page number. You can change the leader character.

E You can choose a format for the TOC.

F You can choose how many outline levels to show.

4 Click OK to generate the TOC with the options you have specified.

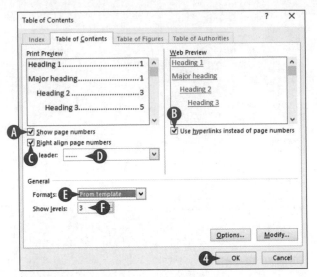

Figure 6-6: Customize the TOC settings.

Insert footnotes or endnotes

One of the simplest ways to provide additional information in a document without cluttering up the main discourse is to create a footnote or endnote. They're the same except that a footnote appears at the bottom of the page on which it is referenced, whereas endnotes appear at the end of the document. I call them *notes* when I'm referring generically to either one.

People use notes for a variety of reasons. A note might include a lengthy paragraph explaining the rationale or details behind a statement, for example. Notes are also sometimes used to cite sources, but source-citing is more properly done using the Citations feature in Word, covered in the next section.

To insert a basic footnote, follow these steps.

1 On the References tab, click Insert Footnote. (If you want endnotes, click Insert Endnote instead.)

2 Type the note text.

To move the reference mark for a note (that is, the little number in the body text of the document), you can drag-and-drop it or cut-and-paste it. If the new position puts it out of sequence, Word automatically renumbers it.

To delete a note, delete the reference mark. The footnote or end-note disappears automatically.

If you change your mind about the footnote versus endnote decision, you can easily switch. Right-click any existing note and choose Note Options. Then click Convert, choose what you want to convert to, and click OK.

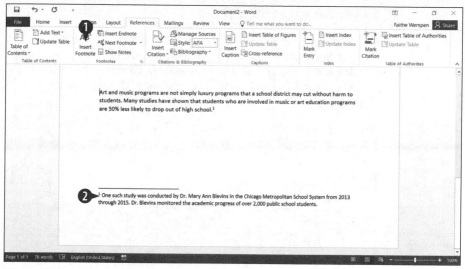

Figure 6-7: Create a footnote.

Cite sources and create a bibliography

When you quote someone else or repeat their ideas, either directly or indirectly, that someone is a *source*. When working with documents, the word *source* typically refers to published material, like a book, web site article, or newspaper story. A source could also be a speech (either live or recorded) or even a private conversation you had with someone.

One of the difficulties that people who write research papers have had for decades is that there are several different formatting systems for citing sources, and each of those systems has complicated, arcane rules for formatting the various source types.

Starting in Word 2007, academics and researchers rejoiced, because Word introduced a formatting tool for citations that took away all that frustration. You can choose the formatting style, and Word will automatically create your in-text and bibliography entries to match your choice.

Citing sources is three-step process.

1. Select a citation style. Make your initial selection upfront; you can change later if needed.

2. Insert in-text references to the sources, and enter the bibliographic information about each source the first time you refer to it.

3. Generate the bibliography. You can update the bibliography later if you add more sources.

The following sections look at each step in more detail.

Select a citation style

You probably already know which style you should be using, because your employer or school will dictate it. But if not, use APA for academic and scientific research, Chicago for journalism, IEEE 2006 for science and technology, or MLA for English literature.

To choose a citation style, open the Style drop-down list on the References tab and make your selection. (See A in Figure 6-8.)

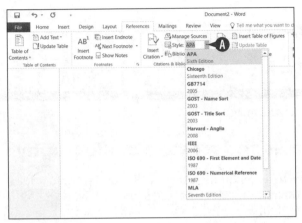

Figure 6-8: Select a citation style.

Cite a source

There are two ways to enter sources. You can enter their bibliographic information at the same time you make your first in-document reference to that source, or you can enter a source ahead of time, in a placeholder, and then refer to the source later.

To enter a source and cite it at the same time:

1 Position the insertion point where the reference should appear in the document.

2 On the References tab, click Insert Citation.

3 Click Add New Source.

4 In the Create Source dialog box, open the Type of Source list and choose the source type (such as Book or Journal Article).

5 Fill in the fields in the dialog box to identify the source.

6 Click OK.

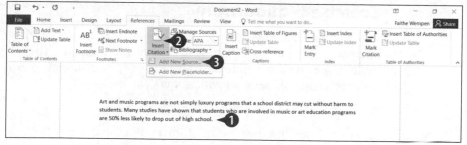

Art and music programs are not simply luxury programs that a school district may cut without harm to students. Many studies have shown that students who are involved in music or art education programs are 50% less likely to drop out of high school.

Figure 6-9: Choose to add a new source.

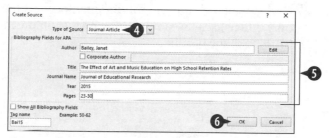

Figure 6-10: Enter the source information.

The article is added to your document's internal database, and a reference to it appears in the text. The format of the reference depends on the citation style you chose.

Here are some variations on that basic process:

Ⓐ After you have entered one or more sources, the Insert Citation button's menu contains those sources on it. You can click a source to insert an additional in-document reference to it.

Ⓑ If you aren't ready to create an in-document reference to the source yet, in step 2 choose Add New Placeholder. The rest of the steps are the same, except you won't get an in-document reference at the end.

Ⓒ If you need to make edits to your source database, choose References ⇨ Manage Sources.

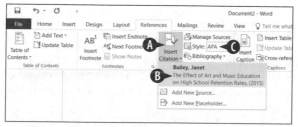

Figure 6-11: Choose an existing source from the Insert Citation button's menu if needed.

Create a bibliography

When the document is complete, and includes all sources and references to them, it's time to generate the bibliography. The bibliography typically appears at the end of the document. Word formats it correctly for the citation style you chose.

To add a bibliography, follow these steps:

1. Position the insertion point at the end of the document.

2 On the References tab, click Bibliography.

3 Click one of the built-in bibliography styles on the list. The only difference between the three presets on the menu is the wording of the heading.

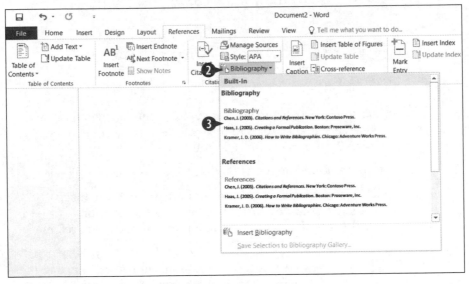

Figure 6-12: Select a bibliography preset.

There aren't a lot of customization options for bibliographies. You can choose Insert Bibliography from the list in Figure 6-12, but it doesn't open a dialog box; it just inserts a bibliography without a heading.

Create an index

An index appears in the back of a book or other long publication. It's an alphabetical listing of important terms, along with the page numbers on which those terms are discussed. This book has one.

The process of creating an index is as follows:

1. Decide on your indexing conventions.

2. Mark each instance to be indexed.

3. Generate the index.

Let's look at each of these steps individually.

Decide on your indexing conventions

Do yourself a favor before you get started, and make some decisions. For example, figure out your policies on the following questions:

- In what forms will action verbs appear? For example, will calibrating equipment be listed in the infinitive form (*calibrate*) or the gerund form (*calibrating*)?

- What will your capitalization policy be? Most indexes capitalize only proper nouns.

- Will you permit multiple forms of the same word? For example, is it okay to have different entries for *mature*, *maturing*, and *maturation*?

- Will you permit entries that begin with adjectives? (Tip: most professional indexers don't.) For example, will *red flowers* be listed under R as *red flowers*, or under F as *flowers, red*?

- How will page numbers be formatted? Bold? Italic? Both?

- Will you use subentries to organize a broad class of words? For example, under *housing*, you might have subentries of *apartment*, *duplex*, *house*, and *townhouse*, as well as indexing each of those words separately.

- Will acronyms be listed by their spelled out version, by the acronym, or both? If both, will they both have the page number, or will one be a cross-reference to the other?

- How will proper names be indexed? Will John Doe be listed under J for John, or D for Doe?

Mark each instance to be indexed

Now comes the tedious part: marking the terms to be indexed. It takes a long time because you have to go through each page of the document and create an index code for each word that you want to appear in the index. If the same word appears on multiple pages, you have to re-mark the word on each page.

To mark an index entry, follow these steps:

1 In the document, select text to include in the index (usually a single word).

2 On the References tab, click Mark Entry.

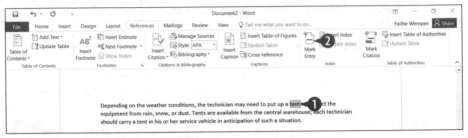

Depending on the weather conditions, the technician may need to put up a tent to protect the equipment from rain, snow, or dust. Tents are available from the central warehouse; each technician should carry a tent in his or her service vehicle in anticipation of such a situation.

Figure 6-13: Select a word to include in the index and choose Mark Entry.

3 Confirm the entry in the Main entry box. By default it is the text you selected in step 1.

4 In the Options section, choose the type of entry. The default is Current page, but you can also create a cross-reference to another entry (no page number) or a page range, which is defined by a bookmark.

To use Page range in step 4, you must define the bookmark ahead of time for the text to which you will be referring. To create a bookmark, select the text to include, and then on the Insert tab, click Bookmark. Type a name for the bookmark and click Add. Then in step 4 above, after selecting Page Range, select the bookmark from the Bookmark drop-down list.

5 (Optional) If you want the page number formatted with bold and/or italic, mark the appropriate check box.

6 Click Mark.

A An XE code is inserted in the document for the index entry, and the Show/Hide ¶ feature is automatically toggled on so you can see the index entry code if it wasn't already on.

B In step 6 if you click Mark All instead of Mark, every instance of the word in the document is marked at once. That might sound like a great time-saver, but it is usually a bad idea because it results in instances being marked that are not significant.

Depending·on·the·weather·conditions,·the·technician·may·need·to·put·up·a·tent{·XE·"t**A**·}·to· protect·the·equipment·from·rain,·snow,·or·dust.··Tents·are·available·from·the·central· warehouse;·each·technician·should·carry·a·tent·in·his·or·her·service·vehicle·in·anticipation·of· such·a·situation.¶

Mark Index Entry ? ✕

Index

Main entry: tent **3**

Subentry:

Options

○ Cross-reference: See

● Current page

○ Page range **4**

Bookmark:

Page number format

☐ Bold **5**

☐ Italic

This dialog box stays open so that you can mark multiple index entries.

6 Mark | Mark All **B** | Close

Figure 6-14: Select a word to include in the index and choose Mark Entry.

7. With the dialog box still open, select another word you want to mark.

8. Click anywhere in the Mark Index Entry dialog box. The word in the Main entry box changes to the word you selected in step 7.

9. Repeat steps 4–6 to mark the additional entry.

10. Keep marking more entries, or click Close to close the dialog box.

Word has an AutoMark feature that enables you to create a list of terms to index as a separate document, and then apply that list to the document to be indexed. It marks every single instance of each word in the document. That can result in a bad index that doesn't allow readers to easily identify where the important discussions are. This book doesn't cover AutoMark, but you can experiment with it on your own.

Generate the index

After all the entries are marked, you can generate the index. To do so:

1. Position the insertion point where you want the index to appear. Usually this is at the end of the document. You might want to start a new page (Ctrl+Enter).

2 On the References tab, click Insert Index. The Index dialog box opens.

3. Set any options as desired for the index.

Ⓐ Mark this check box to right-align page numbers (not common).

Ⓑ Open the Formats list and choose a format if you don't like the default format.

Ⓒ Choose a formatting type for subentries. Indented is the most common.

Ⓓ Choose a number of columns. Two is the default, but three may work better on a wide page.

TIP

The number of columns you choose can make a big difference in the number of pages the index occupies.

④ Click OK. The index appears in the document.

If you realize you left out a few words or want to make other changes, you can edit the index manually as you would any other text. Alternatively, you can delete the index and regenerate it.

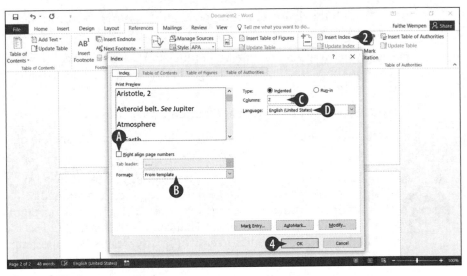

Figure 6-15: Generate an index.

Mail merge: An overview

Mail merging enables you to create personalized copies of a standard document for multiple recipients. You can use mail merge to create letters, envelopes, email messages, mailing labels, and even entries in a directory.

A mail merge consists of two documents: a *main document* and a *data list*. The main document is just like a regular document except in certain spots there are codes that substitute for specific information. For example, a letter might start *Dear <<FirstName>>*.

A data list can be a document that contains a structured list (that is, data in consistently organized rows and columns) in either Word or Excel format, or an Access database table. The mail merge feature can also pull data from the Contacts list in your locally installed copy of Microsoft Outlook. If you do not have a data list already, Word enables you to create one from inside of Word by filling out a form. That process is explained in "Create a data list for mail merge" later in this chapter.

Here's the overview of the mail merge process:

1. Start a new document, or open an existing one, to use for the main document.

2. Use the Start Mail Merge command to select the type of document it will be.

3. Select or create the data list source file.

4. Insert the merge fields in the main document.

5. Perform the merge, either to a new document or directly to a printer.

This process is the same regardless of the type of document (letters, envelopes, labels, or a catalog).

Word has a Mail Merge Wizard feature that walks you through each step in the process, and you might want to try it the first few times you merge, but ultimately you may find that it is faster and easier to complete the steps on your own.

Start a mail merge main document

A main document contains two important things: the text that will remain the same between the personalized copies, and the codes that tell Word what fields to insert at what points.

Follow these steps:

1. Start a new blank document. (Pressing Ctrl+N is a quick way.)

If you're creating letters or email messages, it's generally okay to use an existing document as the main document. Maybe you have a letter or message already written, for example, and you just need to personalize each copy. If you're creating labels, envelopes, or a directory, however, you should start a new document.

2 On the Mailing tab, click Start Mail Merge.

3 Click the type of document you want to merge.

If you choose Letters, Email Messages, or Directory, your work is complete at this point. Move on to the next step in the process: selecting or creating a data list.

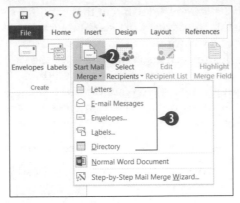

Figure 6-16: Select the type of document.

A directory is just like a letter mail merge except that there is no page break between copies. So, for example, instead of each person's copy being on its own page, a directory runs all the merged data together on a single page, like in a phonebook.

Extra steps for creating envelopes

If you select Envelopes in step 3, the Envelope Options dialog box appears after you complete the steps in the previous section.

④ Choose the envelope size.

The standard U.S. business-size envelope is Size 10, the default.

⑤ Click OK.

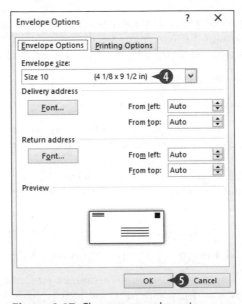

Figure 6-17: Choose an envelope size.

The document's page size changes to reflect the envelope size you chose. An empty text box appears near the bottom of the document, ready to accept the merge codes for addressing the envelopes.

Extra steps for creating labels

If you select Labels in step 3, the Label Options dialog box opens.

④ Open the Label vendors list and choose the brand of label you have.

⑤ On the product number list, choose the label's product number. It should be printed on the package.

The purpose of selecting a manufacturer and product number is to ensure the label size, the number of labels per sheet, and the spacing between labels is accurate in Word. If you don't have the box the labels came in, you might have to enter the information manually. Find a ruler so you can measure your labels. Then click New Label and fill out the dialog box that appears with your label sheet's specifications.

⑥ Click OK.

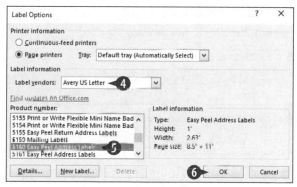

Figure 6-18: Choose a label manufacturer and product number.

If you are creating labels, Word creates a table with the dimensions appropriate to the label size and arrangement you indicated. By default the gridlines of this table do not appear. If you want to see them, Choose Table Tools Layout ⇨ View Gridlines.

Select an existing data list for a mail merge

After you choose the main document type, you next choose the data list. A data list must be in a structured format, such as a Word document containing a table, an Excel workbook, or a database such as the Contacts list in Outlook.

If you plan on using an existing Word or Excel file, it's important to set it up beforehand. You might need to open that file separately to prepare it.

If it's a Word table, keep these points in mind:

(A) Make sure that there is nothing above the table in the document file.

(B) The first row of the table must contain the field names (column labels).

(C) All the rest of the rows must contain the data records.

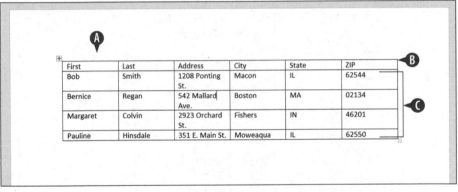

First	Last	Address	City	State	ZIP
Bob	Smith	1208 Ponting St.	Macon	IL	62544
Bernice	Regan	542 Mallard Ave.	Boston	MA	02134
Margaret	Colvin	2923 Orchard St.	Fishers	IN	46201
Pauline	Hinsdale	351 E. Main St.	Moweaqua	IL	62550

Figure 6-19: A Word table suitable for use as a mail merge data list.

If it's an Excel worksheet, keep these points in mind:

(D) Row 1 must contain the field names (column labels).

(E) All contiguous rows below row 1 contain the data records.

	A	B	C	D	E	F	G
1	First	Last	Address	City	State	ZIP	
2	Bob	Smith	1208 Ponting St.	Macon	IL	62544	
3	Bernice	Regan	542 Mallard Ave.	Boston	MA	2134	
4	Margaret	Colvin	2923 Orchard St.	Fishers	IN	46201	
5	Pauline	Hinsdale	351 E. Main St.	Moweaqua	IL	62550	
6							
7							

Figure 6-20: An Excel worksheet suitable for use as a mail merge data list.

When your data source file is ready, follow these steps to connect it to your main document in Word:

1 With the main document open, on the Mailings tab, click Select Recipients.

2 Click Use an Existing List.

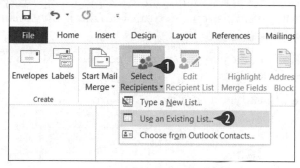

Figure 6-21: Choose to use an existing list.

3 Navigate to the location containing your data file and select it

4 Click Open.

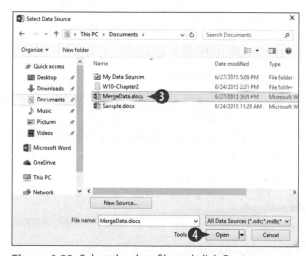

Figure 6-22: Select the data file and click Open.

Congratulations, your data file is now attached. You won't notice anything different yet, though, because you must insert merge fields. Skip down to "Insert merge fields in the main document" later in this chapter.

Create a data list for a mail merge

If the data list doesn't already exist, you can choose to create it in a Word table or in Excel, and then attach it to the main document as you learned in the preceding section.

However, there's another way to create a data list that is a little easier (or at least a little more foolproof), especially if the list you are planning to create contains people's names and addresses:

1. With the main document open, on the Mailings tab, click Select Recipients.

2. Click Type a New List.

Figure 6-23: Choose to type a new list.

3. Type the name and address, pressing Tab to move to the next fields (column).

You don't have to fill in all the fields for every person; just do the ones that pertain to the merge you are going to perform, such as name and mailing address.

4. Click New Entry and then type another person's information on the next row.

5. Repeat step 3 until all the records are entered.

6. Click OK. The Save Address List dialog box opens.

7. Type a name for the list in the File name box.

8. Navigate to a different save location if desired. The default location is My Data Sources in your personal Documents folder.

9. Click Save.

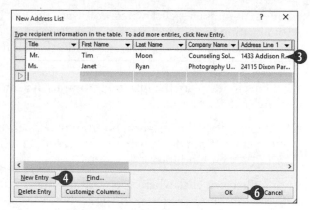

Figure 6-24: Choose to type a new list.

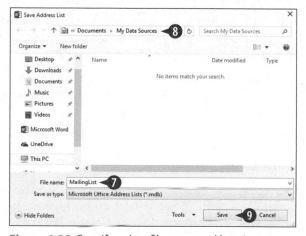

Figure 6-25: Specify a data file name and location.

If you later need to edit that file, choose Mailings ⇨ Edit Recipient List. The saved file is in Microsoft Access database format, so you can also open and edit it with Microsoft Access.

Insert merge fields in the main document

The next step in the merge process is to insert fields where you want the personalization to be. First, position the insertion point appropriately:

- For letters, click where you want the merge code to appear. You will want the recipient's name and address near the top of the document, just below the date. You might also want a greeting like (Dear *name*). You might want other personalization too, such as a mention of the person's city or state in a body paragraph.

- For email messages, click where you want the first bit of personalization to appear. There isn't a customary placement for personalized data in email messages like there is for a business letter.

- For envelopes, place the insertion point in the empty text box in the center of the label.

- For labels, place the insertion point in the upper right cell of the table. If you don't see a table, choose Table Tools Layout ⇨ View Gridlines.

- For a directory, click where you want the merge code to appear. If you want some separator to appear between records, create that (such as a horizontal line or a blank line) and then move the insertion point above that separator.

After positioning the insertion point, you are ready to insert the merge code. To simplify the process of inserting fields, Word offers two special merge codes you can use:

- Address Block inserts all the fields needed to create a properly formatted address block, including the spaces and paragraph breaks between them, something like this:

Amy Jones
3855 W. Main St.
Arcadia, IN 46958

- Greeting Line inserts a greeting such as *Dear* followed by the recipient's name. When you insert the greeting line you can choose whether to use their first name, last name, or both. It might look something like this:

Dear Ms. Jones:

You can also insert individual merge fields. For example, you might mention the person's city in a paragraph like this:

Until June 30, our store in Indianapolis is offering 20% off all clearance items.

Insert an address block

To insert an address block (for example, on an envelope or label, or at the top of a letter), follow these steps:

1 On the Mailings tab, click Address Block.

2 Choose the format in which the person's name should appear.

3 If you do not want the company name (if any) to appear, click the Insert company name check box.

④ Specify how addresses outside of the default country should be shown.

⑤ Check the preview to make sure the address block appears as expected.

If the address preview doesn't look right, click Match Fields and use the dialog box that appears to match up the fields from the merge data file with the fields used for the address block.

⑥ Click OK to insert the code.

The address block code appears in the document with double angle brackets around it, like this: <<AddressBlock>>.

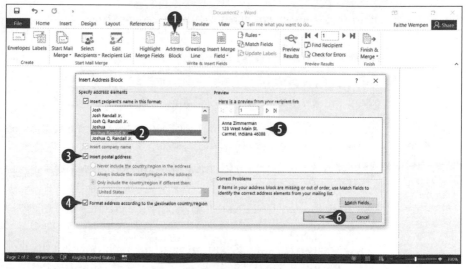

Figure 6-26: Specify options for the address block.

Correct the spacing issue on address blocks

One problem with the default address block is that it leaves too much vertical space between lines, because of the default paragraph spacing. (Each line of the address block is a separate paragraph.) To see this for yourself, choose Mailings ⇨ Preview Results. Repeat that command to turn off the preview.

To correct the problem, follow these steps:

① Select the <<AddressBlock>> code.

② On the Home tab, click the Line and Paragraph Spacing button to open its menu.

③ Click Remove Space After Paragraph.

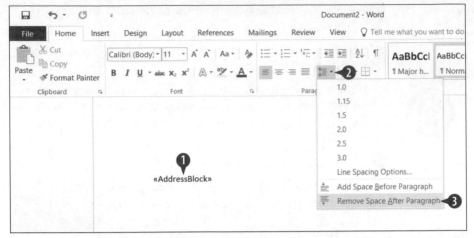

Figure 6-27: Remove extra space after paragraphs within the address block.

Insert a greeting line

To insert a greeting line, follow these steps:

1 On the Mailings tab, click Greeting Line.

2 Use the drop-down lists in the Greeting line format section to specify how the greeting will appear.

3 Specify a greeting line for invalid recipient names (for example, a record where no recipient name was specified).

4 Check the preview area to make sure the greeting line is as you want it.

    A You can click the Next button to move through all the records to check each one.

    B If the fields aren't matching up, click Match Fields and specify which fields from the data list should be included in the greeting.

5 Click OK.

Insert an individual merge field

To insert an individual field, follow these steps:

1 On the Mailings tab, click the arrow on the Insert Merge Field button, opening a menu.

2 Click the desired field to insert.

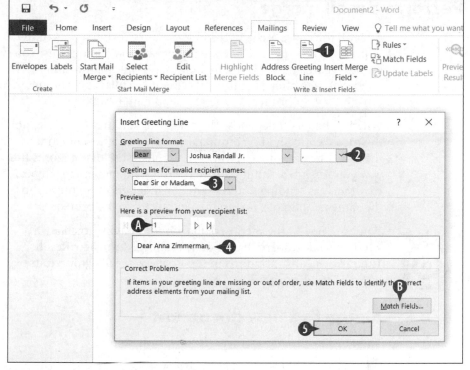

Figure 6-28: Specify the settings for the greeting line.

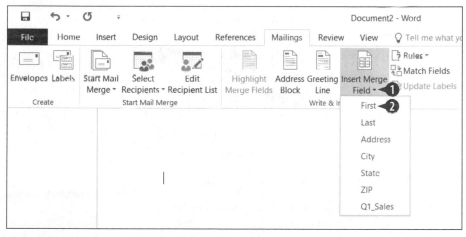

Figure 6-29: Choose an individual field to insert.

 Here's an alternate method. You can click the face of the Insert Merge Field button (the graphical part, not the text and arrow below it) to open the Insert Merge Field dialog box. From there you can choose a field and click Insert.

Perform a mail merge

After all the codes are inserted in the main document, it's time to perform the merge. There are three ways to go about this: you can merge to a new document, and then print that document as a separate step after examining the merge results, you can merge directly to your printer, or you can send email messages.

Which is better? It depends. How sure are you that you've set up the merge correctly? I recommend merging to a new document the first time you run a new merge to make sure that it works the way you intended. But if you are running the same merge repeatedly (such as sending out the same form letters every month to the same people), it's fine to merge directly to the printer.

You can preview the merge results without having to create a whole new document. Just choose Mailings ⇨ Preview Results. Then use the arrow buttons in the Preview Results group to move between results pages.

Merge to a new document

To merge to a new document, follow these steps:

1 On the Mailings tab, click Finish & Merge. A menu opens.

2 Click Edit Individual Documents.

Figure 6-30: Choose to edit individual documents.

3 (Optional) If you want to include only a certain range of records, specify that range. Otherwise leave All selected.

4 Click OK. The new document is created.

Figure 6-31: Choose a range of records.

5. Print and save the new document as you would any document, and then close it.

6. Save your merge main document for later reuse if desired.

Merge to a printer

To merge to a printer, follow these steps:

1 On the Mailings tab, click Finish & Merge. A menu opens.

2 Click Print Documents.

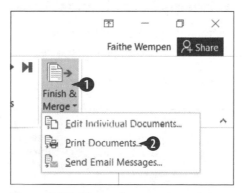

Figure 6-32: Choose to merge to a printer.

3 (Optional) If you want to include only a certain range of records, specify that range. Otherwise leave All selected.

4 Click OK.

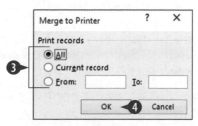

Figure 6-33: Choose a range of records.

5. In the Print dialog box, specify any print options as needed.

6 Click OK.

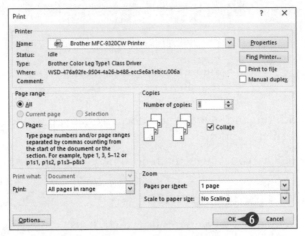

Figure 6-34: Choose printing options and complete the printing.

Send merged email messages

To merge to a printer, follow these steps:

1 On the Mailings tab, click Finish & Merge. A menu opens.

2 Click Send Email Messages.

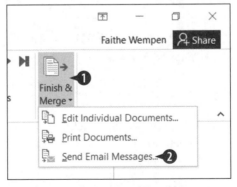

Figure 6-35: Choose Send Email Messages.

3 Open the To: drop-down list and select the field that contains the recipients' email addresses. This field might or might not have been inserted in the message.

4 In the Subject line box, type the desired message subject.

5. (Optional) If you want to include only a certain range of records, specify that range. Otherwise leave All selected.

6. Click OK. The messages are sent using your default email application (probably Microsoft Outlook).

Figure 6-36: Specify email sending options.

CHAPTER SEVEN

Creating Basic Excel Worksheets

Excel has many practical uses. You can use its orderly row-and-column worksheet structure to organize multicolumn lists, create business forms, and much more. Excel provides more than just data organization, though; it enables you to write formulas that perform calculations on your data. This feature makes Excel an ideal tool for storing financial information, such as checkbook register and investment portfolio data.

In this lesson, I introduce you to the Excel interface and teach you some of the concepts you need to know. You learn how to move around in Excel, how to type and edit data, and how to manipulate rows, columns, cells, and sheets.

In This Chapter

⟫ Understanding the Excel interface

⟫ Moving between cells

⟫ Selecting cells and ranges

⟫ Entering and editing text in cells

⟫ Using AutoFill to fill cell content and Flash Fill to extract content

⟫ Copying and moving data between cells

⟫ Inserting and deleting rows, columns, and cells

⟫ Creating and managing multiple worksheets

Understanding the Excel interface

Let's start out with some basic terminology. A *spreadsheet* is a grid composed of rows and columns. Spreadsheet is a generic term, not an Excel-specific one. Excel calls each spreadsheet a *worksheet*. An excel file is called a *workbook*. Here are a few other things to remember about the Excel interface:

A A workbook can have multiple worksheets. Each worksheet has a tab at the bottom of the screen; you can click a tab to switch to that sheet.

B At the intersection of each row and column is a *cell*. You can type text, numbers, and formulas into cells to build your spreadsheet.

C The active cell has a thicker green outline around it called the *cell cursor*. Whatever you type is entered into the active cell.

D The content of the active cell appears in the formula bar. When the cell contains text or a fixed number, the formula bar content is the same as what you see in the cell. However, when the cell contains a formula, the cell shows the results of the formula and the formula bar shows the formula itself.

E A cell's *address* consists of its column letter and row number. The active cell's address appears in the *Name box*.

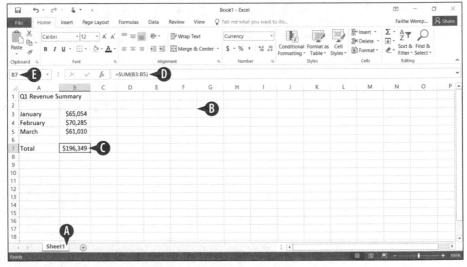

Figure 7-1: Cells are at the intersections of rows and columns.

Excel is very much like Word in many ways. Here are some parts that might seem familiar from previous chapters:

- **F** The Ribbon is a multi-tabbed toolbar of commands to issue. Click a tab to switch to it.

- **G** The Zoom slider controls the magnification of the work area. Drag the slider left or right to zoom out or in.

- **H** Clicking File opens Backstage view, where you can save, open, and print files.

- **I** Scroll bars enable you to move around in the worksheet.

- **J** The Quick Access toolbar provides shortcuts to a few commonly used commands.

- **K** Type in the Tell Me What You Want to Do box to ask a question if you don't know how to do something.

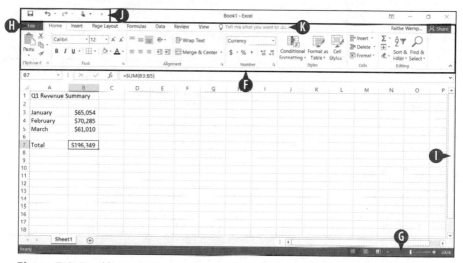

Figure 7-2: Excel has a similar interface to that of other Office applications.

Now that you know what you're looking at, check out the next several sections, which tell you what you can do with it.

Move between cells

To type in a cell, you must first make that cell active by moving the cell cursor there. As shown earlier in Figure 7-1, the cell cursor is a thick green outline. You can move the cell cursor by pressing the arrow keys on the keyboard, by clicking the desired cell, or by using one of the Excel keyboard shortcuts. Table 7-1 provides some of the most common keyboard shortcuts for moving the cell cursor.

Scrolling with the scroll bar does not change which cell is active; it only changes which cells are visible, but it does not move the cell cursor. One common beginner mistake is to scroll to place the desired cell in view and then start typing without first clicking it to make it active.

Table 7-1	Cell Cursor Movement Shortcuts
Press This . . .	**To Move . . .**
Arrow keys	One cell in the direction of the arrow
Tab	One cell to the right
Shift+Tab	One cell to the left
Ctrl+arrow key	To the edge of the current data region (the first or last cell that isn't empty) in the direction of the arrow
End	To the cell in the lower-right corner of the window*
Ctrl+End	To the last cell in the worksheet, in the lowest used row of the rightmost used column
Home	To the beginning of the row containing the active cell
Ctrl+Home	To the beginning of the worksheet (cell A1)
Page Down	One screen down
Alt+Page Down	One screen to the right
Ctrl+Page Down	To the next sheet in the workbook
Page Up	One screen up
Alt+Page Up	One screen to the left
Ctrl+Page Up	To the previous sheet in the workbook

*This works only when the Scroll Lock key has been pressed on your keyboard to turn on the Scroll Lock function.

Select cells and ranges

You might sometimes want to select a multi-cell *range* before you issue a command. For example, if you want to format all the text in a range a certain way, select that range and then issue the formatting command. Technically, a range can consist of a single cell; however, a range most commonly consists of multiple cells. Here are some things to note about cells and ranges:

Ⓐ In Figure 7-3, the range A1:F3 is selected. Range names are written with the upper-left cell address, a colon, and the lower-right cell address.

B The active cell is A1. The active cell's address appears in the Name box.

C The active cell within the range appears white, while all the other cells in the selected range are gray.

This points out the difference between the active cell and a multi-cell range. The active cell is significant when doing data entry; when you type text, it goes into the active cell only. The selected range is significant when you are issuing a command, such as applying formatting.

D To select a row, click its column letter. Drag across multiple column letters to select multiple columns.

E To select a column, click its row number. Drag across multiple row numbers to select multiple rows.

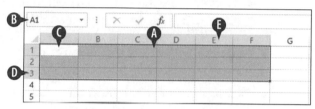

Figure 7-3: The range A1:F3 is selected.

A range is usually *contiguous*, or all the cells are in a single rectangular block, but they don't have to be. You can also select *noncontiguous* cells in a range by holding down the Ctrl key while you select additional cells.

When a range contains noncontiguous cells, the pieces are separated by commas, like this: A1:C3,E3:E5. This range name tells Excel to select the range from A1 through C3, plus the range from E3 through E5. Figure 7-4 shows that range.

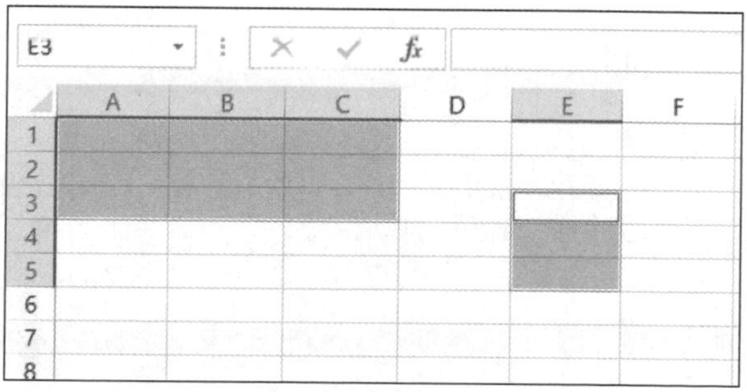

Figure 7-4: A noncontiguous range.

Enter and edit text in cells

Here are some tips for entering and editing text:

(A) To type in a cell, simply select the cell and begin typing. If you make a mistake when editing, you can press the Esc key to cancel the edit before you leave the cell.

(B) Notice that if you type an entry that is wider than the cell, it hangs off into the next column. The solution to that is to widen the column, as you will learn to do in Chapter 8.

When you finish typing, you can leave the cell in any of these ways:

- *Press Enter:* Moves you to the next cell down.

- *Press Tab:* Moves you to the next cell to the right.

- *Press Shift+Tab:* Moves you to the next cell to the left.

- *Press an arrow key:* Moves you in the direction of the arrow.

- *Click in another cell:* Moves you to that cell.

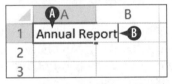

Figure 7-5: Type directly into a cell.

If you need to edit the content in a cell, you can click the cell to select it, and then click the cell again to move the insertion point into it. Edit just as you would in any text program. Alternatively, you can click the cell to select it and then type a new entry to replace the old one.

(C) If you need to undo an edit immediately after you leave the cell, click the Undo button on the Quick Access toolbar, or press Ctrl+Z.

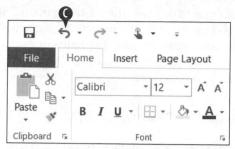

Figure 7-6: Undo an edit

D To clear a cell, select the cell; then choose
Home ⇨ Clear ⇨ Clear Contents.

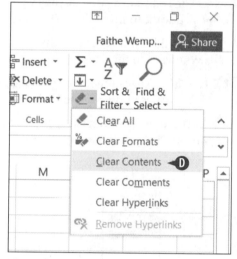

Figure 7-7: Clear a cell's content.

To clear a cell you can also select it and then either press
the Delete key or right-click it and choose Clear Contents.

Don't confuse the Delete key on the keyboard (which issues the
Clear command) with the Delete command on the Ribbon. The
Delete command on the Ribbon doesn't clear the cell content;
instead, it removes the entire cell. You find out more about
deleting cells in the upcoming section, "Insert and delete rows,
columns, and cells."

And while I'm on the subject, don't confuse Clear with Cut,
either. The Cut command works in conjunction with the
Clipboard. Cut moves the content to the Clipboard, and you can
then paste it somewhere else. Excel, however, differs from other
applications in the way this command works: Using Cut doesn't
immediately remove the content. Instead, Excel puts a flashing
dotted box around the content and waits for you to reposition

the cell cursor and issue the Paste command. If you do something else in the interim, the cut-and-paste operation is canceled,
and the content that you cut remains in its original location. You
learn more about cutting and pasting in the section "Copy and
move data between cells" later in this lesson.

Use AutoFill to fill cell content

When you have a lot of data to enter and that data consists of
some type of repeatable pattern or sequence, you can save time
by using AutoFill.

To use AutoFill:

1 Select the cell or cells that already contain an example of
what you want to fill.

2 Drag the fill handle to extend the selection to the range of
cells you want to fill:

A The *fill handle* is the little black square in the lower
right corner of the selected cell or range.

B As you drag, a ScreenTip appears showing what the
value will be in the final cell of the range.

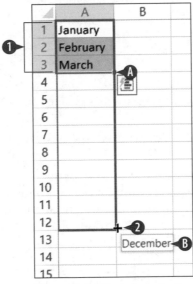

Figure 7-8: Fill a range of cells
by dragging the fill handle.

Depending on how you use it, AutoFill can either fill the same value into every cell in the target area, or it can fill in a sequence (such as days of the month, days of the week, or a numeric sequence such as 2, 4, 6, 8). Here are the general rules for how it works:

Ⓒ When AutoFill recognizes the selected text as a member of one of its preset lists, such as days of the week or months of the year, it automatically increments those. For example, if the selected cell contains Monday, AutoFill places Tuesday in the next adjacent cell.

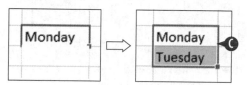

Figure 7-9: AutoFill works on commonly occurring series.

Ⓓ When AutoFill doesn't recognize the selected text, it fills the chosen cell with a duplicate of the selected text.

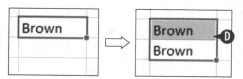

Figure 7-10: AutoFill duplicates the selected text if it's not a recognized series.

Ⓔ When AutoFill is used on a single cell containing a number, it fills with a duplicate of the number.

Ⓕ You can click the AutoFill Options button to open a menu of other choices.

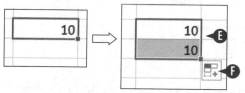

Figure 7-11: AutoFill duplicates a single number.

Ⓖ When Auto Fill is used on a range of two or more cells containing numbers, AutoFill attempts to determine the interval between them and continues filling using that same pattern. For example, if the two selected cells contain 2 and 4, the next adjacent cell would be filled with 6.

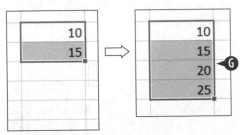

Figure 7-12: AutoFill determines the interval between multiple selected numbers and repeats that pattern.

When you copy formulas or functions (using any method), Excel automatically adjusts the cell references in the copies to the relative positioning of the new locations. For example:

Ⓗ If you have =A1+A2 in cell A3 . . .

Ⓘ . . . and you copy A3's formula into B3 . . .

Ⓙ . . . the resulting formula in B3 will be =B1+B2.

This is called *relative referencing*, and it's covered in more detail in Chapter 8.

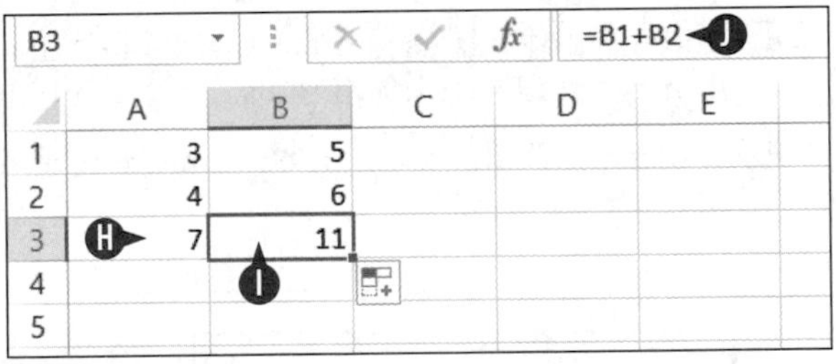

Figure 7-13: AutoFill works when copying formulas and functions.

Copy and move data between cells

When you're creating a spreadsheet, it's common not to get everything in the right cells on your first try. Fortunately, moving content between cells is easy.

Here are the two methods you can use to move content: drag it with the mouse or cut/copy and paste using the Clipboard.

Copy and move using the mouse

Moving or copying with the mouse works well when you can see both the source and the destination locations at once. For example, if you want to move a range of cells a few rows up or down, or a few columns to the left or right, this is the method for you. It's not a good method when moving or copying between different worksheets or workbooks.

To move or copy the contents of a range of cells using the mouse, follow these steps:

1 Select the range of cells to be moved or copied.

2 Position the mouse pointer at the dark outline around the selected range. The mouse pointer changes to a four-headed arrow with a white arrow pointer on top of it.

3. (Optional) If you want to copy (not move), hold down the Ctrl key and keep it down until you are finished with step 4. If you do this, the mouse pointer changes to a white arrow pointer with a small plus sign on it.

4 Drag the selection outline to the new location.

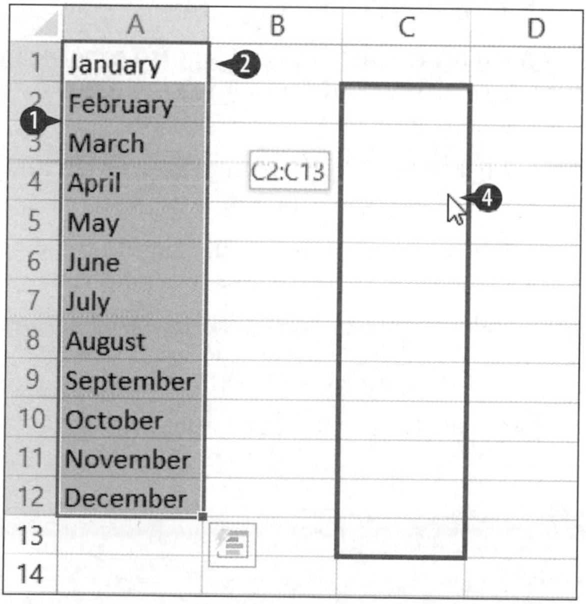

Figure 7-14: Drag a selected range to a new location using the mouse.

Copy and move using the *Clipboard*

The *Clipboard* is a temporary holding area in Windows, designed for moving and copying content from one location to another. That statement is intentionally very broad because the Clipboard works with just about any type of content. You can use it to move files from one folder to another, or to move a selection of data in an application (like Excel) from one spot to another in the same data file or a different one.

You can think of the Clipboard like a real-life clipboard. You place something on it for temporary holding, and then when you get to the desired location, you retrieve the item.

The Clipboard works via a combination of the following commands:

- **Cut:** Removes the item from its original location and places it on the Clipboard.

- **Copy:** Places a copy of the item on the Clipboard, leaving the original in place.

- **Paste:** Places a copy of whatever is on the Clipboard in the active location.

To copy, you use a combination of Copy and Paste; to Move, use Cut and Paste:

1. Select the range of cells to copy or move.

2. On the Home tab, click Copy (to copy) or Cut (to move). The border around the selection becomes dashed temporarily.

3. Click in the cell that is in the upper-left corner of the area into which you want to paste.

If you're moving or copying a multi-cell range with the Clipboard, you can either select the same size and shape of range for the destination in step 3 or you can select a single cell, in which case the paste occurs with the selected cell in the upper-left corner.

4. On the Home tab, click Paste.

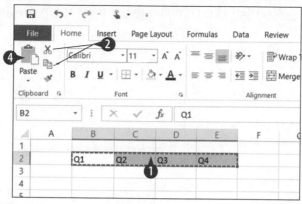

Figure 7-15: Cut or copy, and then paste.

Because the Clipboard is such a popular tool, there are many ways to use it. Table 7-2 summarizes the different ways to issue each of the three basic Clipboard commands.

Table 7-2	Methods of Cutting, Copying, and Pasting with the Clipboard		
Action	**Right-click Method**	**Keyboard Method**	**Ribbon Method**
Cut	Right-click selection and click Cut.	Ctrl+X	Home ➪ Cut
Copy	Right-click selection and click Copy.	Ctrl+C	Home ➪ Copy
Paste	Right-click at the destination and click Paste.	Ctrl+V	Home ➪ Paste

Insert and delete rows, columns, and cells

Even if you're a careful planner, you'll likely decide that you want to change your worksheet's structure. Maybe you want data in a different column, or certain rows turn out to be unnecessary. Excel makes it easy to insert and delete rows and columns to deal with these kinds of changes.

Insert rows or columns

When you insert a new row or column, the existing ones move to make room for it.

1. Select one or more existing rows or columns adjacent to where you want the inserted ones. For example, if you want two new columns, select two adjacent existing columns. See "Select cells and ranges" earlier in this chapter for help if needed.

There is no limit on the number of rows or columns you can insert at once.

2 On the Home tab, click Insert.

Figure 7-16: Insert rows or columns with the Insert command.

Delete rows or columns

When you delete rows or columns, whatever they contained is lost, so be careful with this command. Delete is not the same as Cut. Cut moves the content to the Clipboard, but Delete just destroys it.

If you accidentally delete something you meant to keep, use Undo (Ctrl+Z) to undo commands until you get it back. This works only if you haven't closed the application or the data file since you made the deletion.

3. Select one or more existing rows or columns to delete. See "Select cells and ranges" earlier in this chapter for help if needed.

There is no limit on the number of rows or columns you can delete at once.

4 On the Home tab, click Delete.

Figure 7-17: Delete rows or columns with the Delete command.

Insert or delete cells and ranges

You can also insert and delete individual cells or even ranges that don't neatly correspond to entire rows or columns. When you do so, the surrounding cells shift. In the case of an insertion, cells move down or to the right of the area where the new cells are being inserted. In the case of a deletion, cells move up or to the left to fill in the voided space.

Deleting a cell is different from clearing a cell's content, and this becomes apparent when you start working with individual cells and ranges. When you clear the content, the cell itself remains. When you delete the cell itself, the adjacent cells shift.

When shifting cells, Excel is smart enough that it tries to guess which direction you want existing content to move when you insert or delete cells. If you have content immediately to the right of a deleted cell, for example, Excel shifts it left. If you have content immediately below the deleted cell, Excel shifts it up. You can still override that, though, as needed.

To insert cells:

1. Select a range the size and shape of the range of cells you want to insert, adjacent to where you want to insert them. To insert a single cell, select a single cell.

	A	B	C
1	Tom Jones	Pitcher	
2	Brad Cooper	Shortstop	
3	Bryan Willis	First base	
4	Ed Campbell	Second base	
5	Mary Wilderman	Third base	
6	Josh Peterson	Catcher	
7			
8			
9			

Figure 7-18: Select a range where you want to insert cells.

2. On the Home tab, click the arrow on the Insert button to open its menu.

3. Click Insert Cells.

4. In the Insert dialog box, specify how you want the adjacent cells to move.

5. Click OK.

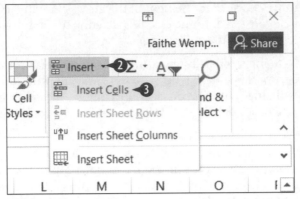

Figure 7-19: Choose Insert Cells from the Insert button's menu.

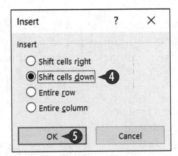

Figure 7-20: Choose where existing content will move to make room for the new cells.

To delete a range of cells or an individual cell:

1. Select the cell(s) to delete.

2 On the Home tab, click the arrow on the Delete button to open its menu.

3 Click Delete Cells.

4 In the Insert dialog box, specify how you want the adjacent cells to move.

5 Click OK.

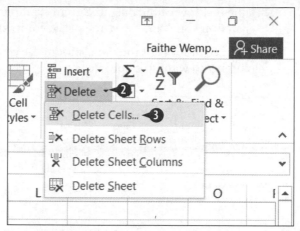

Figure 7-21: Choose Delete Cells from the Delete button's menu.

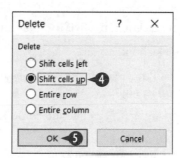

Figure 7-22: Choose where existing content will move when the deleted cells are removed.

Use Flash Fill to extract content

The Flash Fill feature enables you to extract data from adjacent columns intelligently by analyzing the patterns in that data. For example, suppose you have a list of email addresses in one column, and you would like the usernames (that is, the text before the @ sign) from each email address to appear in an adjacent column. You would extract the first few yourself by manually typing the entries into the adjacent column, and then you would use Flash Fill to follow your example to extract the others. You could also use Flash Fill to separate first and last names that are entered in the same column.

To use Flash Fill, follow these steps:

1. Make sure there are enough blank columns to the right of the original data to hold the extracted data. See "Insert and delete rows, columns, and cells" earlier in this chapter if you need help.

2 In the first row of the data, create an example of the separation you want by typing in the empty column(s).

3 In the second row of the data, click in the cell in the column you want to populate.

	A	B	C	D	E
1	Tom Jones	Tom	Jones	Pitcher	
2	Brad Cooper			Shortstop	
3	Bryan Willis			First base	
4	Ed Campbell			Second base	
5	Mary Wilderman			Third base	
6	Josh Peterson			Catcher	
7					
8					

Figure 7-23: Create an example of the separation you want in blank column(s) to the right of the original data.

4 On the Home tab, click the Fill button to open a menu.

5 Click Flash Fill.

The data in the column you selected in step 3 is filled in. (See **A** in Figure 7-24.)

6. Repeat steps 3–5 as needed to populate additional columns.

Step 6 is necessary because you can only Flash Fill one column at a time. If you want to split out data from multiple columns at once, use the Data⇨Text to Columns command. Use the Help system in Excel to find out how to use that command.

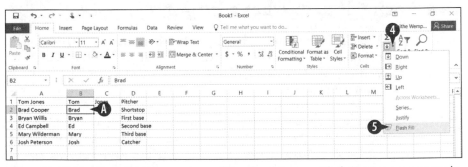

Figure 7-24: The Flash Fill command populates the columns with data using your example.

Create and manage multiple worksheets

Each new workbook starts with one sheet — Sheet1. (Not the most interesting name, but you can change it.) Each worksheet is represented by a tab at the bottom of the Excel window; you can click a tab to switch to that sheet.

You can add or delete worksheets, rearrange the worksheet tabs, and apply different colors to the tabs to help differentiate them from one another, or to create logical groups of tabs.

Add a worksheet

Adding a worksheet gives you an additional page on which to enter your data without having to start a new data file. To add a worksheet:

1 Click the tab that the new worksheet's tab should appear to the *right* of. If your current workbook has only one sheet in it, this is a non-issue.

It's kind of a non-issue anyway, because you can easily reorder the tabs later. See "Reorder worksheet tabs" later in this chapter.

2 Click the New Sheet button (+) to the right of the existing sheet tabs at the bottom of the Excel window.

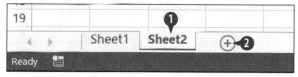

Figure 7-25: Add a worksheet.

Remove a worksheet

Be careful when removing worksheets; whatever was on that sheet is lost when you do so, and you can't use Undo to get it back. If you are deleting a blank sheet, Excel offers no warning, but if the sheet contains anything, you must confirm the deletion.

To delete a worksheet:

1 Right-click the worksheet's tab at the bottom of the screen.

2 Click Delete.

3 If a deletion confirmation dialog box appears, click Delete.

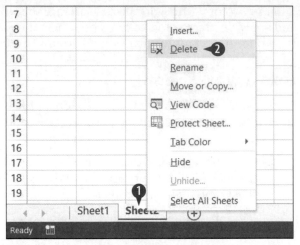

Figure 7-26: Delete a worksheet.

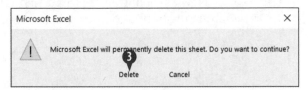

Figure 7-27: Confirm the deletion if the sheet you are deleting is not empty.

Rename a worksheet

As I mentioned earlier, the default sheet names are not terribly useful (Sheet1, Sheet2). You will probably want to rename each sheet's tab to help you remember what is stored on that sheet.

1. Double-click the worksheet tab to place the name in editing mode. Alternatively, you can right-click the tab and choose Rename.

2. Edit the name or type a new name.

3. Click away from the tab to accept the new name.

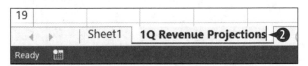

Figure 7-28: Edit the tab's name.

Reorder worksheet tabs

The tab for a new worksheet is always placed to the right of whichever worksheet is active when you create it. You can easily reorder the worksheet tabs, though.

A Drag a tab to the right or left to move it.

B A small black triangle shows where the worksheet tab will be dropped when you release the mouse button.

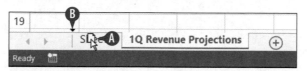

Figure 7-29: Drag a tab to the right or left.

Change the worksheet tab color

If you have a lot of worksheets in a workbook, it can get confusing when you are trying to find the one you want. You can make it easier by color-coding your tabs: gold for management, blue for medical, red for security, and so on. (Yes, those are the *Star Trek* colors. Use your own scheme.)

To change a tab's color:

1 Right-click the tab.

2 Point to Tab Color.

3 Click the desired color.

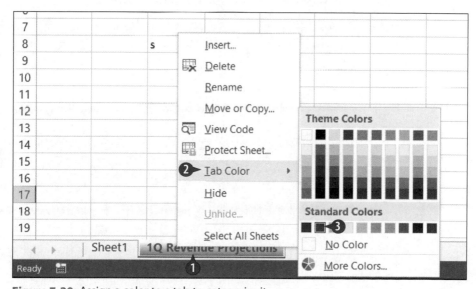

Figure 7-30: Assign a color to a tab to categorize it.

CHAPTER EIGHT

Creating Excel Formulas and Functions

Math. Excel is really good at it, and it's what makes Excel more than just data storage. Even if you hated math in school, you might still like Excel because it does the math for you.

In Excel, you can write math formulas that perform calculations on the values in various cells, and then, if those values change later, you can see the formula results update automatically. You can also use built-in functions to handle more complex math activities than you might be able to set up yourself with formulas. This capability makes it possible to build complex worksheets that calculate loan rates and payments, keep track of your bank accounts, and much more.

In this chapter, I show you how to construct formulas and functions in Excel, how to move and copy formulas and functions (there's a trick to it), and how to use functions to create handy financial spreadsheets.

In This Chapter

⟹ Writing basic formulas

⟹ Copying and moving formulas

⟹ Inserting functions

⟹ Showing the current date or time with a function

⟹ Calculating loan terms

⟹ Evaluating a condition with an IF function

⟹ Referring to named ranges

⟹ Using the Quick Analysis feature

Write basic formulas

A *formula* is a math calculation, like 2+2 or 3*(4+1). In Excel, a formula can perform calculations with fixed numbers or cell contents.

In Excel, formulas are different from regular text in two ways:

- Formulas begin with an equal sign, like this: =2+2.

- Formulas don't contain text (except for function names and cell references). They contain only symbols that are allowed in math formulas, such as parentheses, commas, and decimal points.

Excel also has an advantage over some basic calculators (including the one in Windows): It easily does exponentiation. For example, if you want to calculate 5 to the 8th power, you would write it in Excel as =5^8.

Create formulas that calculate numeric values

To create a basic formula that performs math calculations on numbers:

1 In the desired cell, begin typing the formula to create, starting with an = sign.

2 Type the formula to calculate. Use these math operators:

- + for addition

- – for subtraction

- * for multiplication

- / for division

- ^ for exponentiation

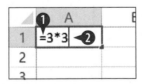

Figure 8-1: Type a formula into a cell.

3. Press Enter. The formula result appears in the cell, and the cell cursor moves down into the next row.

4 (Optional) To see the formula in the cell, click the cell. Its formula appears in the formula bar.

Formula appears in formula bar

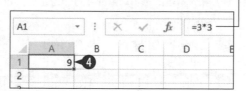

Figure 8-2: The formula result appears in the cell and the formula itself appears in the formula bar.

Control the order of math precedence

Just as in basic math, formulas are calculated by an order of precedence. Table 8-1 lists the order.

Table 8-1	Order of Precedence in a Formula	
Order	**Item**	**Example**
1	Anything in parentheses	=2*(2+1)
2	Exponentiation	=2^3
3	Multiplication and division	=1+2*2
4	Addition and subtraction	=10-4

Here are a few additional examples. Work through them yourself and see if you come up with the same results; if you do, then you understand order of precedence.

3*3+4/2 = 11
3*(3+4)/2= 10.5
3*3+4^2= 25

Reference other cells in a formula

One of Excel's best features is that it can reference cells in formulas. When a cell is referenced in a formula, whatever value it contains is used in the formula. When the value changes, the result of the formula changes too.

To reference another cell in a formula:

1 Begin typing the formula to create, starting with an = sign.

2. When you need to reference another cell, do either of the following:

   A Type the cell's address directly into the formula (for example, A1).

   B Click the cell to fill in its address in the formula being typed.

3. Continue creating the formula normally, adding numbers and math operators as needed. When you are finished, press Enter.

Figure 8-3: Type a formula that includes references to other cells by their column letter and row number.

Reference cells on other worksheets

When referring to a cell on the same sheet, you can simply use its column and row: A1, B1, and so on. However, when referring to a cell on a different sheet, you have to include the sheet name in the formula.

The syntax for doing this is to list the sheet name in single quotes, followed by an exclamation point, followed by the cell reference, like this:

```
='Sheet1'!A2
```

You can also select cells on another sheet by first clicking the sheet tab and then the desired cell as you are creating the formula, as in the following steps:

1 Begin typing the formula to create, starting with an = sign.

2 When you need to reference a cell on another sheet, click the worksheet's tab.

3 Click the desired cell on that sheet.

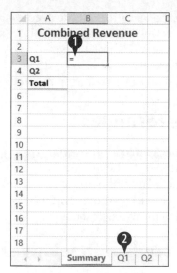

Figure 8-4: Click a tab while typing a formula to reference a cell on that sheet.

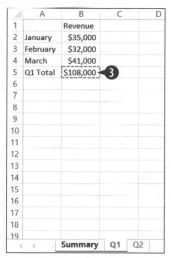

Figure 8-5: Click the desired cell to reference and press Enter.

4. Press Enter to return to the sheet containing the formula you began in step 1. Excel assumes that the formula is complete at this point and moves out of that cell.

5. If the formula is not yet complete, click the cell containing the formula and edit it in the formula bar.

TIP

As you may have noticed in the preceding steps, one of the drawbacks to selecting a cell this way is that Excel ends the formula after you select it. It's not a big deal to edit the formula, but if you would prefer to not have to do so, you can use the typing method instead of the selecting method.

Copy and move formulas

In Chapter 7, you learn how to move and copy text and numbers between cells, but when it comes to copying formulas, beware of a few gotchas. The following sections explain relative and absolute referencing in formulas and how you can use them to get the results you want when you copy.

Refer to cells with relative referencing

When you move or copy a formula, Excel automatically changes the cell references to work with the new location. That's because, by default, cell references in formulas are *relative references*.

For example, in Figure 8-6, suppose you wanted to copy the formula from F2 into F3. The new formula in F3 should refer to values in row 3, not to row 2; otherwise the formula wouldn't make much sense. So, when F2's formula is copied to F3, it becomes =B3+C3+D3+E3 there.

F2 contains =B2+C2+D2+E2

F3		⁝	✕	✓	*fx*	=B3+C3+D3+E3	
◢	A	B	C	D	E	F	G
1		Q1	Q2	Q3	Q4	Total	
2	North	16	15	14	11	56	
3	South	20	21	25	23	89	
4	East	41	4	23	10		
5	West	19	28	17	15		
6							

F2's formula, when copied to F3, changes to =B3+C3+D3+E3

Figure 8-6: Most of the time when you copy a formula, you want its cell references to change.

You don't have to do anything special to move copy with relative referencing. It's the default when you move or copy. See Chapter 7.

Refer to cells with absolute referencing

You might not always want the cell references in a formula to change when you move or copy it. In other words, you want an *absolute reference* to that cell. To make a reference absolute, you add dollar signs before the column letter and before the row number. So, for example, an absolute reference to cell B1 would be =B1.

Figure 8-7 shows an example scenario in which an absolute reference would be appropriate.

A Cell B4 contains the formula =A4*B1. This calculates the tax on the amount in A4, where the tax rate appears in B1.

B If you copy this formula to the range B5:B17, you want the reference to the purchase price to change for each row (A5, A6, A7, and so on).

C However, you want the reference to the tax rate to stay the same for each row.

The dollar signs in the reference B1 ensure that that cell reference will remain static when copied.

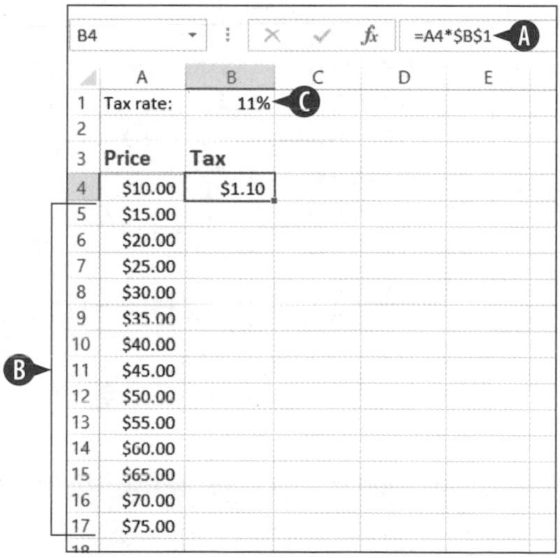

Figure 8-7: An absolute reference ensures the cell reference will not change when copied.

If you want to lock down only one dimension of the cell reference, you can place a dollar sign before only the column or only the row. For example, =$C1 would make only the column letter fixed, and =C$1 would make only the row number fixed. This is called a *mixed reference*.

To create an absolute or mixed reference, you can type the dollar signs directly into the cell where they are needed. Alternatively you can press F4 to cycle through all the available combinations of relative, mixed, and absolute references.

Insert functions

In Excel, a *function* refers to a named type of calculation. Functions can greatly reduce the amount of typing you have to do to create a particular result.

Ⓐ For example, instead of using the `=B2+B3+B4+B5+B6+B7+B8+B9+B10+B11` formula, you could use the SUM function like this: `=SUM(B2:B11)`.

Ⓑ With a function, you can represent a range with the upper-left corner's cell reference, a colon, and the lower-right corner's cell reference. In the case of `B2:B11`, there is only one column, so the upper-left corner is cell B2, and the lower-right corner is cell B11.

	A	B	C
1	Date	Revenue	
2	12/21/2017	$2,500	
3	12/22/2017	$2,200	
4	12/23/2017	$2,100	
5	12/24/2017	$1,800	Ⓑ
6	12/25/2017	$1,700	
7	12/26/2017	$2,400	
8	12/27/2017	$1,900	
9	12/28/2017	$1,200	
10	12/29/2017	$3,000	
11	12/30/2017	$2,800	
12	Total	=sum(B2:B11)	Ⓐ
13			
14			

Figure 8-8: You can specify a range as one of the function's arguments.

Range references cannot be used in simple formulas — only in functions. For example, `=A6:A9` would be invalid as a formula because no math operation is specified in it. You can't insert math operators within a range. To use ranges in a calculation, you must use a function.

An *argument* is a placeholder for a number, text string, or cell reference. Each function has one or more arguments, along with its own rules about how many required and optional arguments there are and what they represent. For example, the SUM function requires at least one argument: a range of cells. So, in the preceding example, B2:B11 is the argument. The arguments for a function are enclosed in a set of parentheses.

C You don't have to memorize the sequence of arguments (the *syntax*) for each function. Excel prompts you for them. When you type a function directly into a cell, a ScreenTip prompts you for that function's arguments.

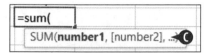

Figure 8-9: Excel prompts you for arguments when you type a function.

Use the SUM function

The SUM function is by far the most popular function; it sums (that is, adds) a data range consisting of one or more cells, like this:

```
=SUM(D12:D15)
```

You don't *have* to use a range in a SUM function; you can specify the individual cell addresses if you want. Separate them by commas, like this:

```
=SUM(D12, D13, D14, D15)
```

If the data range is not a contiguous block, you need to specify the individual cells that are outside the block. The main block is one argument, and each individual other cell is an additional argument, like this:

```
=SUM(D12:D15, E22)
```

The SUM function is so frequently used that it has its own button on the Home tab, in the Editing group. Here's how to use it.

1 Select the cell into which you want to insert the SUM function.

2 On the Home tab, click Sum.

  A The SUM function is placed in the cell.

  B Excel attempts to guess the range you want to sum and places a dashed outline around it.

  C It also fills the range into the SUM function's argument. The range is highlighted so it can be easily removed.

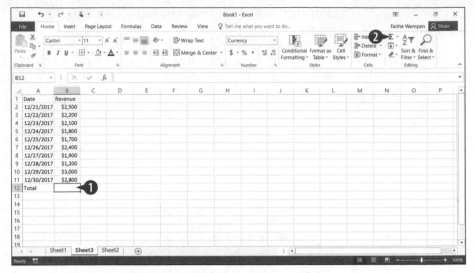

Figure 8-10: Select the cell to hold the function and then click Sum.

	A	B	C	D
1	Date	Revenue		
2	12/21/2017	$2,500		
3	12/22/2017	$2,200		
4	12/23/ⓑ	$2,100		
5	12/24/2017	$1,800		
6	12/25/2017	$1,700		
7	12/26/2017	$2,400		
8	12/27/2017	$1,900		
9	12/28/2017	$1,200		
10	12/29/2017	$3,000		
11	12/30/2017	$2,800		
12	Total Ⓐ	=SUM(B2:B11)Ⓒ		
13		SUM(**number1**, [number2], ...)		
14				

Figure 8-11: Excel tries to complete the function for you.

3A. If the range is correctly selected, press Enter to accept it.

OR

3B. Drag across the correct range to make a different selection and then press Enter.

When you press Enter to complete a function, as in step 3, Excel automatically adds a closing parenthesis to the function if there was not one already entered. You do not have to worry about typing one.

Use AVERAGE, COUNT, MAX, and MIN functions

Perhaps you noticed that the Sum button on the Home tab has an arrow on it. Click the arrow for a list. (See Ⓐ in Figure 8-12.) From this list you can select one of several other common functions to use instead of SUM:

- Ⓑ **Average:** Provides the average of the numeric values within the selected range. Ignores blank and non-numeric values

- Ⓒ **Count Numbers:** Counts the number of cells within the selected range that contain numeric values

- Ⓓ **Max:** Finds and returns the largest numeric value within the selected range

- Ⓔ **Min:** Finds and returns the smallest numeric value within the selected range

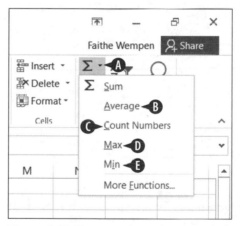

Figure 8-12: You can select other common functions from the Sum button's menu.

Find and insert a function

Typing a function and its arguments directly into a cell works fine if you happen to know the function you want and its arguments. Many times, though, you may not know these details. In those cases, the Insert Function feature can help you.

Insert Function enables you to pick a function from a list based on descriptive keywords. After you make your selection, it provides fill-in-the-blank prompts for the arguments.

To insert a function:

1 Select the cell in which to insert the function.

2 On the formula bar, click the Insert Function button to open the Insert Function dialog box.

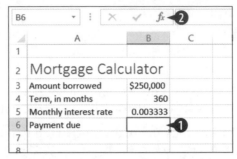

Figure 8-13: Click Insert Function on the formula bar.

3 In the Search for a function describe what you want to do.

4 In the Select a function box, click a function and then read about it below the list.

5 When the appropriate function is selected, click OK.

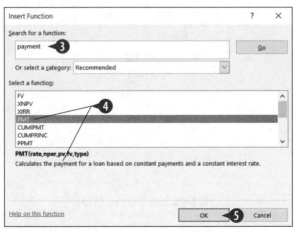

Figure 8-14: Describe the function's purpose, and then browse the list to find the one you want.

6. In the Function Arguments dialog box, type the number or enter the cell reference for each argument. Here are some things to remember about this dialog box:

A You can type directly into any of the argument text boxes.

B You can click in an argument's box and then click a cell on the worksheet behind the dialog box to fill in that cell reference.

C You can click the Collapse Dialog button for any argument to temporarily shrink the dialog box so you can see which cell you want to choose.

D Arguments in bold are required.

E Arguments that are not in bold are optional.

F The Formula Result area previews the formula's result.

7 Click OK to complete the function.

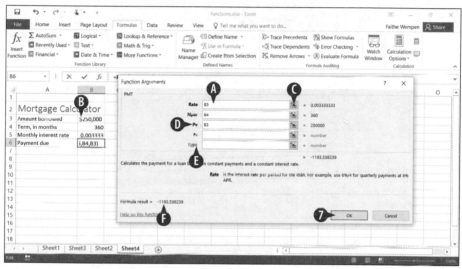

Figure 8-15: Fill in the arguments for the chosen function.

Choose from the Function Library

Once you become familiar with the names of Excel's most common functions, you will not need to look them up every time you need one, as you did in the previous section. Instead you can shortcut the process, either by typing them directly into the cell or by choosing them from the Function Library group on the Formulas tab.

The Formulas tab's Library group organizes functions by their general purpose. There is a separate drop-down list button for each category. There are also extra buttons for AutoSum, which is the same as the Sum button on the Home tab, and Recently Used.

To select a function from the library, follow these steps:

1. Select the cell in which to insert the function.

2. On the Formulas tab, click the button for the category of function you want.

3. Scroll through the list and click the desired function.

You can point at a function on the list to see a pop-up box describing it. (See Ⓐ in Figure 8-16.)

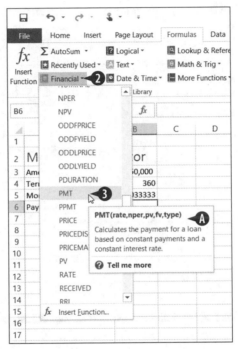

Figure 8-16: Choose the desired function from the category list.

4. Pick up the steps in the preceding section, "Find and insert a function," at step 6 to complete the function.

Show the current date or time with a function

You can use functions to show the current date or time in a cell and have that value be updated automatically every time you open the worksheet. (You can also update the field manually any time by pressing F9 or choosing Formulas ⇨ Calculate Now.) The functions to do this are

- NOW: Reports the current date and time

- TODAY: Reports the current date

Even though neither uses any arguments, you still have to include the parentheses, so they look like this when you use them:

```
=NOW ( )
=TODAY ( )
```

If you want a different format than the default for either of those results, you'll need to apply a different number format to the cell. Here's how:

1 With the cell selected that contains the function, click the dialog box launcher for the Number group on the Home tab.

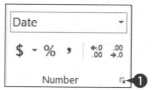

Figure 8-17: Click the dialog box launcher for the Number group.

2 In the Format Cells dialog box, in the Category list, click either Date or Time, whichever you want.

3 Select the desired format from the Type list.

4 Click OK.

You can combine the NOW or TODAY function with a formula to get results that are in the past or future. For example, =TODAY ( ) +7 returns the date that is 7 days in the future. Use decimal points to indicate times. For example, =NOW ( ) -0.5 returns the time that is 12 hours (50 percent of one day) in the past.

There are many other date and time functions available. Check out the functions on the Date & Time button's menu on the Formulas tab.

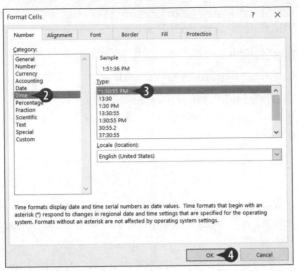

Figure 8-18: Select a specific date or time format.

Calculate loan terms

One of the most common calculation tasks in Excel is to determine the terms of a loan. There is a set of functions designed specifically for this task. Each function finds a different part of the loan equation, given the other parts:

- PV: Short for present value; finds the amount of the loan

- NPER: Short for number of periods; finds the number of payments (the length of the loan)

- RATE: Finds the interest rate per period

- PMT: Finds the amount of the payment per period

Each of those functions uses the other three pieces of information as its required arguments. For example, the arguments for PV are rate, nper, and pmt.

So, let's say, for example, that you want to know the length of a loan in which you borrow $20,000 at 5 percent interest per year (0.417 percent per month) if you make a monthly payment of $350. You can use the NPER function to figure that out. Here's how:

1 In Excel, create the labels needed for the structure of the worksheet, as shown in Figure 8-19. Fill in the information you already know about the loan.

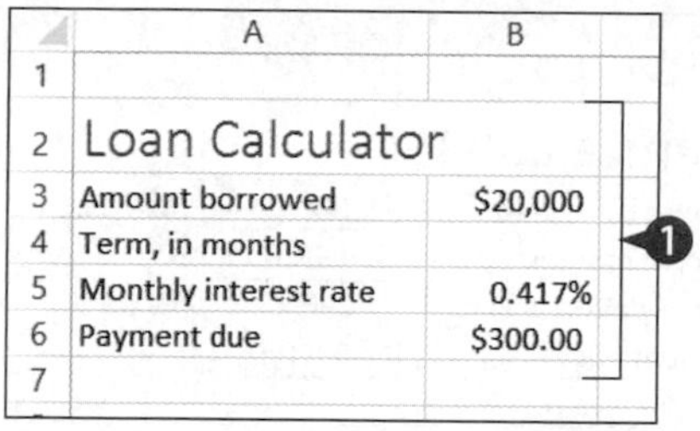

Figure 8-19: Create the structure of the worksheet, including the descriptive labels and any numbers that you already know.

2 Type =NPER(into the cell where the function should be placed.

A ScreenTip reminds you of the arguments to use and their proper order. (See **A** in Figure 8-20.)

3 Click or type the cell that contains the interest rate and then type a comma.

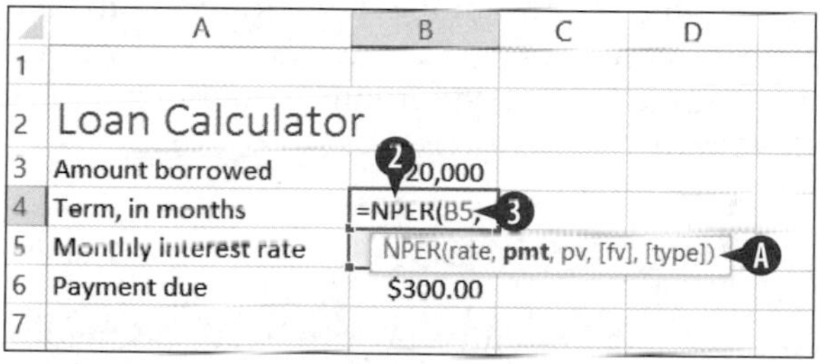

Figure 8-20: Begin entering the function and its arguments.

4 Click or type the cell that contains the payment amount, and then type a comma.

5 Click or type the cell that contains the loan amount, and then press Enter to complete the formula. The closing parenthesis is automatically added for you. If you do the example correctly, the loan term will show as −58.95187.

Besides these four simple functions, there are dozens of other financial functions available in Excel. For example, IPMT is like PMT except it returns only the amount of interest in the payment, and PPMT returns only the amount of principal. Explore the functions on the Financial button's menu on the Formulas tab on your own.

	A	B	C	D
1				
2	Loan Calculator			
3	Amount borrowed	$20,000		
4	Term, in months	=NPER(B5,B6,B3		
5	Monthly interest rate	NPER(rate, pmt, **pv**, [fv], [type])		
6	Payment due	$300.00		
7				

Figure 8-21: Add the remaining arguments, separating them with commas.

The result of the calculation will be negative if the present value (the loan amount) is a positive number. If you want the term to show as a positive number, change the amount borrowed to a negative number, or enclose the function within the ABS function (absolute value), like this: =ABS(NPER(B5,B6,B3)). ABS is short for absolute value.

Since the number of payments must be a whole number, you might choose to use the ROUNDUP function to round that value up to the nearest whole. The ROUNDUP function has two arguments: the number to be rounded and a number of decimal places. For a whole number, use 0 for the second argument. The finished formula would then look like this: =ROUNDUP(ABS(NPER(B5,B6,B3)),0).

Perform math calculations

Technically, all formulas perform math calculations, but there's a specific category of functions called Math & Trig for functions that deal directly with familiar math calculations like finding the square root (SQRT), tangent (TAN), sine (SIN), or cosine (COS) of a number. The ABS and ROUNDUP functions I mentioned at the end of the previous section fall into this category also. Check out the Math & Trig category list on the Formulas tab for a complete list of math functions.

Most of the math-related functions are fairly simple, with just one or two arguments. For example, the SQRT function takes only one argument: the number to be calculated. SQRT(A1) finds the square root of the number in cell A1.

Evaluate a condition with an IF function

The IF function determines whether or not a condition is true and then performs different actions based on that answer. IF is only one of many logical functions that Excel provides; see the list on the Logical button on the Formulas tab for others. For example:

Ⓐ Suppose a customer gets a 10 percent discount if he spends more than $50. You could use the IF function to determine whether his order amount qualifies.

E5			×	✓	f_x	=IF(D5>=50,D5*0.1,0)	
	A	B	C	D	E	F	
1	Order Log						
2							
3	Date	Cust#	Order#	Amount	Discount	Total	
4	12/1/2017	1	C01	$45.20	$0.00	$45.20	
5	12/1/2017	2	C02	$55.60	$5.56	$50.04	
6	12/2/2017	1	C03	$100.22	$10.02	$90.20	
7	12/2/2017	3	C04	$38.50	$0.00	$38.50	
8							Ⓐ

Figure 8-22: The amount of discount is determined using an IF function.

An IF function typically contains three arguments: condition, value_if_true, and value_if_false. Like all arguments, they are separated by commas.

Ⓑ The condition in this example is D5>=50. In other words, is the value in D5 greater than or equal to 50?

Ⓒ The value_if_true in this example is calculated by multiplying D5 by 0.1 (in other words, calculating 10 percent of it).

Ⓓ The value_if_false in this example is zero (0).

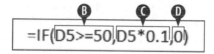

=IF(D5>=50,D5*0.1,0)

Figure 8-23: An IF function with three arguments.

The condition argument is the only required one. If you omit the value_if_true argument, the function returns 1 if the condition is true and 0 if the condition is false. If you omit the value_if_false argument, a value of 0 is assumed for it. Therefore in the above example, technically we did not have to include the value_if_false argument, since we wanted zero for it anyway.

TIP If you want to combine a SUM operation with an IF condition, you can use the SUMIF function, which does both at once. It sums a range of data if the condition you specify in its argument is true. You'll find it on the Math & Trig button's list, rather than under the Logical category.

Refer to named ranges

When constructing formulas and functions, naming a range can be helpful because you can refer to that name rather than the cell addresses. Therefore you don't have to remember the exact cell addresses, and you can construct formulas based on meaning. For example:

Ⓐ Instead of remembering that the number of employees is stored in cell B2, you could name the cell B2 *Employees*.

Ⓑ Then in a formula that used B2's value, such as =B2*3, you could use the name instead: =Employees*3.

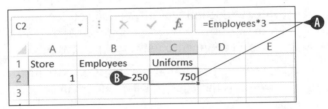

Figure 8-24: You can use range names in formulas.

You can name individual cells, as in the above example, but in some cases it may be more advantageous to name multi-cell ranges. For example, you might name multiple cells in a column that contains the same kind of information. When you then use the range name in a formula or function, Excel assumes that you mean the cell within that range that corresponds to the row or column in which you are typing:

Ⓒ In Figure 8-25, the named range of Employees encompasses B2:B7.

Ⓓ The same formula is used in every cell in column C: =Employees*3.

Ⓔ In each row, Excel assumes that you mean the cell in that same row.

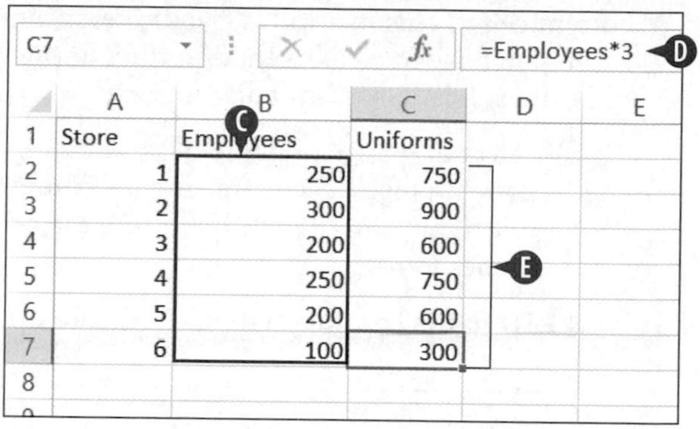

Figure 8-25: When a multi-cell range is named, references to that range are relative to the cell in which the formula is entered.

Excel is rather intelligent about deducing what you mean when you refer to named ranges. When you refer to a range in a calculation like the one shown in Figure 8-25, the reference is to an individual cell in the range. However, if you use the range name in a formula where it makes sense to be referring to the entire range, Excel does so.

For example, =SUM(Employees) would return the sum of *all* values within that range. (See ⓕ in Figure 8-26.)

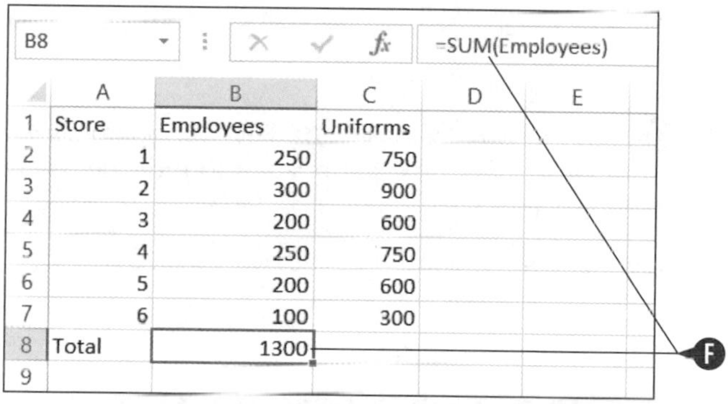

Figure 8-26: When you refer to a multi-cell range in a context that infers the entire range, Excel interprets it that way.

You can name a range in three ways, and each has its pros and cons.

Create range names by selection

If default names are okay to use, you may find automatic naming useful. With this method, Excel chooses the name for you based on text labels it finds in adjacent cells (above or to the left of the current cells). This method is fast and easy, and it works well when you have to create a lot of names at once and when the cells are well labeled with adjacent text:

1. Select the range to name. If you want to create multiple named ranges, each referring to a different column or row, select the entire range, including the cells containing the names to use.

2. From the Formulas tab, click Create from Selection.

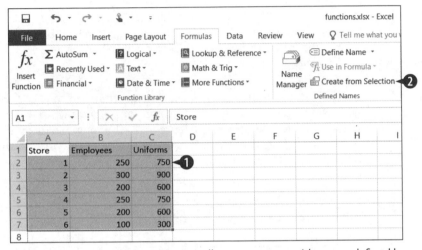

Figure 8-27: Allow Excel to automatically create ranges with names defined by labels in adjacent cells.

3. In the Create Names from Selection dialog box, mark or clear check boxes as needed to indicate where the labels are.

4. Click OK. The range names are created.

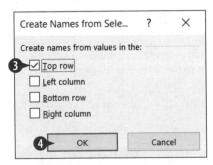

Figure 8-28: Confirm that Excel has correctly guessed where the labels are.

If you aren't sure if the ranges were correctly created, click the Name Manager button on the Formulas tab to see a list of all named ranges and their definitions.

Create range names using the Name box

With this fast and easy method, you get to choose the name yourself. However, you have to do each range separately; you can't do a big batch at a time:

1. Select the cells to include in the named range. Make sure that you select only the cells that contain actual data, not the cell containing text (like the column header).

2. Click in the Name box and type the new range name.

3. Press Enter.

Uniforms ②▾	⋮	✕	✓	ƒx	

	A	B	C
1	Store	Employees	Uniforms
2	1	250	750
3	2	300	900 ①
4	3	200	600
5	4	250	750
6	5	200	600
7	6	100	300
8			

Figure 8-29: Type a range name into the Name box.

Create range names using Define Name

If you want to more precisely control the options for the name, you can use the Define Name command. This method opens a dialog box from which you can specify the name, the scope, and any comments you might want to include:

1. Select the cells to include in the named range. Make sure that you select only the cells that contain actual data, not the cell containing text (like the column header).

2. On the Formulas tab, click Define Name.

3. In the New Name dialog box, type the desired name in the Name box.

④ (Optional) To limit the scope of the name to just the active worksheet, change the Scope setting to a particular sheet (such as Sheet1).

⑤ (Optional) Type any comments in the Comment box. This can help you remember why you created the range.

⑥ Click OK.

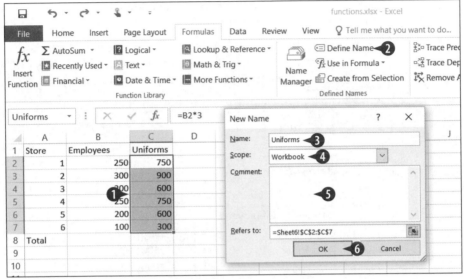

Figure 8-30: Define a range using the Define Name command.

Use Quick Analysis features

Here are some points to keep in mind about Quick Analysis:

Ⓐ When you select a range of cells, a small icon appears in the lower right corner of the selected area. This is the Quick Analysis icon, and clicking it opens a panel containing shortcuts to several types of common activities related to data analysis.

Ⓑ Click on the five headings to see the shortcuts available in that category. Then hover over one of the icons in that category to see the result previewed on your worksheet.

Ⓒ *Formatting:* These shortcuts point to conditional formatting options, which you will learn about in Chapter 9. For example, you could set up a range to make values under or over a certain amount appear in a different color or with a special icon adjacent.

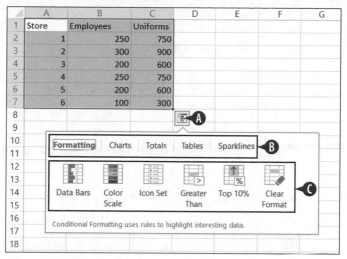

Figure 8-31: Open the Quick Analysis panel by clicking its icon. Then choose a category heading and click an icon for a command.

D *Charts:* These shortcuts generate common types of charts based on the selected data. You will learn about charts in Chapter 11.

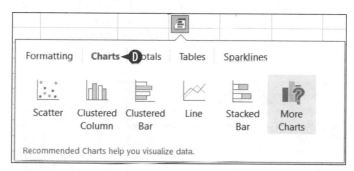

Figure 8-32: Quick Analysis offers shortcuts for creating several common chart types.

E *Totals:* These shortcuts add the specified calculation to adjacent cells in the worksheet. For example, Sum adds a total row or column.

F Notice that there are separate icons here for rows versus columns.

G Notice also that in this category there are more icons than can be displayed at once, so there are right and left arrows you can click to scroll through them.

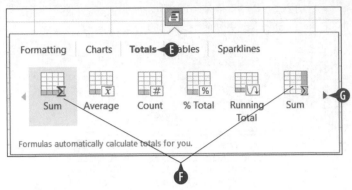

Figure 8-33: You can use Quick Analysis to add summary rows or columns.

H *Tables:* You can convert the range to a table (covered in Chapter 10) for greater ease of analysis. You can also generate several different types of PivotTables via the shortcuts here. A *PivotTable* is a special view of the data that summarizes it by adding various types of calculations to it.

I The PivotTable icons aren't well differentiated, but you can point to one of the PivotTable icons to see a sample of how it will summarize the data in the selected range. If you choose one of the PivotTable views, it opens in its own separate sheet.

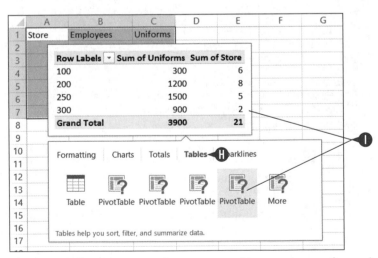

Figure 8-34: You can convert the range to a table or apply one of several PivotTable specifications.

J *Sparklines:* Sparklines are mini-charts placed in single cells. They can summarize the trend of the data in adjacent cells. They are most relevant when the data you want to trend appears from left to right in adjacent columns.

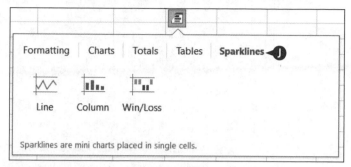

Figure 8-35: Choose Sparklines to add mini-charts that show overall trends.

CHAPTER NINE

Formatting and Printing Excel Worksheets

Face it: Plain worksheets aren't that much to look at. A worksheet packed full of rows and columns of numbers is enough to make anyone's eyes glaze over. However, formatting can dramatically improve a worksheet's readability, which in turn enables the reader to understand its meaning much more easily.

You can apply formatting at the whole-worksheet level or at the individual-cell level. This lesson focuses on formatting entire worksheets — or at least big chunks of them. You learn how to adjust rows and columns, apply worksheet backgrounds, create headers and footers, and format ranges as tables, complete with preset table formatting. You also learn how to print your work in Excel.

Apply and customize themes

Themes are formatting presets that you can apply to entire worksheets to change their formatting without having to select each formatting aspect manually. A theme includes font, color, and effect choices. You learned about themes in Word in Chapter 2, and

In This Chapter

➠ Applying and customizing themes

➠ Applying a worksheet background

➠ Resizing rows and columns

➠ Applying cell borders and shading

➠ Formatting cells using styles

➠ Using conditional formatting

➠ Setting up headers and footers

➠ Printing a worksheet

themes work basically the same way in Excel, too (and also in PowerPoint, as you'll see in Chapter 15). The theme choices are the same across those three applications, so you can standardize your formatting across all the documents you create, regardless of application used.

A theme doesn't override manually applied formatting. It simply redefines the default values for fonts, colors, and effects. In order for a theme's fonts to apply to a certain cell, you must not have changed its font manually, or you must have changed it to one of the fonts in the Theme Fonts section of the Font drop-down list. Similarly, in order for colors to take effect, you must have recolored objects only with the theme colors placeholders, not with fixed colors. See Chapter 2 for more information. If a cell or object doesn't appear to be working with the applied theme, select it and choose Home ⇨ Clear ⇨ Clear Formats.

Apply a theme

To apply a theme, do the following:

1 On the Page Layout tab, click Themes. The Themes menu appears.

2 Click the desired theme.

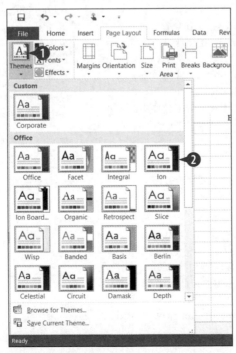

Figure 9-1: Choose a different theme to change the formatting.

Each aspect of a theme can also be individually changed, using the Colors, Fonts, and Effects buttons on the Page Layout tab. Each one opens a menu from which you can make your selection. These color, font, and effect schemes do not correspond one-to-one with the themes on the Themes button's list; there are more color, font, and effect schemes than there are themes. You can change these as follows:

Ⓐ Click Colors and choose a different set of colors.

Ⓑ Click Fonts and choose a different set of fonts.

Ⓒ Click Effects and choose a different effect type.

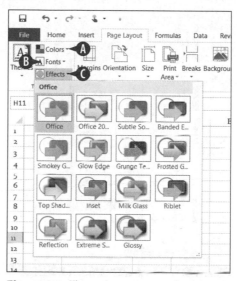

Figure 9-2: Change one aspect of a theme individually from the Design tab.

Effects apply only to certain graphic objects, such as drawn lines and shapes and SmartArt. Therefore, you should not expect to see an immediate, dramatic difference in your worksheet when you apply a different Effect setting unless your worksheet contains graphic objects *and* those graphic objects have not been manually formatted with specific effects.

Create a custom theme

You can create your own custom themes and then save them and share them with other people. This is handy when your company has specific fonts and colors that you are expected to use in your work-related projects; you can create a theme that uses the right formatting, and then everyone in your company can use that same theme, ensuring consistency.

To create a custom theme, follow these steps:

1. Make your selection of Color, Fonts, and Effects, as in Figure 9-2. If none of the font and color themes are suitable, you can create your own custom schemes, as I explain in the next two sections.

2 On the Page Layout tab, click Themes, and then click Save Current Theme.

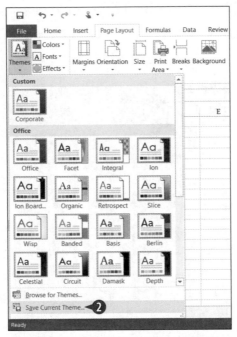

Figure 9-3: Select the Save Current Theme command from the menu.

3. In the Save Current Theme dialog box, type a name in the Filename box for the new theme. Leave the save location as-is.

4 Click Save.

From now on, your custom theme appears on the Themes button's menu, in the Custom section, as shown at **A** in Figure 9-5.

If you want to share the theme with others, repeat steps 1–4 but this time navigate to a shared location before clicking Save. Excel will save a copy of it there.

If you want to use someone else's custom theme, click the Themes button and click Browse for Themes. Navigate to the file's location and click Open. (See **B** in Figure 9-5.)

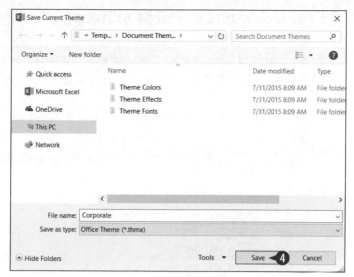

Figure 9-4: Save a custom theme to Excel's default location for themes.

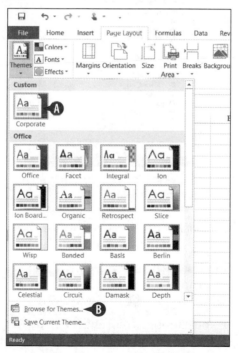

Figure 9-5: Custom themes appear at the top of the menu.

Create a custom color scheme

As you learned in Chapter 2, each color scheme in Office applications consists of values for 12 color placeholders. Each of the preset color combinations is represented on the Colors button's menu.

To create your own color combination, follow these steps:

1 On the Page Layout tab, click Colors.

2 Click Customize Colors.

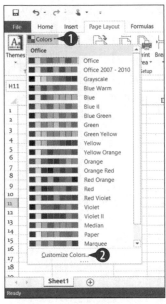

Figure 9-6: Choose Customize Colors from the menu.

3 For each of the 12 placeholders, click its arrow and then choose the desired color.

In most cases you will want to choose one of the colors in the Standard Colors area, or click More Colors for a wider selection. (See Ⓐ in Figure 9-7.)

If you choose a color that is in the Theme Colors section, the color choice will not hold when you apply a different color theme or choose different colors for the other placeholders. (See Ⓑ in Figure 9-7.)

4 In the Name box, type a name for the custom color scheme.

5 Click Save.

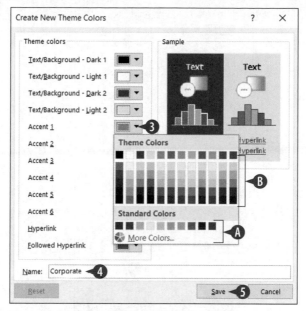

Figure 9-7: Select the desired color for each of the placeholders.

Create a custom font scheme

A font scheme consists of font choices for two types of text: Headings and Body. You can define these placeholders with the same font or two different fonts.

To create a custom font scheme:

1. On the Page Layout tab, click Fonts.

2. Click Customize Fonts.

3. Open the drop-down list for the Heading font and choose a font.

4. Open the drop-down list for the Body font and choose a font.

5. Type a name for the scheme in the Name box.

6. Click OK.

Should you wish to share your custom font or color schemes with others, you can find them in C:\Users\username\AppData\Roaming\Microsoft\Templates\Document Themes, in the Theme Colors or Theme Fonts folders, respectively. (Replace username in that path with your Windows username. Browse the C:\Users folder if you don't know the exact name.)

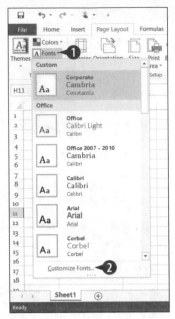

Figure 9-8: Choose the Customize Fonts command.

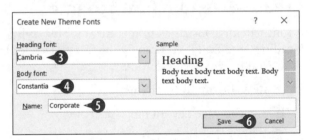

Figure 9-9: Define the fonts for the custom scheme.

Apply a worksheet background

A worksheet background is a background picture that appears only onscreen; it doesn't print. Some people use a background to dress up the appearance of a sheet, but be careful not to impede readability when using one.

As Excel defines it, a "background" is a picture. If you want a solid-color background, apply the same shading to the entire worksheet. You'll learn about cell shading later in this chapter, in "Apply cell borders and shading."

A background picture repeats (tiles) itself as needed to fill the entire worksheet. You can't modify that behavior to stretch the picture or make it repeat only once. (Are you getting the idea yet that a background is a pretty simple, limited feature? It is.)

To apply a picture background:

1 On the Page Layout tab, click Background. The Insert Pictures dialog box opens.

2. Do one of the following:

A Click Browse next to From a File to browse your computer for the picture to use.

B Click in the Search Bing box, type a keyword to use for an Internet image search, and press Enter to initiate the search.

C Click Browse next to OneDrive to browse your OneDrive storage for the picture to use.

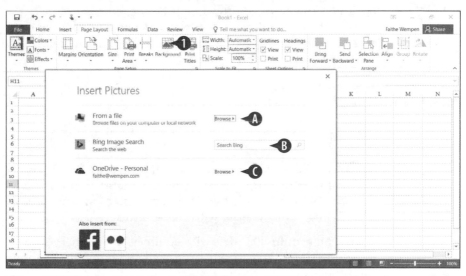

Figure 9-10: Select a source from which to locate an image.

3 Select the desired picture. (If you chose option **A** or **C** in step 2, you might need to browse for it.)

4 Click Insert.

To remove a background image, choose Page Layout ⇨ Remove Background.

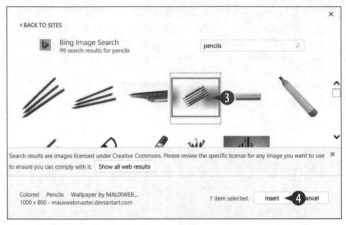

Figure 9-11: Select the desired image.

If you want a background picture that prints, add a picture to the header or footer. You'll learn about headers and footers later in this chapter, in "Set up headers and footers." After entering the header/footer for editing, use the Header & Footer Tools Design ⇨ Picture command to insert a picture in the header or footer. A code appears in the header or footer, but the image itself appears behind the worksheet.

Apply cell borders and shading

Borders and shading are two ways of dressing up a cell's plain appearance. Here are some tips for using them:

Ⓐ A *border* is a line around one or more sides of a cell. Not all sides of a cell necessarily have a border. For example, in Figure 9-12 only the top and bottom of this cell have a border. Borders print with the worksheet.

Ⓑ Don't confuse borders with gridlines, which are the lines onscreen that mark where one cell ends and the next one begins.

Ⓒ To turn off the display of gridlines onscreen, clear the View check box in the Gridlines section of the Page Layout tab.

Ⓓ Gridlines do not print by default. To force gridlines to print, mark the Print check box in the Gridlines section.

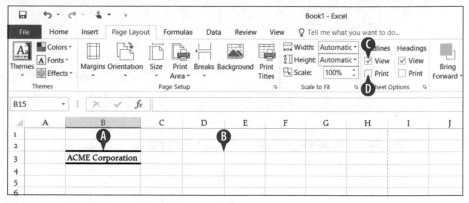

Figure 9-12: Borders versus gridlines

To apply a border:

1. Select the cell or range that should receive the border.

2. Click the arrow on the Borders button on the Home tab, opening a menu.

3. If you don't want the default colored line (black), point to Line Color and then select the desired color (if not black, the default).

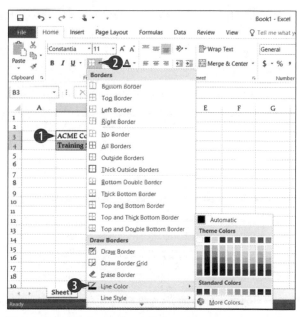

Figure 9-13: Select a line color.

4. If you don't want the default line style (solid thin line), reopen the Borders button's menu, point to Line Style, and click the desired line style.

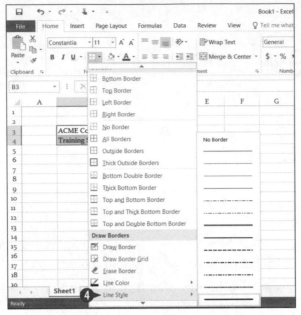

Figure 9-14: Select a line style.

5. Reopen the Borders button menu if needed. Then click the type of border in the Borders section of the menu:

(A) The Outside border, when applied to a multi-cell range, creates a single border around the range.

(B) All Borders applies the border to every side of every cell in the range.

(C) Some of the possible styles include solid (thin), solid (thick), dotted, and dashed (in various patterns).

	A	B	C	D	E	F
1						
2	(A) March					
3						
4		Week 1	52			
5		Week 2	48			
6	(B)	Week 3	42			
7		Week 4	58	(C)		
8						
9		Note: All figures are preliminary				
10						
11						

Figure 9-15: Some border examples.

Format cells using cell styles

As you learned in Chapter 3, in Word you can apply formatting preset called *styles* to individual paragraphs. You can do the same thing to individual cells in Excel, except in Excel they are called *cell styles.*

Excel provides a number of styles with names that reflect their suggested uses. For example, there are Heading 1 and Heading 2 styles, a Total style, and a Title style. There are also styles that apply shading using the theme's color placeholders.

To apply a cell style to one or more cells:

1 Select the cell(s) to affect.

2 On the Home tab, click Cell Styles.

3 Click the desired style.

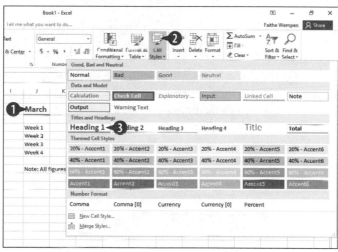

Figure 9-16: Apply a cell style.

You can also create your own custom cell styles. To do so:

1 Format a cell the way you want it, with font, color, alignment, border, and fill settings. Make sure that cell is selected.

2 On the Home tab, click Cell Styles.

3 Click New Cell Style.

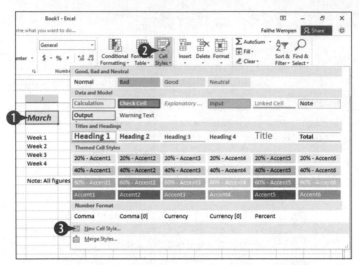

Figure 9-17: Format a cell the way you want the style, and then choose New Cell Style.

④ Type a name for the style in the Style name box.

⑤ Review the style definition in the six categories listed.

⑥ If there is any additional formatting you need to define for the style, click Format. Make your choices in the Format Cells dialog box and click OK to return to the Style dialog box.

⑦ Click OK to create the style.

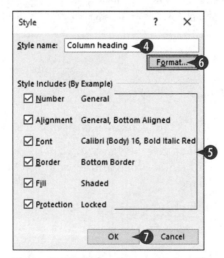

Figure 9-18: Define the new style with six categories of formatting.

After you have defined a custom style, it appears at the top of the Cell Styles button's gallery, in the Custom group. (See **A** in Figure 9-19.)

To manage a custom style (modify, delete, or duplicate it), right-click it and choose the appropriate command. (See **B** in Figure 9-19.)

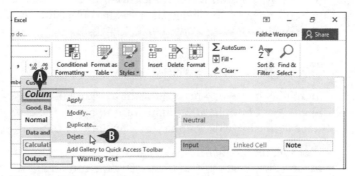

Figure 9-19: Custom styles appear at the top of the Cell Styles gallery.

Resize rows and columns

Each column in a worksheet starts with the same width, which is 8.43 characters (based on the default font and font size) unless you've changed the default setting. That's approximately seven digits and either one large symbol (such as $) or two small ones (such as decimal points and commas).

You can define the default width setting for new worksheets: Choose Home ➪ Format ➪ Default Width and then fill in the desired default width.

As you enter data into cells, those column widths may no longer be optimal. Data may overflow out of a cell if the width is too narrow, or there may be excess blank space in a column if its width is too wide. (Blank space is not always a bad thing, but if you're trying to fit all the data on one page, for example, it can be a hindrance.)

In some cases, Excel makes an adjustment for you automatically, as follows:

- **For column widths:** When you enter numbers in a cell, Excel widens a column as needed to accommodate the longest number in that column, provided you haven't manually set a column width for it.

- **For row heights:** Generally, a row adjusts automatically to fit the largest font used in it. You don't have to adjust row heights manually to allow text to fit. You can change the row height if you want, though, to create special effects, such as extra blank space in the layout.

The units of measurement are different for rows versus columns, by the way. Column width is measured in characters of the default font size. Row height is measured in points. A point is $1/72$ of an inch.

Change a row's height

There may be times when you want to manually adjust a row's height. For example, you might want to add some extra blank space vertically between one row's text and another's.

After you manually resize a row's height or a column's width, it won't change its size automatically for you anymore. That's because manual settings override automatic ones.

To manually change row height to a specific value, do the following:

1. Select any cell in the row.

2 Choose Format ⇨ Row Height to open the Row Height dialog box.

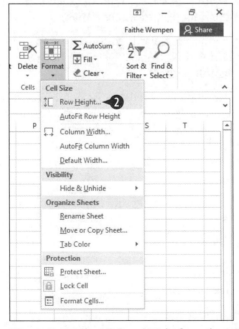

Figure 9-20: Choose Row Height from the menu.

③ Enter the desired row height in points. You can use decimal points for precise sizing if needed.

④ Click OK.

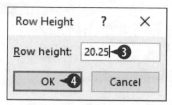

Figure 9-21: Specify a row height.

You can also adjust a row's height manually by dragging the divider below the row's number up or down. (See Ⓐ in Figure 9-22.)

A ScreenTip shows the height as you are dragging. (See Ⓑ in Figure 9-22.)

If you manually adjust a row height, that row will no longer autofit its height to content. To autofit row height, double-click the divider below the row's number. (See Ⓒ in Figure 9-22.)

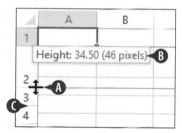

Figure 9-22: Adjust row height by dragging.

Change a column's width

You can adjust a column width any time you need it to be wider or narrower to achieve the look you want. Most often this will be because the content of one or more cells in the column overflows its cell (or is truncated), but you can also widen or narrow columns to create specific layout effects, such as adding more space between columns of text or numbers.

To manually change column width to a specific value, do the following:

1. Select any cell in the row.

2 Choose Format ⇨ Column Width to open the Column Width dialog box.

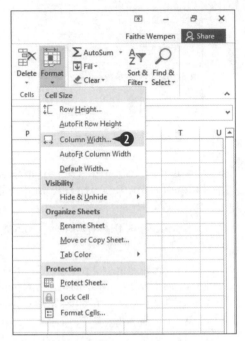

Figure 9-23: Choose Column Width from the menu.

3 Enter the desired column width in characters (of the default font and size).

4 Click OK.

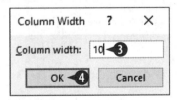

Figure 9-24: Specify a column width.

To autofit a column's width to the widest entry in that column, double-click the divider below the column's letter and the one to its right.

You can also adjust a column's width manually by dragging the divider to the right of the column's letter to the left or right. (See **A** in Figure 9-25.)

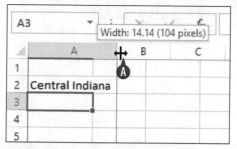

Figure 9-25: Adjust column width by dragging.

Make text wrap in a cell

When you have an entry that overflows its cell but you don't want to widen the column for some reason (perhaps it would interfere with the worksheet's layout, for example), you might choose to wrap the text in that cell to multiple lines. The row height increases automatically as much as needed to display the multiple lines and decreases again later if conditions change such that the additional height is no longer needed.

To wrap text in a cell:

1. Select the cell(s) that should be set for wrapping. You can set a cell for text wrapping even if it doesn't have anything in it at the moment that requires wrapping.

2. On the Home tab, click Wrap Text.

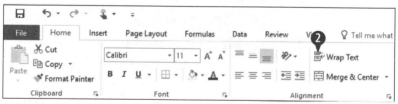

Figure 9-26: Wrap text to multiple lines in a cell.

To remove the setting for a cell (or multiple cells), repeat the steps to toggle the option off.

Use conditional formatting

Conditional formatting is formatting that appears only if certain conditions are met in the cell's content. It can help readers understand the data they are seeing more easily. For example, you might have a cell display a green background if the value is over a certain amount and a red background if the value is under a certain amount. A reader can quickly scan a long column of numbers and zero in on just the red or green shaded cells as being especially small or large.

Excel provides several preset types of conditional formatting, including these:

- **Data bars:** Each cell has left-to-right shading proportionate to the value of the number. The end result is that each cell functions as a mini-chart. See Figure 9-27 for an example.

	A	B
3	Date	Volume
4	10/1/2017	27129
5	10/2/2017	44147
6	10/3/2017	13337
7	10/4/2017	57161
8	10/5/2017	55422
9	10/6/2017	84140
10	10/7/2017	71997
11	10/8/2017	18513

Figure 9-27: Data bars.

- **Color scales:** Each cell has a background color that reflects its content. For example, in Figure 9-28, lower numbers are red, average numbers are yellow, and higher numbers are green.

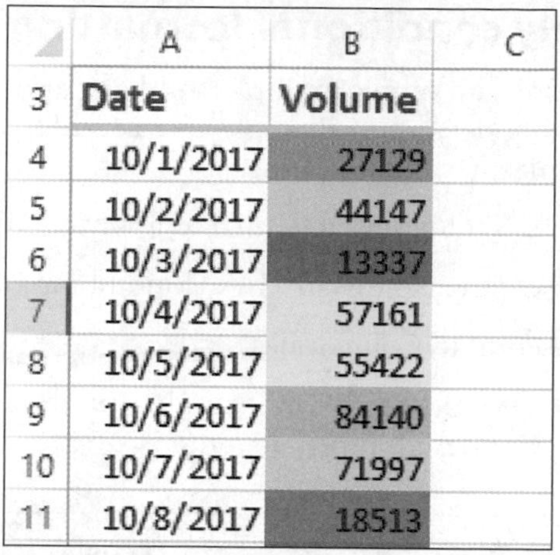

	A	B	C
3	**Date**	**Volume**	
4	10/1/2017	27129	
5	10/2/2017	44147	
6	10/3/2017	13337	
7	10/4/2017	57161	
8	10/5/2017	55422	
9	10/6/2017	84140	
10	10/7/2017	71997	
11	10/8/2017	18513	

Figure 9-28: Color scale.

- **Icon sets:** Each cell has an icon that varies depending on its content. In Figure 9-29, higher numbers have green check marks, average numbers have yellow exclamation points, and lower numbers have red Xs.

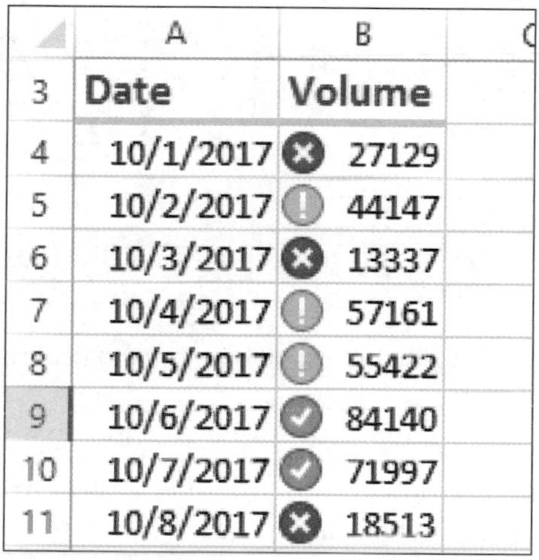

	A	B	C
3	**Date**	**Volume**	
4	10/1/2017 ✖	27129	
5	10/2/2017 ❗	44147	
6	10/3/2017 ✖	13337	
7	10/4/2017 ❗	57161	
8	10/5/2017 ❗	55422	
9	10/6/2017 ✔	84140	
10	10/7/2017 ✔	71997	
11	10/8/2017 ✖	18513	

Figure 9-29: Icon set.

You can also define your own custom conditional formatting.

Apply conditional formatting

Let's look at a simple example: applying a color scale. In the following steps you will apply a preset color scale and then customize it.

1. Select the cells to which to apply conditional formatting.

2 On the Home tab, click Conditional Formatting.

3 Point to Color Scales.

4 Click the desired color scale—or one that is close to what you want if none are right.

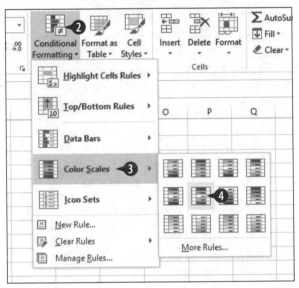

Figure 9-30: Choose a conditional formatting preset.

Next, you'll customize the preset that you just applied.

5 With the same range still selected, click Conditional Formatting again.

6 Click Manage Rules.

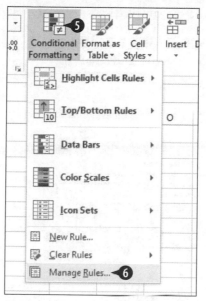

Figure 9-31: Choose Manage Rules.

7 Select the rule you just created.

8 Click Edit Rule.

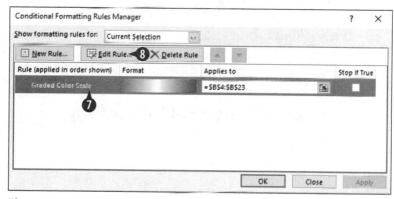

Figure 9-32: Select the rule to edit.

9 Open the Color palette under Minimum and choose the desired color.

10 Open the Color palette under Maximum and choose the desired color.

11 Change any other aspects of the rule as desired. For example, you can define exact minimum and maximum values, change the midpoint, choose more or fewer colors for the scale, and so on.

12 Click OK.

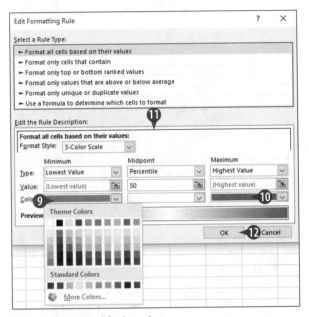

Figure 9-33: Modify the rule.

13. Click OK to close the Conditional Formatting Rules Manager.

Remove conditional formatting

To remove the conditional formatting from cells:

1. Select the cells from which to remove conditional formatting.

2 On the Home tab, click Conditional Formatting.

3 Point to Clear Rules.

4 Click Clear Rules from Selected Cells.

Figure 9-34: Clear conditional formatting.

Set up headers and footers

If you plan to print your worksheet, you might want to set up a header and/or footer. Headers and footers are lines of information that repeat at the top and bottom of each page. These lines can contain any text you want plus codes that print page numbers, the current date and time, or other information.

The header and footer areas exist on all worksheets, but by default they are blank so you don't notice them. Follow these steps to display the header and footer areas and place text and codes in them as desired:

1 On the Insert tab, click Header & Footer.

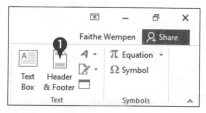

Figure 9-35: Choose Header & Footer from the Insert tab.

The display changes to Page Layout view. The worksheet is displayed as it will print, with header and footer areas at the top and bottom. Consider Figure 9-36:

Ⓐ Notice that the Header area consists of three boxes. Depending on which box you choose to enter content into, it will appear left-aligned, centered, or right-aligned at the top of the page.

Ⓑ The Header & Footer Tools Design tab appears, containing buttons for inserting various types of content into the header and footer.

❷ (Optional) If you want to work with the footer, click Go to Footer.

❸ Click in the placeholder area in which you want to enter header or footer content. The insertion point appears in it.

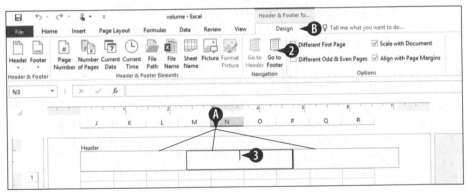

Figure 9-36: The Header area in Page Layout view.

❹ If you want text to appear, type it. Any text you type will appear the same on all pages.

❺ Click to move the insertion point to a different section if desired.

6. Click a button on the Header & Footer Tools Design tab to insert a code:

Ⓐ Page Number shows the page number of each printed page.

Ⓑ Number of Pages shows the total number of pages in the printout.

Ⓒ You might want to type *of* between the Page Number and Number of Pages codes.

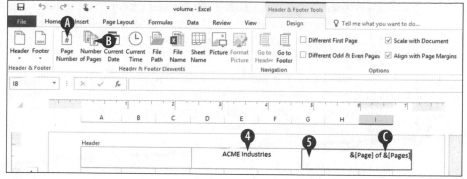

Figure 9-37: Codes inserted in a header.

D Current Date inserts an automatically updating date code.

E Current Time inserts an automatically updating time code.

F File Path prints the entire path and file name of the workbook.

G File Name prints only the file name (not the path) of the workbook.

H Sheet Name prints the sheet name (as represented on the sheet tab).

I Picture prompts you to select a picture to include. Note that this picture will not be confined to the header or footer area.

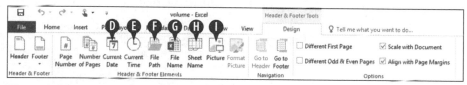

Figure 9-38: Other types of codes you can insert.

The Picture code is somewhat different from the other codes. You are prompted for the picture to use when you insert this code. You can choose a picture from your own files, or you can search online for a picture.

Depending on its size, the picture may overflow out of the header and footer, into the background of the worksheet itself. The picture starts out in whatever area of the header or footer you place it in. So, for example, if you want a picture to start in the lower right corner of the page and extend upward and to the left from there, place its code in the right-hand section of the footer.

To change the picture's size, click Format Picture. In the Format Picture dialog box, on the Size tab, you can set its height and width. You can also crop the picture using the controls on the Picture tab of that dialog box.

If you don't see the picture immediately after inserting the code, click in some other section of the header or footer to move the insertion point out of the one where the picture code resides, and the picture should appear.

Print a worksheet

You can print your work in Excel on paper to share with people who may not have computer access or to pass out as handouts at meetings and events. You can print the quick-and-easy way with the default settings or customize the settings to fit your needs.

By default, when you print, Excel prints the entire active worksheet — that is, whichever worksheet is displayed or selected at the moment. But Excel also gives you other printing options:

- **Print multiple worksheets:** If more than one worksheet is selected (for example, if you have more than one worksheet tab selected at the bottom of the Excel window), all selected worksheets are included in the printed version. As an alternative, you can print all the worksheets in the workbook. To select more than one worksheet, hold down the Ctrl key as you click the tabs of the sheets you want.

- **Print selected cells or ranges:** You can choose to print only selected cells, or you can define a print range and print only that range (regardless of what cells happen to be selected).

Print entire worksheets

To print the active worksheet, and optionally other worksheets too in the same workbook, follow these steps:

1 If you want to print only one worksheet, click its tab to make sure it is active.

OR

If you want to print multiple worksheets, hold down Ctrl and click each of the worksheet tabs of the desired sheets to group them.

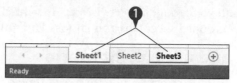

Figure 9-39: Select the tabs of the sheets to print, if more than one.

2 Choose File ⇨ Print.

If you chose more than one sheet in step 1, [Group] appears in the title bar. (See **A** in Figure 9-40.)

3 Make sure the correct printer appears in the Printer setting; click to change it if needed.

4 Specify a number of copies in the Copies box.

5 Change any additional print settings as needed. For example, you can change the collation options if you are printing multiple copies, and you can change the margins and paper size. These options are like the ones you learned about in "Print your work" in Chapter 2.

6 (Optional) Click the left and right arrows to preview the pages of the print job.

7 Click Print.

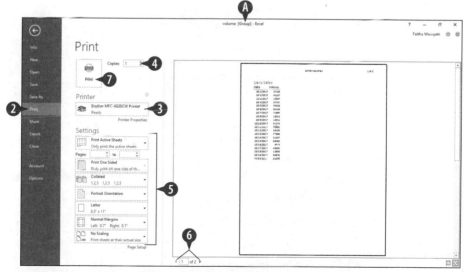

Figure 9-40: Set print options and then click Print.

8. If you grouped sheets in step 1, right-click one of the grouped sheet tabs and choose Ungroup Sheets.

Set and use a print range

If you want to select a range for a one-time print job, you can select the range of cells and then choose to print only the selection. Here's how:

1. Select the cells to print.

2. Choose File ⇨ Print.

3 Click Print Active Sheets to open a menu.

4 Click Print Selection.

5. Continue printing normally, as in the previous section's steps.

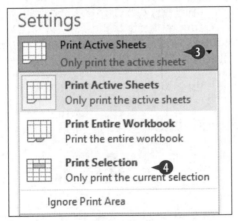

Figure 9-41: Choose to print only the selected cells.

If you want to print a certain range every time you print that sheet, it may make more sense to set a print range. When you do so, Excel prints only the cells included in your specified range, even when you don't select that range before printing.

To set a print range:

1. Select the desired cells to include.

2 On the Page Layout tab, click Print Area.

3 Click Set Print Area.

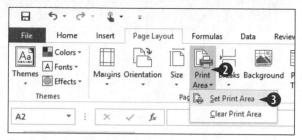

Figure 9-42: Set the print area.

When a print area is set, nothing outside of that area will print on that sheet. If you want to override this behavior temporarily to print the entire sheet, choose the Ignore Print Area command on the menu shown in Figure 9-41.

To clear the print area, repeat the steps for setting the print area, but in step 3 choose Clear Print Area instead.

If you want the same cells (only) to print each time you print this worksheet in the future too, you can select them as a print range, and Excel remembers them.

CHAPTER TEN

Storing and Managing Databases in Excel

Besides its calculation capabilities, Excel also has some great features for managing databases. You can store, search, sort, and filter large lists of information with ease in Excel. And by converting a range to a table in Excel, you can access certain sorting and filtering commands even more easily.

In this chapter, you learn some database concepts and find out how to create and manage tables in a workbook. You'll also learn how to create and save a query, remove duplicates from a dataset, and use data validation to minimize data entry errors.

Create an Excel database

Here are a few terms you need to know. A *database* is a collection of information stored in a consistent, structured way. An address book is a database, for example, because it stores the same pieces of information about each person: name, address, city, state, and ZIP code. In that example, each type of information is a *field*. Each person's complete entry (all fields) is a *record*. The collection of data as a whole is called a *table*, or *dataset*.

In This Chapter

- ➡ Entering database data in Excel
- ➡ Converting between a range and a table
- ➡ Sorting a table
- ➡ Filtering a table
- ➡ Referring to named ranges in formulas in a table
- ➡ Creating and saving a query
- ➡ Removing duplicates from a dataset
- ➡ Validating data to minimize entry errors

In a database table in Excel:

A Each column is a field. The field names appear in the first row.

B Each record appears in a separate row beneath the column headings.

▲	A	B	C	D	E	F
1	First ▼	Last ▼	Address ▼	City ▼	State ▼	ZIP ▼
2	Anna	Zimmerman	12 West Main St.	Carmel	Indiana	46088
3	Beth	Yoder	345 SR 234 West	Noblesville	Indiana	46060
4	Carl	West	50818 Highway 37	Indianapolis	Indiana	46240
5	Dan	Turner	577 W. Walnut Street	Franfort	Ohio	43291
6	Ed	Sanchez	9881 Maple Lane	Franklin	Ohio	42199
7	Frank	Richards	91 Mockingbird Drive	Noblesville	Indiana	46060
8	Gary	Perry	456 North Carmel Drive	Indianapolis	Indiana	46211
9	Hank	Niederman	2847 Wilson Parkway	Carmel	Indiana	46088
10	Inez	Montoya	1991 Ponting Street	Fishers	Ohio	46115
11	Jaqui	Keith	998 Madison Trail	Fishers	Ohio	46115
12	Kim	Jones	789 Williams Lane	Greenwood	Indiana	47281
13	Larry	Illes	1811 Scout Street	Greencastle	Indiana	49828
14	Mort	Hausman	5917 Bluff Falls Way	Greenwood	Indiana	49828
15	Norman	Gordon	1084 Riverview Drive	Fishers	Ohio	46115
16						

Figure 10-1: A simple database in an Excel table.

Tables have several advantages over ranges:

● You can filter by columns using an easy drop-down list.

● You can add a Totals row that adds summary calculations without having to manually enter the formula for it.

● You can apply table formatting presets.

● You can publish a table to a SharePoint server.

Convert a range to a table

Before you convert a range to a table, make sure you have properly prepared the range. Specifically, you need to do the following:

● Make sure that the first row contains the field names you want to use. The entries in the first row will become column headings.

● Make sure that each row contains one and only one record.

● Make sure that there are no blank rows between rows containing records

When the data is cleaned up and ready to go, follow these steps:

1. Select the range of data that should become a table.

2. On the Insert tab, click Table. The Create Table dialog box opens.

3. Confirm that the range is correct.

4. Click OK. The range is converted to a table and the default table formatting style is applied to it.

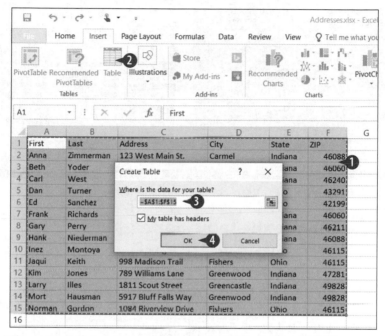

Figure 10-2: Convert a range to a table using the Insert tab's Table command.

Convert a range to a table and choose a table style

Here's an alternate method that enables you to specify the table formatting style you want:

1. Select the range of data that should become a table.

2. On the Home tab, click Format as Table.

3. Click the desired format. The Format as Table dialog box opens. (It's exactly the same as the Create Table dialog box shown in Figure 10-2 except for its name.)

4. Confirm that the range is correct.

5. Click OK. The range is converted to a table and the chosen table formatting style is applied to it.

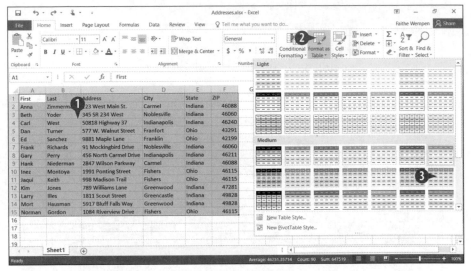

Figure 10-3: Convert a range to a table by applying table formatting to it.

Change the table appearance

After a range has been converted to a table, you can modify its appearance by adjusting the table style.

To choose a different table style, on the Table Tools Design tab, choose a different style from the Table Styles gallery. (See **A** in Figure 10-4.)

Fine-tune the table's appearance by marking or clearing check boxes in the Table Style Options group:

B Header Row turns the display of the header row on/off.

C Total Row toggles a total row at the bottom of the table. In tables with numeric data that can be summarized, this is great, but in a database that is purely unrelated records, like in an address book, it makes no sense to use this.

D Banded Rows and Banded Columns toggle the use of shading in alternate rows or columns to make the data easier to browse.

E First Column and Last Column make their respective columns formatted differently from the others in the table; this is useful if those columns contain headings or summary data.

F Filter Button toggles the down-pointing arrow button on each field name at the top of the table.

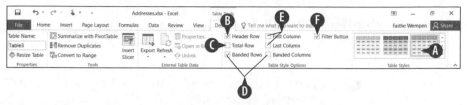

Figure 10-4: Control table formatting on the Table Tools Design tab.

Convert a table to a range

If you decide you want the dataset to go back to being a regular range, you can easily restore that status. Here's how:

1 Select any cell within the table.

2 On the Table Tools Design tab, click Convert to Range.

3 Click Yes to confirm. The range is no longer a table; however, it retains any formatting that it had as a table.

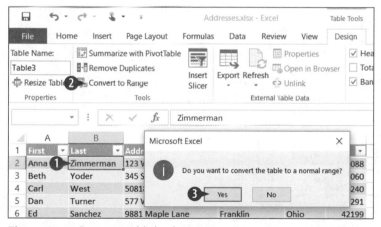

Figure 10-5: Convert a table back to a range.

If you want to remove the table formatting, select the range and choose Home ⇨ Clear ⇨ Clear Formats.

Sort a table

You can sort a table's data by a single field or by multiple fields.

Sort by a single field

When you sort by a single field, Excel rearranges the records in A to Z (ascending) or Z to A (descending) order based on the field you specify.

There are several ways to sort by a single field, including the following:

Ⓐ Click any cell in the desired column and then click the AZ or ZA button on the Data tab.

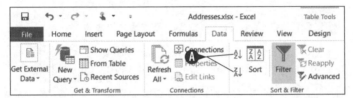

Figure 10-6: Use the Sort Ascending (AZ) or Sort Descending (ZA) button for a quick one-column sort.

Ⓑ Right-click any cell in the desired column, point to Sort, and then click Sort A to Z or Sort Z to A. (The wording of the choices is different if the column contains numbers or dates.)

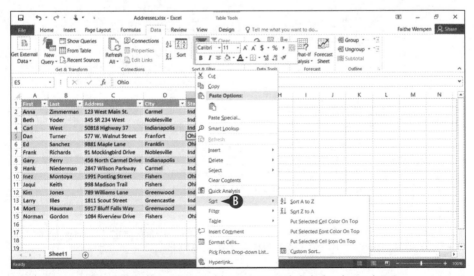

Figure 10-7: Right-click in the column, choose Sort, and click the desired sort.

C Click the arrow at the top of the column to open its menu, and then click Sort A to Z or Sort Z to A. (Again, the wording of the choices is different if the column contains numbers or dates.)

Figure 10-8: Open the column's menu and choose a sort option.

Sort by multiple fields

When you sort by multiple fields, it does a single sort by the first field you specify, and then in the event of a tie for that field, it relies on the additional field(s) you specify to break the tie. For example, if you sort first by City and then by State, Decatur GA will come before Decatur IL.

To sort by multiple fields:

1. Click anywhere within the table to sort. It does not have to be within a specific column.

2. On the Data tab, click Sort. The Sort dialog box opens.

3. Open the Sort by drop-down list and choose the first field on which to sort.

4. Open the Order drop-down list and choose the desired order.

5. Click Add Level.

6. For the newly added level, repeat steps 3–4.

7. Add more levels if needed; click OK when finished.

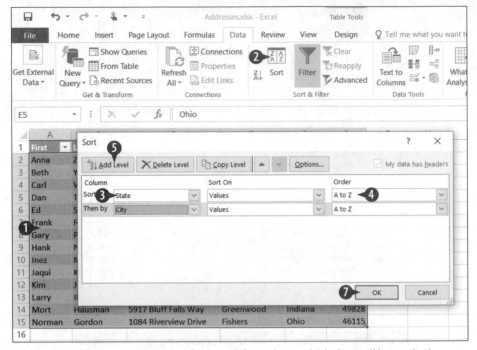

Figure 10-9: Choose multiple sort fields and the order in which they will be applied.

Remove a sort or filter

When a table has been sorted, the button at the top of the column shows an up-pointing or down-pointing arrow on it, depending on whether you sorted in ascending or descending order. (See **A** in Figure 10-10.)

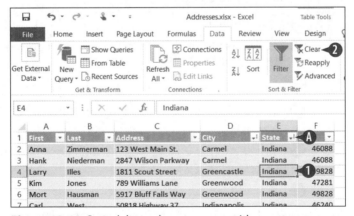

Figure 10-10: Sorted data columns appear with an extra arrow on their button.

To clear the sort (and also clear any filters that have been applied):

1 Click any cell in the table.

2 Click the Clear button on the Data tab.

Filter a table

Filtering data means to hide certain records, displaying only the ones that match criteria you specify. There are several ways to specify filter criteria.

Filter by selection

Perhaps the easiest filtering technique is *to filter by selection*, which hides all records where the specified field does not contain a sample value you select. Here's how to do it:

1 Click a cell in the table that contains the value by which you want to filter. For example, to show only addresses with Indianapolis as the city, select a cell in the City column that contains Indianapolis.

2 Right-click the cell, and then point to Filter.

3 Click Filter by Selected Cell's Value.

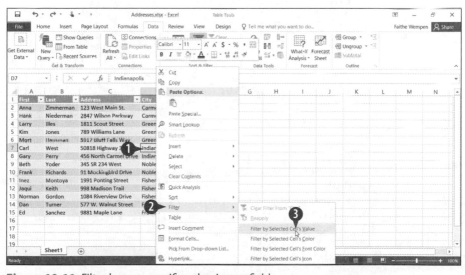

Figure 10-11: Filter by one specific value in one field.

A filter is immediately applied so that only records that match that value in that field are shown.

Filter by choosing values from a list

If you want to filter by more than one value in a field, here's a technique that enables you to do so:

1 Click the arrow on the column containing the values by which you want to filter.

2 Clear the check boxes for each value that you do not want to include.

In step 2, if you want only a few values to be selected, click the (Select All) check box to clear all check boxes, and then mark just the few you want.

3 Click OK. The filter is applied.

4. (Optional) To filter the data even further, repeat steps 1–4 for additional columns.

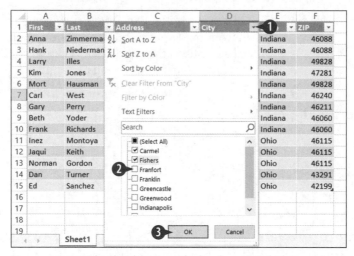

Figure 10-12: Filter by choosing which values to include or exclude.

Filter using conditions

Depending on the content of the field (text, date, number, etc.) you can also use conditions for that type of data, such as Begins With, Ends With, or Contains (for text) or Greater Than, Less Than, or Between (for numbers).

For a field that contains text, do the following:

1 Click the arrow on the column containing the values by which you want to filter.

2 Point to Text Filters (if it's a text field) or the equivalent command for number or date field if appropriate.

3 Click the desired logical condition, such as Begins With.

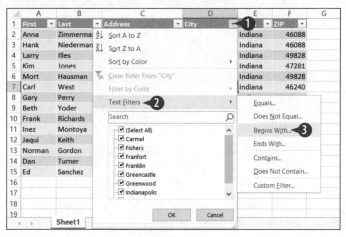

Figure 10-13: Choose a condition.

4 In the Custom AutoFilter dialog box, specify the condition value. You can optionally enter a second condition, too.

Use ? to represent a single character or * to represent any number of characters.

5 Click OK. The filter is applied.

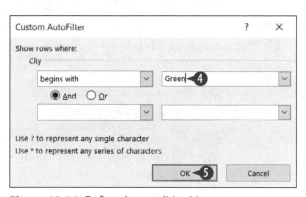

Figure 10-14: Define the condition(s).

Add a Total row to a table

One of the advantages of making a data range into a table is the ability to show a Total row as part of the table, summarizing one or more columns that you specify. Contrary to its name, a total row can do more than just total (add). A total row performs a summary operation of your choice on any field(s) in the table. For example, you can average, count, sum, or find the minimum, maximum, or standard deviation of that column's data.

1 To enable the total row, on the Table Tools Design tab, mark the Total Row check box.

Figure 10-15: Enable the total row by marking the Total Row check box.

The Total row appears at the bottom of the table. Each of the cells in that row now have their own arrow that opens a menu.

TIP

② At the bottom of a column that contains data you want to summarize, click the arrow to open the drop-down list.

The arrow for a cell appears just outside the cell to its right.

TIP

There are more options available when working with a numeric field, but even text fields have some totals they can display, such as a count of the number of records. You can use any function in Excel for this, but the most common ones are available from a menu for easy access.

If a column has a calculation in the Total row that you don't want, click the arrow on that cell to open its menu and choose None. (See Ⓐ in Figure 10-16.)

③ Click the kind of calculation you want.

④ (Optional) Type a text label in an adjacent cell to describe the calculation you chose.

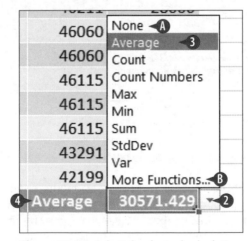

Figure 10-16: Select the desired calculation. Use text labels to make sure your meaning is clear.

If you want a function that isn't on the list in Figure 10-16, choose More Functions, and then choose from the Insert Function dialog box, just as you would if you used the Insert Function command on the Formulas tab in a normal range. (See ⓑ in Figure 10-16.)

Create queries

When you sort and filter a table in a certain way, it may take you a few minutes to set up those conditions. Wouldn't it be nice to be able to save that sorting and filtering specification to use again later? A query does that and can also do much more. For example, a query can also temporarily hide certain columns as well as sort and filter rows.

Although the full query capabilities of Excel are beyond the scope of this book, the following steps give you a little taste of it.

To create a query:

➊ Click anywhere within the table.

➋ On the Data tab, click From Table. A Query Editor window opens.

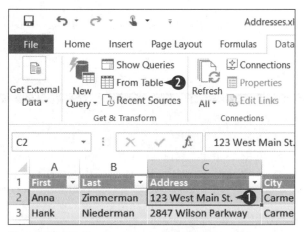

Figure 10-17: Start a new query based on a table.

➌ Sort the data the way you want it. Use the AZ and ZA buttons on the Home tab or open a column's menu and choose a sort order for that column.

➍ Filter the data to include only the records you want. Use a column's menu to set up the filter, as you learned earlier in this chapter.

If you want to remove one of the instructions, click it in the Applied Steps box and then click the X to its left. (See A in Figure 10-18.)

5 If you want to exclude certain columns, click Choose Columns. Clear the check box for each column to exclude and click OK.

6 Change the name in the Name box to something meaningful for the instructions you specified.

7 Click Close & Load. The query results appear on a new sheet in the workbook.

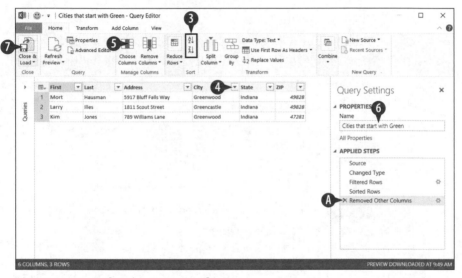

Figure 10-18: Define the query specification.

The query results sheet becomes a permanent part of your workbook. Any time you want to view the query results, just display that worksheet. However, the data on the query results sheet doesn't automatically update when the data changes on the original sheet. Therefore you will want to refresh the query whenever the original data changes. To do this, on the Data tab, click Refresh All. (See B in Figure 10-19.)

Figure 10-19: Click Refresh All to refresh all results.

Remove duplicates from a dataset

A dataset may contain records for which certain fields are identical, and usually that is not a problem. For example, you might have multiple people with the same last name, address, and phone number if they all live in the same household.

In some cases, though, duplicate values in multiple fields may signal that the same record has been accidentally entered multiple times. For example, if two people both have the same Social Security number, that's probably an entry error.

You can define a Remove Duplicates operation so that multiple fields must all be identical in order for a deletion to occur. For example, you might delete records with the same phone number only if both the first name and last name are identical.

When removing duplicates, you don't get to select which of the duplicates will be deleted; the first instance is kept and all others are deleted. Therefore if it's important that the most recently entered record be kept, sort the table in descending order by a Date field first.

To find duplicates:

1 Click anywhere in the table.

2 On the Data tab, click Remove Duplicates.

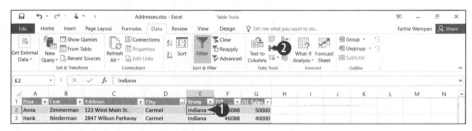

Figure 10-20: Click Remove Duplicates.

3 Mark or clear check boxes as needed to define which fields must *all* be duplicate in order for records to qualify for deletion.

4 Click OK.

5. At the confirmation box, click OK.

If the deletion results are not what you expected—for example, if some records were deleted that you meant to keep—use Undo (Ctrl+Z) immediately after the deletion to get them back.

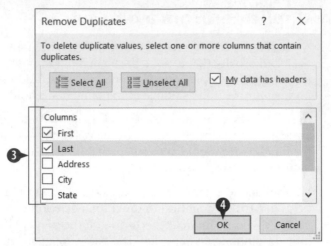

Figure 10-21: Choose which fields to check for duplication.

Restrict data entry with validation rules

Data entry errors can cause big headaches in database management. When two entries vary, is it because they are truly different, or did someone just make a mistake? It's hard to know.

Data entry inconsistencies can also plague a database, especially if multiple people are entering records. For example, should states be entered with their full names or as two-character abbreviations? If the data isn't consistent, you won't get accurate results when you query, sort, or filter on a certain state.

A validation rule can limit entry to only certain types of values, such as only integers or dates. It can also limit text entry to a certain number of characters.

Create a validation rule

To create a data validation rule:

1 Select the cells for which the rule will apply. For example, to restrict entries in a certain field in a table, select that field's column.

2 On the Data tab, click Data Validation.

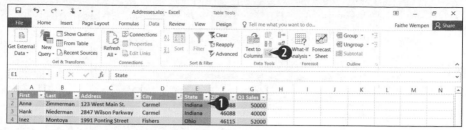

Figure 10-22: Click the Data Validation button.

3. On the Settings tab, open the Allow drop-down list and choose a restriction. Then enter any parameters for that restriction.

For example, if you wanted states to be entered as two-character codes, you might choose Text length and then enter 2 as both the minimum and maximum length, as in Figure 10-23. (See **A** in Figure 10-23.)

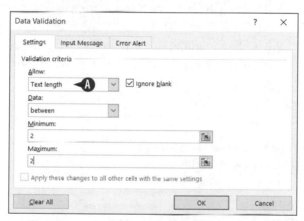

Figure 10-23: A text length validation rule.

Or, if you choose a certain type of entry, such as Whole Number, you can enter a range of whole numbers into which the value must fall, as in Figure 10-24. (See **B** in Figure 10-24.)

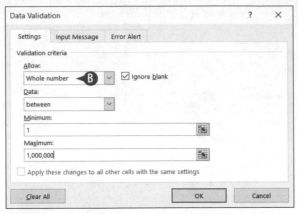

Figure 10-24: An integer validation rule where the number is positive.

④ Click the Error Alert tab.

⑤ In the Title box, enter text to appear in the title bar of an error message box that will appear if the rule is violated.

⑥ In the Error message box, enter text to appear as the body of the error message.

⑦ Click OK.

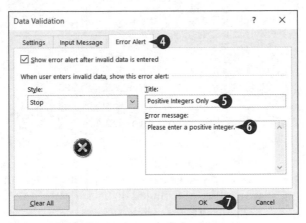

Figure 10-25: Create the error dialog box text.

When someone violates the rule, the error box appears that you set up in steps 4–6. (See 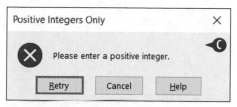 in Figure 10-26.)

Figure 10-26: The error message appears in a dialog box when the validation rule is broken.

Remove a validation rule

To remove data validation, follow these steps:

1. Select the cell(s) from which to remove data validation.

2. On the Data tab, click Data Validation.

3. Click Clear All.

4. Click OK.

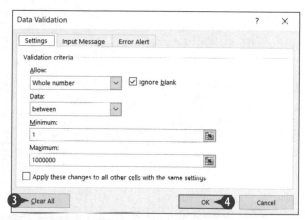

Figure 10-27: Clear data validation rules from the selected cell(s).

CHAPTERELEVEN

Creating Charts in Excel

Is a picture really worth a thousand words? Just ask anyone who has been faced with a spreadsheet full of numbers to analyze. Creating charts that summarize data is a quick way to make sense of data — or to present data to someone else.

In this lesson, you learn how to create several types of charts and how to add and remove chart elements such as legends, data labels, and data tables. You learn how to move and resize charts, how to place a chart on its own separate tab in a workbook, and how to apply a variety of formatting to a chart.

Choose the correct chart type

Excel offers various chart types, each suited for a different type of data analysis. Here are some things to note about Excel's chart types:

A Pie charts are good for situations in which the relationship among the values being charted is the most significant thing. For example, suppose Bill sold 15 cars, Dave sold 7, and Tom sold 8. If the important thing is that Bill sold 50 percent of all the cars, a pie chart is ideal. Pie charts are limited in that they can handle only one data series.

In This Chapter

⟹ Creating a chart

⟹ Moving and resizing a chart

⟹ Switching rows and columns

⟹ Modifying the data range for a chart

⟹ Changing the axis scale

⟹ Applying a chart style

⟹ Changing a chart's colors

⟹ Adding, removing, and formatting chart elements

The key that tells what each color represents is called a *legend*.

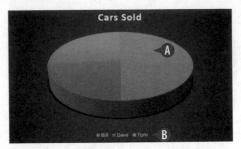

Figure 11-1: A pie chart shows the relationship of each data point to the whole.

C A column chart is good for showing multiple data series on a two-axis grid. This particular sub-type is called a clustered column chart; each data point has its own bar, and the bars are clustered together into groups.

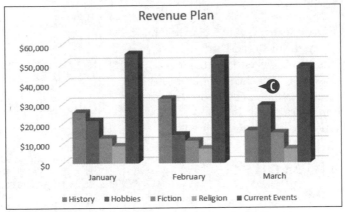

Figure 11-2: A column chart summarizes multiple data series.

D When a column chart is horizontal, it's called a bar chart.

E The sub-type shown here is called a stacked chart; instead of having a separate bar for each month, it combines all three months in a single bar. This makes it easier to see their cumulative value.

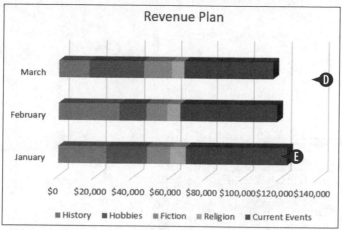

Figure 11-3: A bar chart is a horizontal version of a column chart.

A few of the other chart types available include:

- **XY (Scatter):** Plots each data point as a small dot on a two-dimensional (XY) grid, like in geometry class

- **Stock:** Plots the high, low, open, and close price of a stock on a particular day or range of dates

- **Line:** Plots each data point as a small dot, and then connects the dots of each series with a different color of line

- **Area:** Like a line chart, except the area beneath each line is filled in solid with color

- **Surface:** Like an area chart only three-dimensional

There are many other types, and you might want to explore them on your own. For the rest of this chapter, though, I stick with the basic column and pie charts for the examples.

Create a chart

Here's how to create a chart:

1. Select the data to include. Make sure you include any labels that go with that data too. The labels will become label text on the chart.

To select noncontiguous cells, hold down Ctrl as you drag across them. For example, if the labels aren't contiguous with the data you want to include, you might need to use Ctrl to select the labels.

If there are total rows or columns in your data, don't include them in your selection in step 1 unless you are *only* charting the total row or column. (See **A** in Figure 11-4.)

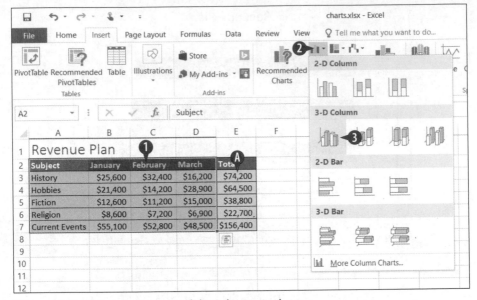

Figure 11-4: Click a chart type, and then choose a sub-type.

② On the Insert tab, in the Charts group, click the button for the chart type you want. You can change the chart type later if you change your mind.

③ On the menu that appears, click the desired sub-type.

A preview of the chart appears behind the menu as you move the mouse pointer over the various sub-types.

Move and resize a chart

After creating a chart, you can move it around on the worksheet or resize it by dragging it:

Ⓐ Position the mouse pointer over any part of the chart except a selection handle, so that the pointer becomes a four-headed arrow, and drag it where you want it.

Ⓑ To resize a chart, drag one of the selection handles (white circles) on its border.

Resizing a chart may change its *aspect ratio* (its ratio of height to width), and the chart may stretch or compress as you drag.

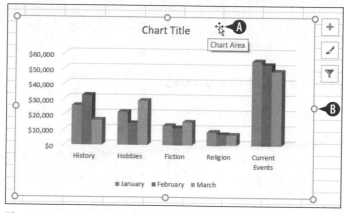

Figure 11-5: Drag a chart to move or resize it.

You can also place a chart on its own separate sheet in the workbook. Here's how to do that:

1 Select the chart.

2 On the Chart Tools Design tab, click Move Chart.

3 Click New Sheet.

4 (Optional) Change the sheet name if desired.

5 Click OK.

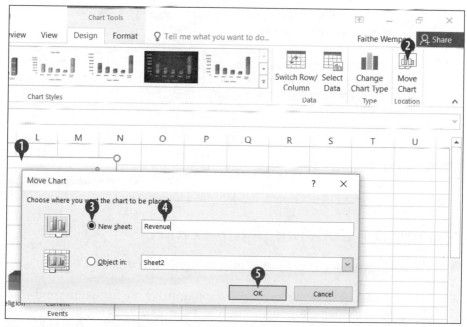

Figure 11-6: Move a chart to its own sheet.

To reverse that process, display the chart's sheet and repeat steps 2–5, but in step 3 choose Object in and then choose the desired existing worksheet.

Switch rows and columns

When you create a chart that includes multiple data series, the chart might not plot that data in the way that you expect by default. For example, take a look back at the chart in Figure 11-5. What if you had intended for the different column colors to represent the different book categories, as in Figure 11-7?

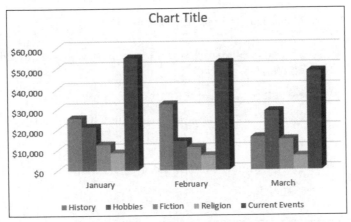

Figure 11-7: This chart uses the same data as Figure 11-5 but plots it by columns rather than by rows.

On the Chart Tools Design tab, click Switch Row/Column to switch back and forth between the two ways of plotting the data. (See **A** in Figure 11-8.)

Figure 11-8: Click Switch/Row/Column to change the plot orientation.

Modify the data range for a chart

If you need the chart to plot different data than you originally chose, there are two ways to go. One is to delete the chart and start over. If you haven't invested much time formatting and customizing the chart, this may be your quickest option.

The other method is to modify the data range for the chart, as follows:

1 On the Chart Tools Design tab, click Select Data.

2. To select a different range for the chart:

A Click in the Chart data range box.

B On the worksheet, drag to redefine the range.

3 Clear the check box for any series or category that you want to temporarily exclude.

4 Select any series that you want to remove permanently from the chart and then click Remove.

5 Click OK.

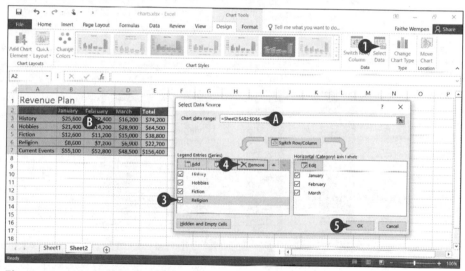

Figure 11-9: Modify the data range.

Change the axis scale of a chart

The axis scale is the numeric scale on the chart on which the values are plotted. In Figure 11-6, for example, the axis scale is $0 to $60,000.

Excel sets the axis scale automatically based on the values in the data range. However, you might sometimes want to adjust the axis scale strategically to give the audience a different impression of the data. For example, check out the following charts:

A In this chart, the axis scale is automatically set by Excel. The lower value is 16150 and the upper value is 16650. The differences among the bars are obvious.

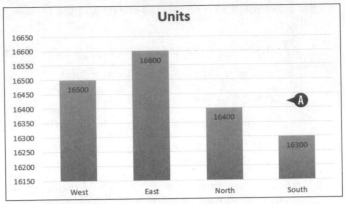

Figure 11-10: With the default axis scale, the differences are clear.

B In this version, the axis scale has been manually changed to 0 as the lower value and 16650 as the upper value. In this version, the values appear to be nearly identical.

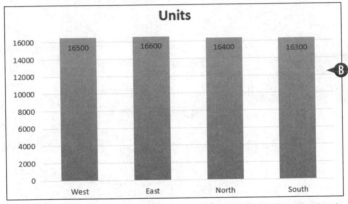

Figure 11-11: You could manually modify the axis scale to make the differences seem less significant.

Here's how to set the axis scale:

1A Click the vertical axis on the chart to select it.

OR

1B On the Chart Tools Format tab, open the Select Object drop-down list and choose Vertical (Value) Axis.

2 On the Chart Tools Format tab, click Format Selection. The Format Axis task pane opens.

3 Click Axis Options text hyperlink if it is not already selected.

4 Click the Axis Options icon.

⑤ Click the Axis Options heading to expand its options if it is not already expanded.

⑥ In the Bounds area, change the Minimum and Maximum values as desired.

If you decide to go back to the default value, click Reset. (See Ⓒ in Figure 11-12.)

⑦ Click Close to close the task pane.

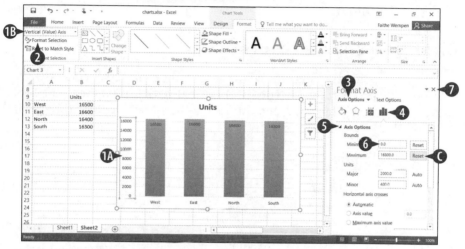

Figure 11-12: Change the axis scale in the Format Axis task pane.

Apply a chart style

Excel provides many *chart styles*, which are formatting presets for charts. Rather than manually formatting a chart, you may wish to save yourself some time by applying a chart style to improve a chart's appearance. (If you do want to do manual formatting, though, it's covered later in this chapter.) Some things to note about applying chart styles:

Ⓐ To apply a chart style, choose one from the Chart Styles gallery on the Chart Tools Design tab.

Ⓑ As with other galleries, you can click More to open up a list of additional choices.

Some chart styles have more or fewer chart elements (that is, helper objects such as titles, legends, labels, and so on). In the next section you learn how to add and remove chart elements, so you aren't tied to the particular combination of elements that a particular chart style uses.

Figure 11-13: Apply a chart style.

Here's another way to apply a chart style. With the chart selected, click the Chart Styles button (the paintbrush button) to the right of the chart's frame. Then select a style from the palette that appears.

Change a chart's colors

You can change the colors used in the chart, independently of the chart style. To do so, click Change Colors on the Chart Tools Design tab, and then choose a different set of colors. (See (A) in Figure 11-14.)

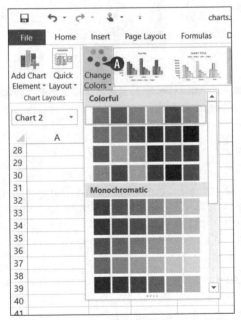

Figure 11-14: Change the colors used in the chart.

Note that these are not really different color schemes in the same sense as the overall color scheme for the entire workbook. The colors that appear on the Change Colors button's menu are just different combinations, tints, and shades of the overall workbook's colors.

Here's another way to change the colors. With the chart selected, click the Chart Styles button (the paintbrush button) to the right of the chart's frame. At the top of the pane that appears, click Colors, and then choose the desired colors.

If you want to change the overall colors of the workbook, do the following:

1 On the Page Layout tab, click Colors.

2 Click the desired color scheme. This changes all the color placeholders for the workbook and also affects the chart colors.

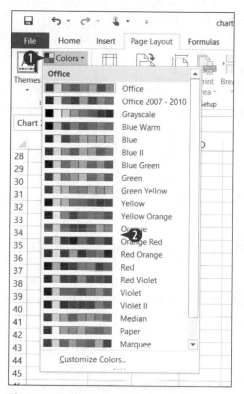

Figure 11-15: Apply a different color scheme to the entire workbook.

If you want to individually customize a particular chart element, such as making a certain data series or data point a specific color, see "Format a chart element" later in this chapter.

Add or remove chart elements

Chart elements refers to the individual parts of a chart that you can enable, adjust, and format separately. Figure 11-16 points out some of the most common chart elements. Most of these elements are optional and can be turned on/off.

In Figure 11-16, I have increased the size of some of the text-based chart elements so you can see them better. To increase the size of a text-based element, such as data labels or a legend, select that element and then use the Grow Font button on the Home tab. Keep in mind, though, that if you manually change the size of some text, it won't change automatically anymore if you resize the chart.

Here are some things to remember about chart elements:

Ⓐ The *chart area* is the entire chart.

Ⓑ A *chart title* describes the entire chart.

Ⓒ The *plot area* is the section of the chart area that contains the actual plotted data. It is usually set to the same background color as the chart area, so it's not that noticeable, but in Figure 11-16 I've made it a different color so you can see it.

Ⓓ The *legend* is a key that describes the meaning of each series color or pattern.

Ⓔ A *data table* shows the data on which the chart is based; it can be helpful to use a data table if the chart is not near the data.

Ⓕ An *axis* contains the scale on which the data is plotted. When the axis contains numeric values, it's called the value axis. When the axis contains labels, like the months in Figure 11-16, it's called the category axis.

Ⓖ An *axis label* explains the unit of measurement or the meaning of the axis values.

Ⓗ *Data labels* report the exact value of each data point.

Ⓘ An individual bar, column, slice, or other data marker is a *data point*.

Ⓙ The set of bars, columns, or other data markers of a common color or pattern is a *data series*.

K A 3D-style chart, like the one in Figure 11-16, has *walls* behind the data series, and a *floor* on which the bars sit. The walls and floor can be formatted separately from the chart or plot area and can even be formatted separately from one another.

L *Gridlines* appear behind the columns or bars to help make the height of the columns or bars easier to read on the axis.

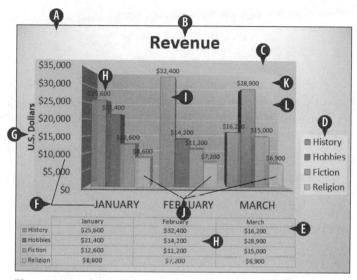

Figure 11-16: Parts of a chart.

A few of the elements of a chart are fairly essential, like the data points and the value axis, and you couldn't remove them without the chart losing its meaning. Most of the other elements, however, are optional. A chart can still make sense without a data table, data labels, or even a legend, in some cases.

Some chart elements can be removed by selecting them (by clicking) and then pressing the Delete key on the keyboard. The chart title and legend are that way, for example.

To add or remove a chart element:

1. Select the chart, so that icons appear in its upper right corner.

2 Click Chart Elements. A menu of the optional chart elements appears.

3 Mark or clear the check box for each element to turn it on or off.

4. When you are finished, click Chart Elements again to close the menu.

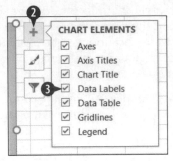

Figure 11-17: Add or remove chart elements.

Going the above route is the quickest and easiest way to enable or disable a certain element. However, if you are enabling an element, you might want a bit more control over how it appears. For some additional options, use the following method instead:

1. Select the chart.

2 On the Chart Tools Design, tab, click Add Chart Element.

3 Point to the desired chart element to see a submenu.

4 Click the desired option on the submenu.

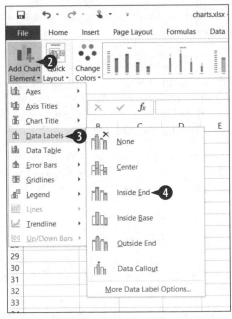

Figure 11-18: Add a chart element with specific options.

TIP

In Figure 11-17, if you hover over one of the items on the menu, you see a right-pointing triangle. Click that, and a submenu appears that contains many of the same options as in Figure 11-18.

Format a chart element

Now let's look at some ways to change a chart element's appearance.

Reposition a chart element

As you saw in Figure 11-18, each element has a submenu on the Add Chart Element button's menu. Some of these, like the ones for Legend and Chart Title, contain options for different positions within the chart area.

You can also drag-and-drop some of the chart elements to move them within the chart area:

1. Select the chart element, so that selection handles appear around that element.

2. Position the mouse over it so the pointer turns into a four-headed arrow.

3. Drag the element to a new location.

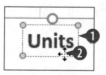

Figure 11-19:
Add a chart
element with
specific options.

Not all chart elements can be repositioned. For example, the data points and the axes are in fixed locations, and a data table can't appear anywhere other than below the chart.

Change the properties of a chart element

Each chart element has its own unique customizable properties. It's hard to generalize about these, as they vary so dramatically depending on the element. For example, for a data series (a set of colored bars) in a 3D column chart, you can adjust the width of the bars, the gaps between them, and the shape of the bars (box, pyramid, cylinder).

To access an element's properties, do the following:

1A Click the chart element to select it.

OR

1B On the Chart Tools Format tab, open the Select Object drop-down list and choose the desired element.

2 On the Chart Tools Format tab, click Format Selection. The Format task pane opens for that element.

3 Click the rightmost icon on the task pane. Its name and appearance varies, but this is the one that shows the properties that are specific to the chosen element type.

4 Adjust the properties as desired.

5 Close the task pane.

Figure 11-20: Change the chart element's properties from its task pane.

While you're in the task pane, check out the other sections to see what else you can do to change the appearance of that element. There are dozens of settings available.

Resize chart element text

To adjust the size of some text in a chart, do the following:

1 Select the desired chart element. You can do this by clicking it or by using the Select Object drop-down list on the Chart Tools Format tab.

2A On the Home tab, click the Increase Font Size or Decrease Font Size button to change the font size.

OR

2B Open the Size drop-down list and select a specific size.

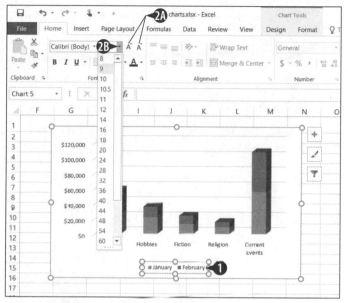

Figure 11-21: Use the Home tab controls to change the text size.

Format chart element text

You can also change the attributes of the text (bold, italic, and so on). From the Home tab, use the buttons in the Font group, as shown in Figure 11-22, or use keyboard shortcuts:

Ⓐ Bold (Ctrl+B)

Ⓑ Italic (Ctrl+I)

Ⓒ Underline (Ctrl+U)

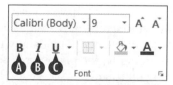

Figure 11-22: Apply bold, italics, or underline to a text element on a chart.

To apply further special effects to the text, use the Text Effects settings in the element's task pane. Here's how:

1. Select the desired chart element.

2. On the Chart Tools Format tab, click Format Selection to open the element's task pane.

3. At the top of the task pane, click the Text Options hyperlink.

4. Click the Text Effects icon.

5. Click an effect category to expand its settings.

6. Adjust the settings as desired.

7. Repeat steps 5–6 as needed, and then close the task pane.

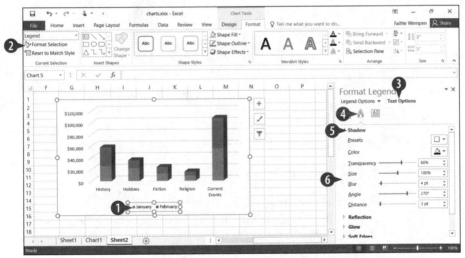

Figure 11-23: Apply special effects to a text-based element from the Text Effects section of its task pane.

Change a chart element's border and fill

Most of the chart elements have their own rectangular frames around them, although by default that frame may not have any border or fill so the element blends in with the background behind it. For example, the plot area is its own separate rectangular area, but you usually don't see it. The same is true for the legend, the axes, and the axis labels.

First, here's a quick way to apply border and fill combinations to a chart element — apply a shape style to it:

1. Select the chart element.

2 On the Chart Tools Format tab, click the More button in the Shape Styles group to open the Shape Styles gallery.

Figure 11-24: Click More to open the Shape Styles gallery.

3 Click one of the shape styles to apply it.

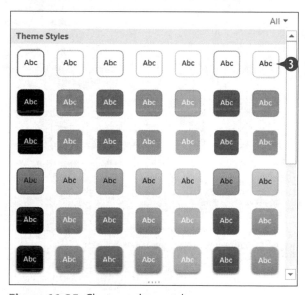

Figure 11-25: Choose a shape style.

Want more control? To manually change the fill and/or border of an element, follow these steps:

1 Select the chart element.

2 On the Chart Tools Format tab, open the Shape Fill button's menu.

3. Select a fill color:

A Automatic allows Excel to choose the color based on the background color, and is the default.

B You can choose one of the theme colors.

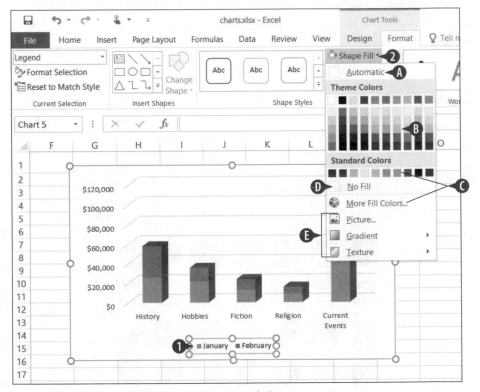

C You can choose a standard color. Click More Fill Colors for additional choices.

D To remove the fill, click No Fill.

E You can also choose a picture, gradient, or texture fill.

Figure 11-26: Choose a fill effect for the selected element.

4 Open the Shape Outline button's menu.

5. Select an outline color:

F Automatic allows Excel to choose the color based on the background color, and is the default.

G You can choose one of the theme colors.

H You can choose a standard color.

I To remove the outline, click No Outline.

After selecting an outline color, you can optionally adjust the line style and thickness:

⑥ Click the Shape Outline button again to reopen its menu.

⑦ If you want a different line thickness, point to Weight and select a line weight.

⑧ The default is a solid outline; if you want a dotted or dashed line, point to Dashes and select a line style.

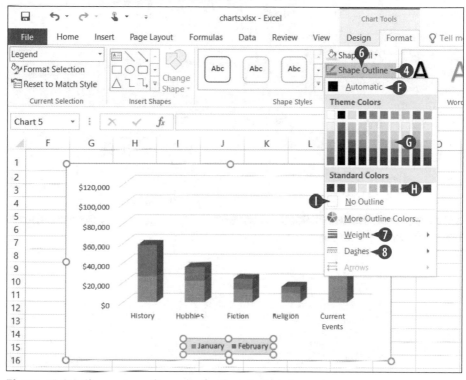

Figure 11-27: Choose an outline color for the selected element.

Apply special effects to a chart element

Special effects that you can add to an element include shadow, glow, soft edges, bevel, and 3D rotation. Most people don't take the time to apply such effects, but you may encounter situations where it is worthwhile to do so.

To apply an effect:

① Select the chart element.

② On the Chart Tools Format tab, open the Shape Effects button's menu.

③ Point to an effect to open its submenu.

④ Click the desired effect.

To remove an effect, click the selection in the No area of the menu, such as No Bevel for a bevel. (See Ⓐ in Figure 11-28.)

5. Repeat steps 2–4 to apply additional effects as desired.

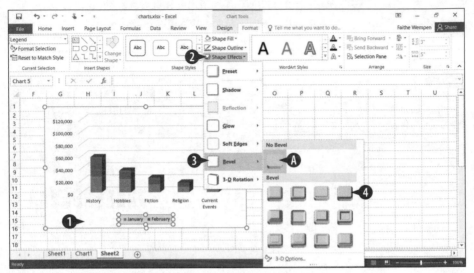

Figure 11-28: Apply special effects to a chart element.

CHAPTER TWELVE

Managing Email with Outlook

Outlook is a multipurpose program. It's an address book, a calendar, a to-do list, and an email handling program, all in one. The most popular Outlook feature, though, is the email handling. Millions of people use Outlook as their primary email program, and for good reason! It's fast, full-featured, and easy to use and customize.

In this chapter, I show you how to set up an email account in Outlook and then how to use it to send and receive email messages.

Understand the Outlook interface

Outlook 2016 is like other Office 2016 applications in many ways. For example, it has a Ribbon, a File tab that opens Backstage view, and a status bar that shows status messages and provides a Zoom slider for changing the magnification of the application's content. The following sections explain what is unique about Outlook, and what you might not pick up on immediately on your own.

In This Chapter

➡ Navigating the Outlook interface

➡ Setting up a mail account

➡ Receiving and reading email

➡ Composing and sending email

➡ Attaching a file to a message

➡ Creating folders for managing email

➡ Creating a message-handling rule

➡ Configuring the junk mail filter

TIP If you've never used Outlook before this, you might be prompted to set up an email address before Outlook starts working normally. See "Set up a mail account" later in this chapter if you need help with the initial setup.

Understand the Mail section's layout

The Mail section consists of three panes. From left to right, they are:

Ⓐ **Navigation:** Lists different locations you can click to make the active location. The default location is Inbox, where your incoming mail is located.

Ⓑ **List:** Provides a list of emails stored in the active location.

Ⓒ **Reading:** Shows a preview of whatever message is selected in the Mail list pane.

Figure 12-1: The Mail area of the Outlook application.

• You can move the Reading pane to the bottom of the screen, or turn it off altogether. On the View tab, click Reading Pane, and then make your selection from the menu. (See Ⓓ in Figure 12-2.)

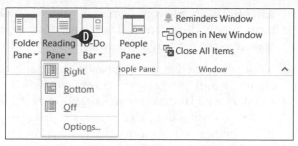

Figure 12-2: Change the location of the Reading pane if desired.

Switch between folders

In the navigation pane, you can click any folder to view its contents in the center (List) pane. The exact folders that appear depend somewhat on the type of email account you have set up and the folders on its server, but will probably include these:

A Inbox: This is where incoming email arrives. You will probably spend most of your time in this folder.

B Drafts: Any messages that you partially compose and then quit working on for some reason wait here for you to complete and send them.

C Sent Items: Outlook saves a copy of every message you send in this folder, for your reference.

D Deleted Items (or Trash): When you delete a message from any other folder, it goes here instead of being destroyed. To permanently delete a message, delete it from Deleted Items. For some mail accounts this folder is called Trash.

E Junk Email: If Outlook's junk mail filter identifies a message as potentially unwanted, it moves it here.

F Outbox: Messages that you have sent but that have not yet been uploaded to the mail server wait here. If a message stays here for more than a few minutes, there may be a problem with your mail server or Internet connection.

G RSS Feeds: RSS stands for Really Simple Syndication. It's a technology for aggregating updates from multiple websites in a single, easy-to-read location. It's not very popular anymore, but if you use this service, messages appear here.

H Search Folders: If you have any saved searches, you can run them from here.

You can also create your own mail folders, as you will learn later in this chapter. If you have done so, they will appear in the Navigation pane also.

I Notice at the very top of the Navigation pane in Figure 12-3, it says *Drag Your Favorite Folders Here.* You can drag a folder from the main section of the navigation pane and drop it there to create easily accessed shortcuts to the folders you use most often. This is not that big a deal if you just have a few folders, as in Figure 12-3, but if you start creating your own custom folders, over time you may have dozens of folders, with one inside another, and navigating to the correct folder may become not so simple anymore.

J If more than one email account is configured in Outlook, you might have multiple sections in the Navigation pane. At the top of each section is the email address to which it pertains. Other email accounts might have their own sections beneath that. Alternatively, all email accounts might use the same set of folders under a generic heading like Outlook or Mail, depending on how they are set up.

Figure 12-3: Navigate among the available mail folders.

Navigate to other areas of the application

Outlook has several diverse areas, each providing a different service, and each area has a different interface. These areas are Mail, Calendar, People, Tasks, and Notes. (Two other items that are also listed aren't really separate areas: Folders and Shortcuts.)

Even though this lesson covers only the email component of Outlook, it's a good idea to familiarize yourself with the entire application so you can get an idea of how the areas fit together.

You click a button in the lower-left corner of the Outlook application window to switch to the area you want to work with, as shown in Figure 12-2:

(A) **Mail:** Send, receive, and manage email

(B) **Calendar:** Record and display appointments and events

(C) **People:** Store and retrieve information about people and businesses

(D) **Tasks:** Record and track the progress of to-do items

(E) **More:** Open a menu of other areas of Outlook, such as Notes

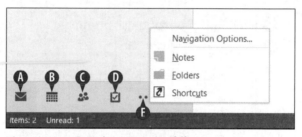

Figure 12-4: Switch among the different Outlook areas using the buttons in the lower left corner.

Set up a mail account

The first time you start Outlook, you're prompted to complete several setup operations. The most important of these is to set up your email account.

If you are not prompted to set up a mail account, and Outlook simply opens up, your mail account may already be configured. If that's the case, you don't have to do anything other than start enjoying it. See the rest of this chapter to learn what to do.

If you are not prompted but you also don't have a valid email account set up, *or* if you want to set up additional accounts, use the following steps. If you *are* prompted, jump into the following steps at step 3.

Setting up an account automatically

First, let Outlook try to configure your account automatically. If it works, you've just saved yourself some time and effort:

1. In Outlook, click File to open Backstage view.

2 Click Add Account. The Add Account dialog box opens.

Figure 12-5: Choose to add a new account.

3 Fill in the information as prompted.

4 Click Next.

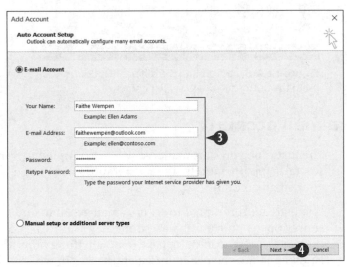

Figure 12-6: Enter the basic information about your email address.

5 Wait for Outlook to attempt to configure the account. If it is successful, you see a Congratulations message. Click Finish and you're done.

Outlook is usually successful if you have a Microsoft Exchange account on the network to which your computer is connected, or if you are using an Outlook.com or Hotmail.com address. That's because those are Microsoft account types.

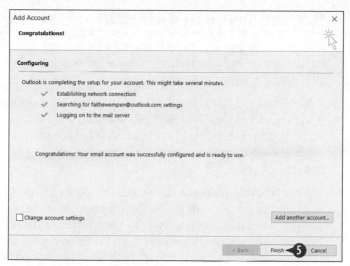

Figure 12-7: Click Finish if Outlook was successful in automatically configuring your mail account.

6. If the initial attempt failed, you might see the following:

   An encrypted connection to your mail server is not available. Click Next to attempt using an unencrypted connection.

   If you see that message, click Next to try the alternate, unencrypted method.

7. Wait for Outlook to try the alternate method. You might see a success message, like in Figure 12-7, or another failure message.

8. If you see another failure message, mark the Change account settings check box at the bottom of the dialog box, and then click Next.

Figure 12-8: Choose to change the account settings manually.

9. Go on to the next section to continue your mail setup attempt.

Setting up an account manually

If the preceding procedure didn't work out for you, you'll need to manually enter the settings for your account. That means you'll need to know a bit more *about* your email account.

These are different kinds of mail servers. You need to know which type you have before you start setting up your email account in Outlook. Ask your Internet service provider or IT department if needed. If that information is not available, try POP3 first; it's the more common type.

POP3 (Post Office Protocol 3) is the most common for home use and for most offices. With a POP3 account, mail is stored on the server until you retrieve it, and then it's downloaded to your PC (and deleted from the server). This is called a store-and-forward system.

With an IMAP (Internet Mail Access Protocol) account, the mail stays on the server at all times. This is convenient because you can get your email from anywhere (and review old messages from anywhere), but it's slower than POP3 to access and more labor-intensive for the company managing the server. Some companies provide IMAP to their employees who travel a lot so they can get their email from different PCs.

A third kind of email account is available: a web-based account, such as Yahoo! Mail, Gmail, and so on. These are also known as HTTP accounts (HyperText Transfer Protocol). Generally speaking, Outlook doesn't support this type of email account. However, Outlook does support web-based accounts through Outlook.com, its own service, as well as Microsoft email accounts ending in hotmail.com or live.com.

 Workarounds are available for many of the web-based email services, like Gmail and Yahoo! mail that enable Outlook to work with them. Check the provider's Support section on their website for information.

You not only need to know what kind of account you have, but also the incoming and outgoing mail server addresses. An incoming email server might be something like pop.provider. net or imap.provider.net. An outgoing email server usually starts with *smtp* (Simple Mail Transfer Protocol), as in smtp.provider. net. Don't try to guess, though; get the information from the mail provider.

Depending on the account type and provider, you might also need to know the following:

- What kind of authentication does the outgoing mail server require?

- What ports are used (numeric codes) for incoming and outgoing mail? For example, a mail server might use 110 for incoming and 3535 for outgoing mail.

After arming yourself with all that information, follow these steps.

1. If you didn't come here directly from the previous section, do the following to get caught up so that you see what's in Figure 12-9: Click File ⇨ Add Account ⇨ Add Account. Then click Manual setup or additional server types, and click Next.

❷ At the Choose Service screen, make your selection of your account type.

If you have a Web-based email account or an Exchange server account, choose the first option; if you have an account from an ISP such as through your cable or DSL service, choose the second option.

❸ Click Next.

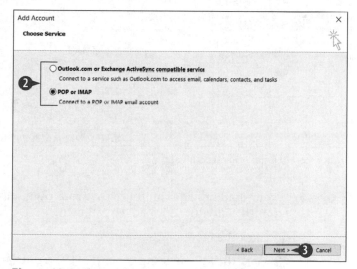

Figure 12-9: Choose the appropriate account type.

4. Fill in the information about your email account using the data you gathered from your provider or IT department. Some of the important fields include:

Ⓐ Account Type: Choose POP3 or IMAP.

Ⓑ Enter the incoming and outgoing mail servers.

Ⓒ For your username, enter your entire email address, not just the portion before the @ sign.

Ⓓ Enter the password you were assigned for your email account.

E If you choose POP3 as the account type, you have a choice of using an existing Outlook data file or creating a new one to store the received mail for this account. This choice isn't available for IMAP because IMAP stores messages on the server.

REMEMBER

5 Click More Settings.

Some of the fields will be different depending on the account type.

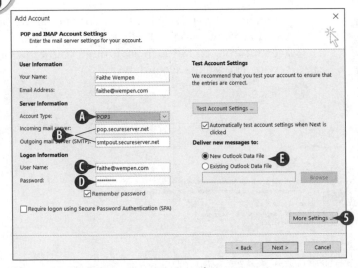

Figure 12-10: Enter your account settings.

6. If your mail provider indicated that your outgoing server requires authentication, do the following:

A Click the Outgoing Server tab.

B Mark the My outgoing server (SMTP) requires authentication.

C Choose and configure the authentication method as directed by your provider.

7. If your mail provider indicated that you should use specific ports for mail sending and receiving, do the following:

D Click the Advanced tab.

E Enter the correct port numbers in the Incoming server and Outgoing server text boxes.

F Adjust any other settings as directed by your provider.

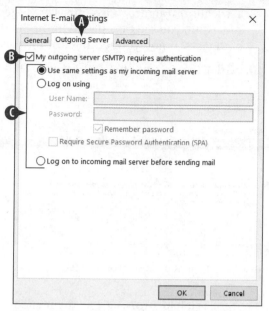

Figure 12-11: Allow Outlook to send authentication to the outgoing mail server.

⑧ Click OK.

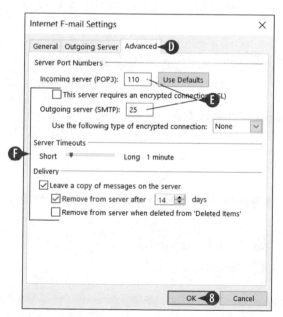

Figure 12-12: Specify port numbers and any other advanced settings.

⑨ Click Next. Your account settings are tested. If the test is successful, you see Completed in the Status column for both tasks. If not, you see an error message.

10. Click Close to close the Test Account Settings box.

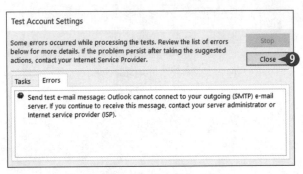

Figure 12-13: Check the results of the test.

11. If the test had errors, correct them and then return to step 10 to try again, or click Cancel to give up for now and go get help.

OR

If there were no errors, click Finish to finalize the account setup.

Modify an account's settings

If an account isn't working right, check with your provider to make sure your settings haven't changed. For example, my email provider changed the default port for outgoing mail, and I didn't know until I suddenly couldn't send mail one day.

To modify an account's settings:

1. Click File to open Backstage view.

② Click Account Settings to open a menu, and then click Account Settings on the menu.

③ Click the account you want to change.

④ Click Change.

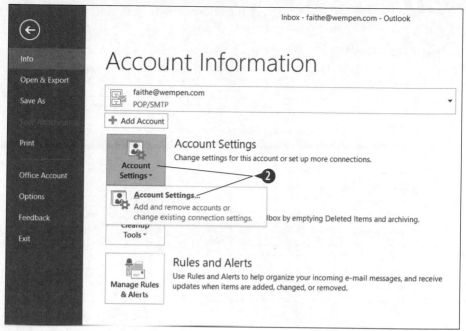

Figure 12-14: Choose Account Settings.

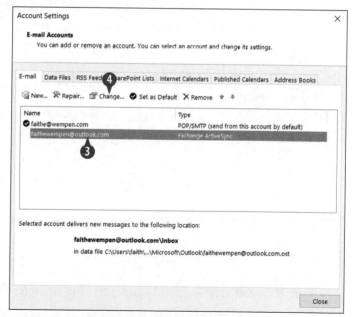

Figure 12-15: Choose the account to change.

⑤ Modify the account's settings. You cannot change the account type (Exchange, POP3, IMAP), but you can change most other properties.

TIP

If you need to change the account type, remove and recreate the account in Outlook.

6 Click Next. Outlook performs a test send and receive operation.

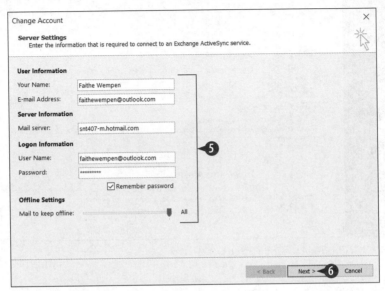

Figure 12-16: Modify the account settings.

7 Click Close.

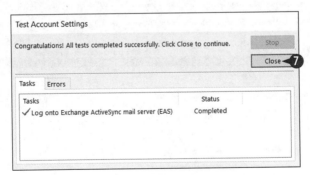

Figure 12-17: Click Close to accept the test results.

8. If the test was successful, click Finish. If not, return to step 5.

9. Click Close to close the Account Settings dialog box.

Compose and send email

You can send a new email message to anyone for whom you have an email address. Just fill in the recipient, subject, and message and then send it off.

If you have stored contacts in the People section of Outlook, you can look up recipients' email addresses from there. If you are on an Exchange server, you can also use the directory or address book provided on that system.

Compose and send a message

Follow these steps to compose and send a message:

1. On the Home tab, click New Email.

2. If you have more than one email account set up in Outlook, click From and choose the account from which you want to send this message.

3. In the To box, type the recipient's email address. For multiple recipients, separate them with semi colons. Or, alternatively, look up addresses, as explained in the section "Address an email" later in this chapter.

4. (Optional) If you want to send copies to anyone else, enter their email addresses in the Cc box.

You can also send blind copies (Bcc) from Outlook. To do so, click the Cc button and then enter them in the Bcc text box in the dialog box that appears.

5. In the Subject box, type the email subject. This text will appear in the recipient's inbox.

6. Type the body of your message.

7. If desired, format the text in the message body using the Basic Text group on the Message tab. The controls are nearly the same as on Word's Home tab.

8. Click Send.

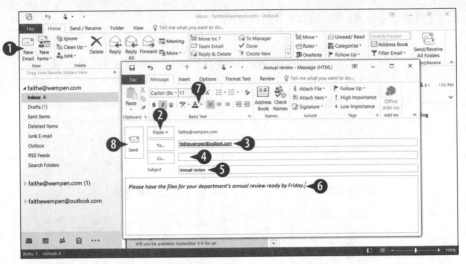

Figure 12-18: Compose and send an email.

Address an email

You can look up recipient email addresses as you compose a message. You can place recipients into one of three categories:

- **To:** Main recipients

- **Cc:** Recipients that should receive a courtesy copy

- **Bcc:** Recipients that should receive a courtesy copy without other recipients knowing about it

Follow these steps to select recipients in one or more of these categories from your company's address list on its mail server or from your own private list of addresses stored in the Contacts section of Outlook (covered in Chapter 13):

1 Click the To button in the message composition screen.

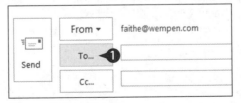

Figure 12-19: Click To.

2 Double-click the desired name. Repeat this as needed for additional recipients.

The name moves to the To line in the dialog box. (See **A** in Figure 12-20.)

If the names that appear on the list in the dialog box aren't the ones you expect, or if the list is empty, you might need to change which address book is shown. To do so, open the Address Book drop-down list and select another source. (See Ⓑ in Figure 12-20.)

③ (Optional) If you want to choose recipients to receive a Cc copy, move the insertion point into the Cc box and then double-click the desired name.

④ (Optional) If you want to choose recipients to receive a Bcc copy, move the insertion point into the Bcc box and then double-click the desired name.

⑤ Click OK.

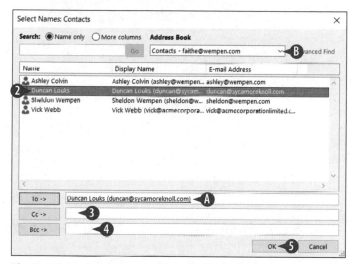

Figure 12-20: Select names for the To field, and optionally for Cc and/or Bcc.

Attach a file to a message

You can attach a file to an email, such as a word processing document or a photo. There is no limit on the number of attachments you can add to an email, although some mail servers have a limit on the size of an email message being sent or received (usually somewhere between 2 and 10MB).

For your safety, Outlook does not allow you to receive attachments with certain file extensions, such as exe, com, and vbs. That's because those executable formats can carry viruses. Other people's email programs may have the same restriction, so any files you send with those extensions might not be received. Therefore if you need to send such files, compress them in a ZIP file or use a file sharing service such as OneDrive or Dropbox.

To attach a file as you are composing an email, follow these steps:

1 From the message composition window, on the Message tab, click Attach file.

2 From the menu that appears, click Browse This PC.

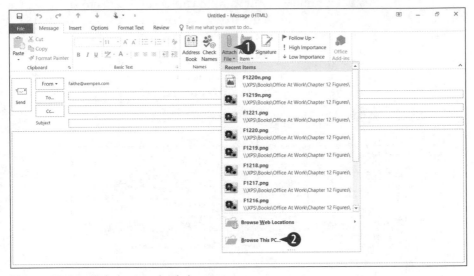

Figure 12-21: Click the Attach File button.

3 Navigate to and select the desired file to attach.

4 Click Insert.

5. Finish sending the message as you normally would.

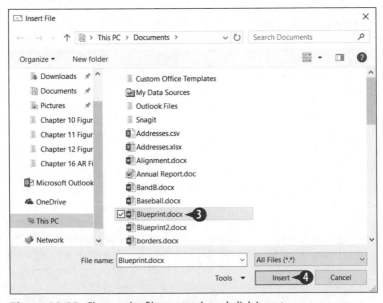

Figure 12-22: Choose the file to attach and click Insert.

Receive and read email

After you configure your email account(s) in Outlook, receiving mail is an automatic process. Outlook automatically sends and receives mail when you start it and also at 30-minute intervals (by default) whenever Outlook is running. Your incoming mail comes automatically into the Inbox folder. You can also initiate a manual send/receive operation at any time.

Send and receive email manually

When you manually send and receive mail, Outlook connects to the mail server(s), sends any mail you have waiting to be sent, and downloads any waiting mail for you.

To send and receive manually, you can either press F9 or do one of the following:

(A) On the Quick Access toolbar, click Send/Receive All Folders.

(B) On the Send/Receive tab, click Send/Receive All Folders.

Figure 12-23: Perform a manual send/receive.

Change the send/receive automatic interval

If you would like to change the interval at which Outlook automatically sends and receives mail, or disable automatic send/receive altogether, do the following:

1. On the Send/Receive tab, click Send/Receive Groups.

2. Click Define Send/Receive Groups.

3. Select the default group name (All Accounts) if it is not already selected. There might not be any other groups.

4. Increase or decrease the value in the Schedule an automatic send/receive every ____ minutes box.

   You can also turn the automatic send/receive off altogether by clearing its check box. (See (A) in Figure 12-25.)

   There are separate settings for when Outlook is offline; this might happen if you were on a dial-up connection that was not always on. Scheduling an automatic send/receive to occur when Outlook is offline would tell Windows to establish the dial-up connection each time, get the mail, and then disconnect. (See (B) in Figure 12-25.)

Figure 12-24: Select Define Send/Receive Groups.

⑤ Click Close.

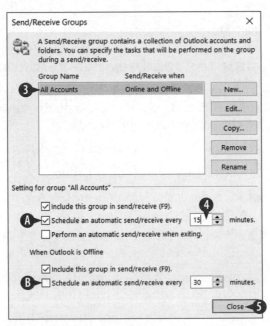

Figure 12-25: Change the interval for automatic sending and receiving.

Read a received email message

Ⓐ Unread messages appear with bold and blue subject lines in the Inbox.

Ⓑ You can read the selected message in the Reading pane.

Ⓒ You open a received message in its own separate window by double-clicking the message.

Figure 12-26: Read a message.

Work with a received attachment

After receiving an attachment, you will want to do something with it, such as view it or save it. Here are some tips for working with received attachments:

Ⓐ If the received message has an attachment, a paperclip icon appears in the message list.

Ⓑ In the Reading pane, the attachment file name appears above the message.

Ⓒ To open the attachment in whatever program is the default for its type on your system, double-click it. Doing so does not automatically save the attachment to your PC, although it remains available via the message in Outlook until you delete that message.

Ⓓ To save the attachment to your PC, or to perform other actions on it such as printing or previewing, click the arrow on the file name in the reading pane.

E Choose Quick Print to print a copy of the attachment on your default printer using default settings.

F If you choose Save As, the Save Attachment dialog box opens. Navigate to a storage location and click Save.

G If there are multiple attachments and you want to save them all to the same location, use Save All Attachments to save them all at once.

H Remove Attachment is not common, because normally you would want to keep a record of having received the attachment. You might use it if the attachment contained sensitive information, or a virus.

I Copy places the attachment on the Windows Clipboard; you can then use Paste (Ctrl+V) to paste it somewhere (such as in a location in File Explorer).

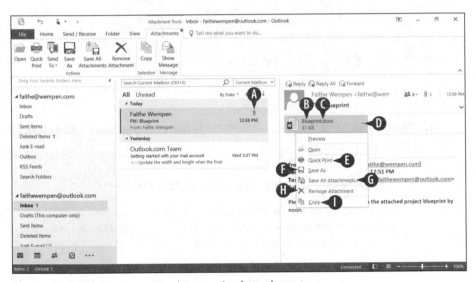

Figure 12-27: You can save or print a received attachment.

Reply to a message

Email messages often consist of multiple back-and-forth exchanges. Rather than starting a new message each time, you can use the Reply feature. Here's how:

1 To reply to a message, select the message and then click Reply on the Home tab.

Use Reply All if you want the reply to also go to anyone who was also a recipient of the original message. (This doesn't include Bcc recipients.) (See A in Figure 12-28.)

You can also use the Reply or Reply All button in the Reading pane. (See B in Figure 12-28.)

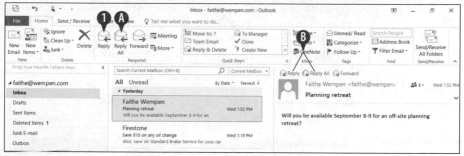

Figure 12-28: Click Reply or Reply All.

When you reply to a message, the original attachments are not included. That's because the original recipient probably doesn't want to get his or her attachment back.

The reply message begins in the Reading pane by default, but you can pop it out into its own window if you want by clicking Pop Out. (See Ⓒ in Figure 12-29.)

The recipient is already filled in, based on the sender of the original message. (See Ⓓ in Figure 12-29.)

The subject is already filled in; it's the original subject with RE: at the beginning. (See Ⓔ in Figure 12-29.)

❷ Type your reply in the message body.

The original message appears quoted. You can delete any portion of it that you don't want to include in your reply. (See Ⓕ in Figure 12-29.)

❸ Click Send when you are finished composing the reply.

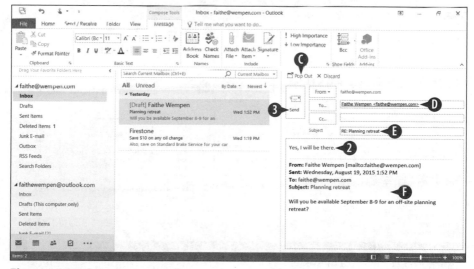

Figure 12-29: Compose your reply.

Forward a message

Forwarding is mostly the same as replying (see the previous section) except the recipient isn't filled in automatically for you.

To forward a message, follow these steps:

1. To forward to a message, select the message and then click Forward on the Home tab.

   You can also use the Forward button in the Reading pane. (See Ⓐ in Figure 12-30.)

Figure 12-30: Click Forward to begin forwarding a message.

2. Enter the recipient(s) in the To box, or click To and select them.

3. (Optional) Type any comments or notes you want to include in the message body.

4. Click Send.

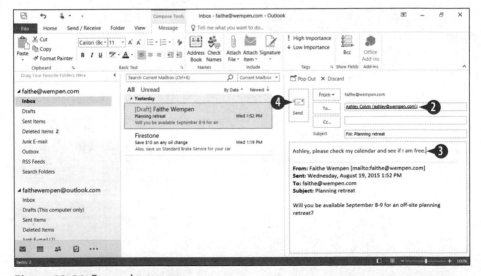

Figure 12-31: Forward a message.

TIP

Unlike when replying, forwarding includes any attachments that the original contained in the forwarded copy.

Delete a message and recover deleted messages

Most of the email you receive will eventually be deleted, just as most of the postal mail you receive ultimately ends up in your wastebasket.

To delete a message, select the message and then do any of the following:

- On the Home tab, click Delete.
- Press the Delete key on the keyboard.
- Right-click the message and choose Delete.

If you make a mistake and delete the wrong thing, you can recover it from the Deleted Items folder:

1 In the navigation bar, click Deleted Items. (Or, depending on your mail account, it may be Trash.)

2 Drag the message from the message list to the desired folder in the navigation pane, such as to the Inbox.

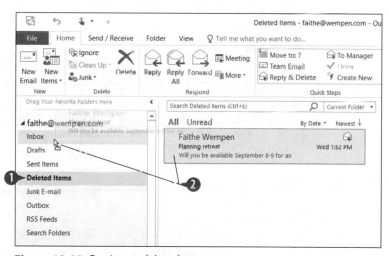

Figure 12-32: Retrieve a deleted message.

Create folders for managing email

As you receive more and more messages, messaging handling becomes increasingly important. You don't want to have to wade through thousands of messages in your Inbox just to find the one you need in a hurry.

To create a mail folder:

TIP

1 On the Folder tab, click New Folder.

Instead of step 1 you can right-click the Inbox folder and choose New Folder from the shortcut menu.

Figure 12-33: Choose New Folder from the Folder tab.

2 Type the folder name in the Name box.

3 Click Inbox to make the folder a subfolder of your inbox.

TIP

It's not required, but it's a good idea to make all of the folders that will hold received mail subfolders of Inbox. That way when you act upon the Inbox folder (for example, archiving it), all your subfolders will be included in that operation.

4 Click OK. The new folder appears in the navigation pane.

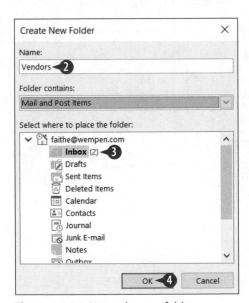

Figure 12-34: Name the new folder.

Moving messages between folders

The main point of creating new folders (covered in the preceding section) is so you can move messages into them for storage.

To move a message, select the message in the message list, and then drag-and-drop it on a different folder in the navigation pane. (See Ⓐ in Figure 12-35.)

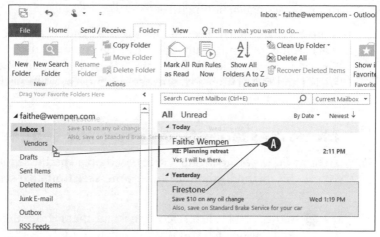

Figure 12-35: Drag a message from its current location to a different folder in the navigation bar.

If drag-and-drop isn't your thing, here is another way to move a message:

1. Select the message.

❷ On the Home tab, click Move.

❸ Click the desired folder.

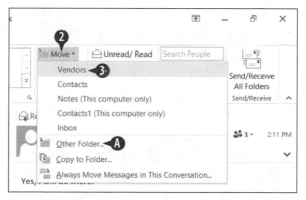

Figure 12-36: Move a folder using the Ribbon.

If the folder you want doesn't appear, click Other Folder to browse a more complete list. (See Ⓐ in Figure 12-36.)

Create a message handling rule

You may find it tedious to be constantly moving messages into different folders manually. Outlook can help with that chore by running message handling rules.

A message handling rule evaluates the mail and then processes it according to your instructions based on criteria you specify. For example, you might have a rule that evaluates mail when it arrives and, if it is from a certain sender, moves it into a certain subfolder.

Move messages from a specific sender

Here's a quick way to set up a rule based on a specific sender. To use this method, you must have a message from that sender available to select:

1 In the message list, select a message that is from the sender for which you want to create a rule.

2 On the Home tab, click Rules.

3 Click Always Move Messages From *Sender* where *Sender* is the person's name.

Figure 12-37: Select a message from that sender.

4 Select the folder into which you want to move the messages.

If the folder doesn't exist yet, you can click New to create it on-the-fly. (See A in Figure 12-38.)

5 Click OK. The rule is created and the message moves to the new folder. All other messages from that same sender also move.

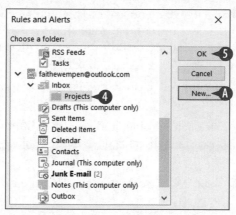

Figure 12-38: Choose a folder to which to move the messages.

Create a message handling rule

The following steps show a method that works for multiple types of criteria, not just the sender's name. You can use this procedure to filter by subject line, sender, and/or recipient account (if you have more than one email account set up in Outlook).

1. Select a received message that matches the criteria you want to specify.

2. On the Home tab, click Rules.

3. Click Create Rule.

Figure 12-39: Choose to create a new rule.

4. Mark the check boxes for the conditions which must apply for the message. The message must match *all* of the criteria you choose.

   If you want to set up a rule that applies if one condition *or* the other is met, create two separate rules.

⑤ Specify what you want to happen when a message matches the criteria. You can make Outlook play a sound, display an alert, and/or move the message.

⑥ If you want the item to be moved to a certain folder, make sure the Move check box is marked and make sure the correct folder appears in its text box.

Click Select Folder and choose a different folder if needed. (The dialog box for selecting the folder is the same as shown in Figure 12-38.) (See Ⓐ in Figure 12-40.)

⑦ Click OK to create the rule. The rule runs.

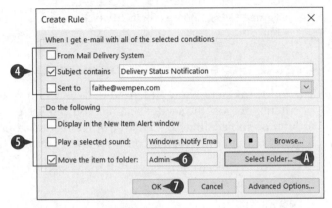

Figure 12-40: Define the rule.

Modify or delete a message handling rule

Over time, your rule needs may change. Some rules may no longer be applicable, and others may need modification. If you later need to make changes to a rule, here's how.

1. On the Home tab, click Rules, and then click Manage Rules & Alerts.

② Select a rule.

The rule's description appears in the lower part of the dialog box. (See Ⓐ in Figure 12-41.)

You can delete the selected rule by clicking Delete. (See Ⓑ in Figure 12-41.)

3 Click an underlined portion of the rule description to modify that section of the rule. For example, to change where to move the message, click the underlined folder name.

4. Make a change in the dialog box that appears. The dialog box that appears depends on what portion of the rule you are modifying.

5. Then click OK to return to the Rules and Alerts dialog box.

6 When you are done modifying the rule, click OK.

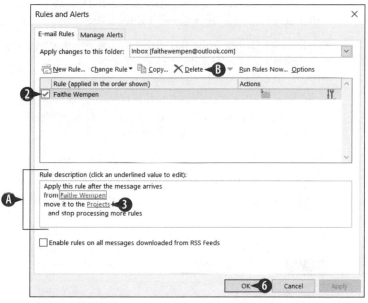

Figure 12-41: Manage rules from the Rules and Alerts dialog box.

Configure the junk mail filter

Outlook isn't a great tool for spam filtering. You will probably want to add on another one, unless your company's email server or your ISP has its own spam filter.

Nevertheless, Outlook's tools do provide some measure of filtering and control. Here's what Outlook has to offer.

Enable junk mail filtering

Outlook's junk mail filtering tool evaluates incoming mail and then moves some of it to a Junk Email folder based on its evaluation.

Outlook's junk mail filtering is disabled by default. You can enable it with your choice of three levels of filtering:

- **Low:** Moves only the most obvious junk mail to the Junk Email folder.

- **High:** Moves nearly all junk mail to the Junk Email folder, but some regular mail may be accidentally moved too, so you should check the Junk Email folder frequently.

- **Safe Lists Only:** Only mail from recipients that you designate as safe senders will appear in your Inbox; everything else will move to the Junk Email folder.

If you opt for Safe Lists Only, you'll need to set up your list of never-blocked senders, as described in "Manage the blocked and unblocked sender lists" later in this chapter.

To enable junk mail filtering, follow these steps:

1. On the Home tab, click Junk.

2. Click Junk Email Options.

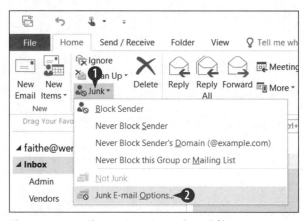

Figure 12-42: Choose to open junk mail filtering options.

3. On the Options tab, select your preferred level of filtering.

4. Click OK.

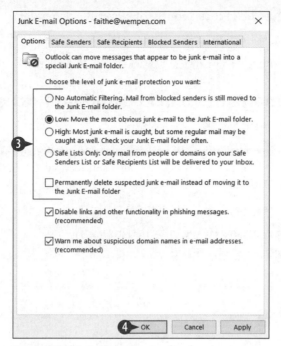

Figure 12-43: Select a filtering level.

Block or never block a certain sender

You can quickly block a particular email address from sending you mail. When you get mail from that address, Outlook will automatically move it to the Junk Email folder. You can also set a particular address to never be blocked.

To block (or never block) a certain sender, follow these steps:

1. Select an email you have received from that sender.

2. On the Home tab, click Junk.

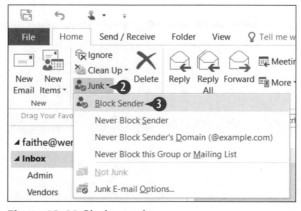

Figure 12-44: Block a sender.

③ Click Block Sender (or Never Block Sender).

4. Click OK at the confirmation message.

If you need to unblock a blocked sender, see the next section.

Manage the blocked and unblocked sender lists

You can manually add and remove addresses from the lists of blocked and never-blocked (safe) senders; you don't have to wait until you have an email from one of them.

To access the lists, follow these steps:

① On the Home tab, click Junk.

② Click Junk Email Options.

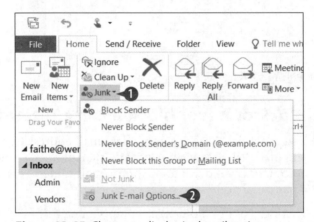

Figure 12-45: Choose to display junk mail options.

③ Click the Blocked Senders tab.

4. To block an email address or domain, do the following:

Ⓐ Click Add.

Ⓑ Type the address or domain to block.

The domain is the name that follows the @ sign in an address. You can block or allow entire domains with one entry; for example, you might add your company's domain to your Safe Senders tab.

C Click OK.

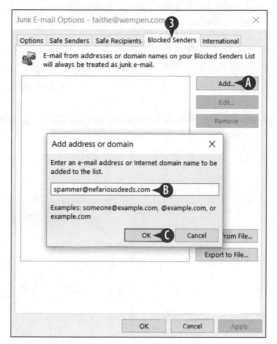

Figure 12-46: Choose to display junk mail options.

5. To remove the block on an address or domain, do the following:

D Select the address or domain.

E Click Remove.

6 (Optional) To add to or remove from the list of never-blocked senders, click the Safe Senders tab and then repeat steps 4 and 5 on that tab.

Addresses you add on the Safe Senders tab will *not* be blocked; you are approving the addresses you place here.

7 Click OK to close the dialog box.

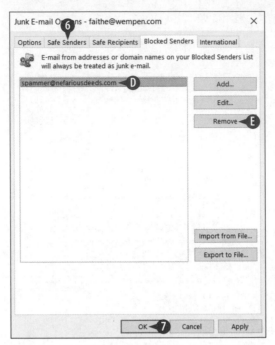

Figure 12-47: Choose to display junk mail options.

Use an automatic signature

Many companies like their employees to append a certain signature block to the end of every message they send from their work email accounts. This could include the company's name and address, their job title, and/or a privacy notice.

To set up an automatic signature block, follow these steps:

1. Choose File ⇨ Options.

2 Click Mail.

3 Click Signatures.

4 Click New.

5 Type a name for the signature.

6 Click OK.

7 Type the desired signature text in the Edit signature box.

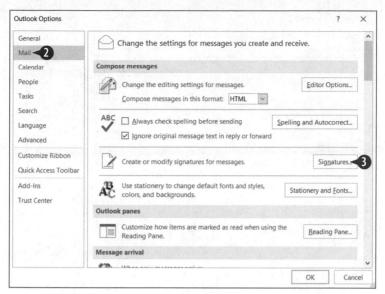

Figure 12-48: On the Mail tab of the Options dialog box, click the Signatures button.

Figure 12-49: Create a new signature.

Use the formatting buttons to format the text as desired. (See Ⓐ in Figure 12-50.)

8. Repeat steps 4–7 to create additional signatures if needed.

⑨ Open the Email account drop-down list and choose one of your email accounts that should use a signature.

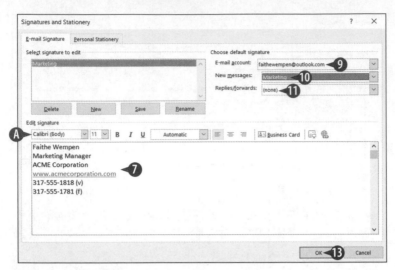

Figure 12-50: Create a new signature.

⑩ Open the New messages drop-down list and choose the signature you just created.

⑪ (Optional) If you want to use a signature on replies and forwards, choose it from the Replies/forwards drop-down list.

12. Repeat steps 8–10 as needed if you have additional email accounts for which you want to use a signature.

⑬ Click OK.

14. Click OK to close the Outlook Options dialog box.

As you are composing an email message, Outlook places the signature in the message body when you open the message composition window. You can manually delete or change the signature as you wish before you send. (See Ⓐ in Figure 12-51.)

You can also open the Signature drop-down list from the Message tab and choose a different signature for the current message. (See Ⓑ in Figure 12-51.)

You can also reopen the Signatures and Stationery dialog box (Figure 12-50) by choosing Signatures. (See Ⓒ in Figure 12-51.)

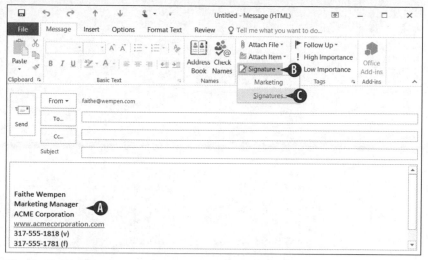

Figure 12-51: Using signatures when composing new messages.

CHAPTER THIRTEEN

Using Outlook Contacts and Tasks

Outlook is much more than just an email program. It excels at storing information that you need for your daily business and personal dealings, such as contact information and to-do lists. If you can't keep yourself organized with all these tools available to you, don't blame Outlook!

In this chapter, I show you how to enter and use contact information in the People area of Outlook. I also show how to create and manage tasks and to-do items in the Tasks area.

Add and edit contacts

The People area of Outlook stores a *contact* (also called a *record*) for each person or business that you want to save for later use.

You can access the People area by clicking the People icon in the lower left corner of the Outlook window. (See **A** in Figure 13-1.)

If you have more than one email account set up in Outlook, you might have multiple separate Contacts listings. If so, you'll see them listed in the navigation pane. Click the one you want to see. (See **B** in Figure 13-1.)

In This Chapter

➤ Adding and editing contacts

➤ Viewing and searching the People list

➤ Sending a message to a contact

➤ Forwarding contact data via email

➤ Creating and managing tasks

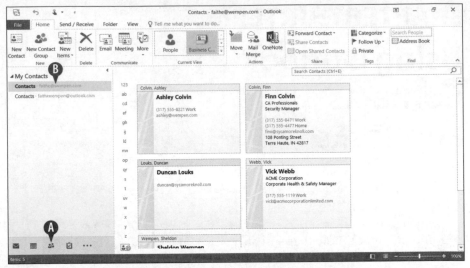

Figure 13-1: Click People to open the People area of Outlook, where contacts are stored.

Create a new contact

Outlook stores complete contact information about the people you want to keep in touch with. You can store not only mailing addresses but also phone numbers, email addresses, pager numbers, and personal information such as birthdays, spouse names, departments, and professions.

To create a new contact, follow these steps:

1 From the People area of Outlook, on the Home tab, click New Contact.

2 Fill in the fields with all the information you want to record about that contact.

A summary of the person's contact information appears in the upper right corner. (See **A** in Figure 13-2.)

Figure 13-2: Start a new contact.

TIP

You can store as much or as little information as you like about each contact, and it need not be consistent between contacts. For some people, all you need is an email address. For others, you might need multiple ways to contact the person, as well as personal details such as spouse's name and birthday.

When creating a contact, the window in which it appears may truncate the available fields at the bottom if the window is not tall enough. You can increase the window size, but if you are using a very small screen size or low resolution, you might not be able to make the window large enough to see all the fields, and you can't scroll down to see them because there's no scroll bar in this window. The bottommost field is the Addresses area, so if you can see that, you're good.

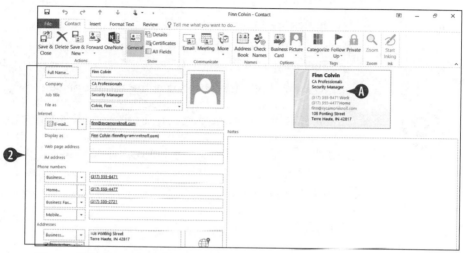

Figure 13-3: Enter the information to store about that contact.

3 (Optional) If you need to enter additional information about the contact, click Details and fill in any of the additional fields.

4 Click Save & Close.

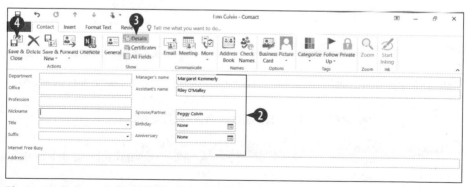

Figure 13-4: Record any additional details as needed.

If you need to make changes to a contact, you can double-click it to reopen it.

Change how a contact is filed

If someone asked you how contacts were alphabetized in Outlook, you would probably say that they're done by last name, right? And you'd be absolutely . . . *wrong*.

The File As setting determines the sort order in the People list. By default, when you create a new contact, the File As setting for it is set to *Last Name, First Name*. But you can change that to some other setting if you prefer, such as the company name or the first name. Here's how:

1. Double-click the contact to reopen it for editing.

2 Open the File as drop-down list and choose a different filing method for the contact.

If you want both the company name and the person's name to show, choose one of the File As options that includes both. The one that appears first will be how it is alphabetized. For example, Strong, Terry (ACME Corporation) alphabetizes by Strong but also includes ACME Corporation in the title.

3 Click Save & Close.

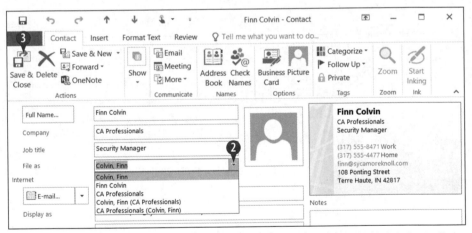

Figure 13-5: Change the File As setting to control how the contact is filed alphabetically.

Delete and restore a contact

With Outlook, you don't have to tear pages out of a paper address book to get rid of a person's information; just delete the contact:

Ⓐ To delete a contact, select the contact and then click Delete on the Home tab.

Ⓑ Alternatively, you can right-click the contact and click Delete.

Ⓒ You can also select the contact and then press the Delete key on the keyboard.

Figure 13-6: Delete a contact.

To restore an accidentally deleted contact, follow these steps:

❶ Click the More (. . .) button in the lower left corner to open a menu.

❷ Click Folders. The navigation pane is replaced by a list of folders.

❸ Click Deleted Items.

❹ Select the deleted contact.

❺ Drag the deleted contact and drop it on the Contacts folder in the navigation pane.

6. Click the People icon in the lower left corner to return to the People area.

Figure 13-7: Find a deleted contact in the Deleted Items folder.

Figure 13-8: Find a deleted contact in the Deleted Items folder.

View and search the People list

Depending on the view you're using at the moment, each contact may be displayed as a card, a business card, or an item in a list. Consider Figure 13-9:

A To change the view, make a selection from the Home tab's Current View group.

B You might need to click the More button to see all the choices, depending on the window size.

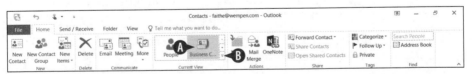

Figure 13-9: Choose between different views of the People list.

As your list of contacts grows, you might need some help finding a particular contact.

Ⓒ You can click a letter to jump to the corresponding section in the listing. This is a good way to look up a contact if you know what it was filed under (for example, the company name, or the person's last name).

Ⓓ If you aren't sure how the contact was filed, you can search by entering any piece of information you know in the Search Contacts box and pressing Enter. For example, you might search by entering the person's first name or the city in their mailing address.

Figure 13-10: Locate a contact.

Send a message to a contact

You can easily address an email message to a contact in your People list. You can initiate this process either from the Contacts area of the program or from the Mail area.

To send from the People area, do the following:

❶ Select the contact.

❷ On the Home tab, click Email. Outlook starts a new message with the recipient's email address pre-entered.

3. Compose and send the email as you would normally.

Figure 13-11: Send an email from the People area of Outlook.

To send from the Mail area, do this:

1 Click New Email.

2 In the new message window, click Address Book, or click the To button.

3 In the Select Names window, click the contact's name.

4 If the name does not immediately appear in the To box, click the To button.

5. Add other names to the To, Cc, and/or Bcc lines as desired.

6 Click OK.

7. Compose and send the email as you would normally.

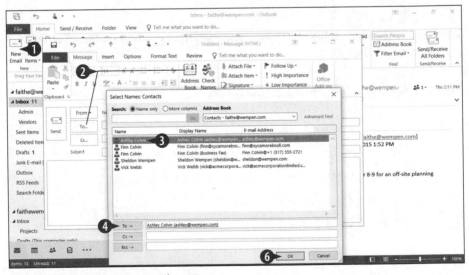

Figure 13-12: Address an email message.

Forward contact data via email

You can share a contact by attaching the contact record to an email in one of these formats:

- **Outlook contact:** The attachment is an Outlook contact, which only Outlook can accept. The recipient must have Outlook to make use of the attachment.

- **Business card:** The attachment is in vCard format (.vcf), a standard format for personal data that many programs can accept.

Sharing contact data can be a quick way of transferring information about vendors and customers between employees; you can also use this feature to share your own contact information with people, so they can import your contact info into their address book without having to manually type it in.

To attach contact information to a message:

1 In the People area, select the contact to send.

2 On the Home tab, click Forward Contact.

3 Click either As a Business Card or As an Outlook Contact.

Figure 13-13: Forward a contact to an email recipient.

4 In the New Message window that appears, enter or select the recipient(s).

The contact's name appears on the Subject line, but you can change this. (See **A** in Figure 13-14.)

The contact information is already attached. (See **B** in Figure 13-14.)

5 Click Send to send the email.

Figure 13-14: Compose and send the message.

Create and manage tasks

A *task* is a database record that contains information about something that you need to accomplish. For example, when I was writing this book, I used a task in Outlook to keep track of my deadlines and progress.

Don't confuse tasks with appointments. A staff meeting would be an appointment, and you would enter that in the Calendar area of Outlook. A task, on the other hand, is something that you need to complete *by* a certain date or time, but not necessarily *at* that exact date or time. For example, a task might be to turn in your time card before 5 p.m. on Friday.

The Tasks area in Outlook helps you create and manage action items for yourself and others. Not only can Outlook keep track of what you need to do, but it can also remind you of upcoming deadlines, record what percentage of a large job you've completed, and even send out emails that assign certain tasks to other people.

Click the Tasks icon to switch to the Tasks area. (See Ⓐ in Figure 13-15.)

It's important to understand the difference in Outlook between Tasks and the To-Do list:

Ⓑ *Tasks* are specific items you created in the Tasks area of Outlook. Something isn't technically a *task* unless it was created in the Tasks section. If you click Tasks, you see only tasks created in the Tasks section.

C If you have more than one email account, each one may have its own Tasks entry, which opens a separate task list.

D *The To-Do list* contains everything from the Tasks list as well as other items you have marked for action, such as email messages you flag for follow-up. If you click To-Do List, you get all your tasks plus any other flagged items from other areas.

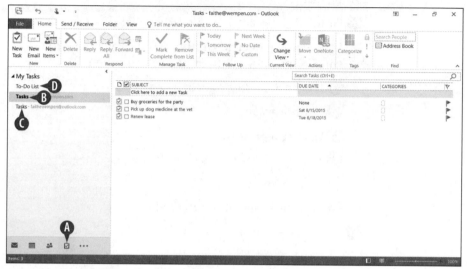

Figure 13-15: Work with the Tasks list.

Enter a new task

Here's a very simple way to enter tasks. If you have a lot of tasks to enter, and you don't need to record much information about them, this method is your best bet:

A Enter a new task by typing it in the *Click here to add a new task* box at the top of the task list.

B You can enter a due date in the DUE DATE column or leave it blank for no due date.

C The fields available depend on the view you have chosen. See "Change the Tasks view" later in this chapter. Simple List view is shown here.

D After entering a task this way, you can double-click the task to open it in its own window and enter additional details.

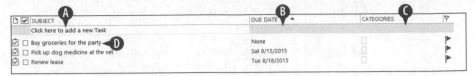

Figure 13-16: Click in the box and begin entering the task.

To enter more information about a task as you create it, use the following method instead:

1 From the Tasks area, on the Home tab, click New Task.

2. Enter data in the fields in the New Task window. You can enter as much or as little information as you like:

Ⓐ Enter a Start date and/or a Due date.

Ⓑ Choose a status.

Ⓒ Choose a priority.

Ⓓ Estimate the project's completion percentage.

Ⓔ Set a reminder.

Ⓕ Type any notes about the task.

3 Click Save & Close.

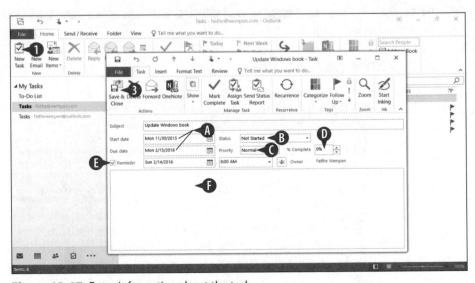

Figure 13-17: Enter information about the task.

To reopen a task for editing, double-click it.

Change the Tasks view

There are many different views available for the Tasks list. Here are some tips for working with different views of your tasks:

Ⓐ To choose among the available views, on the Home tab, click Change View and then click the desired view.

Ⓑ Some views show different fields. For example, Detailed view has several more columns than Simple List view.

Ⓒ Some views also filter the task list to show only items with certain statuses. For example, Active shows only uncompleted tasks, and Overdue shows only overdue tasks.

Ⓓ Some views place the tasks in a certain order. For example, Prioritized arranges them by their priority status.

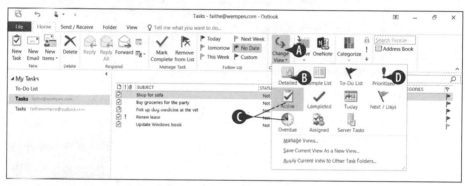

Figure 13-18: Change the view if desired.

Set up a recurring task

You can set up a task once in Outlook and then tell it to reoccur at a defined interval. This can save you a lot of time reentering tasks that are the same every day, week, or month. Here's how:

1. Double-click an existing task to open it for editing, or start a new task.

❷ On the Task tab, click Recurrence.

❸ Set the task to recur daily, weekly, monthly, or yearly.

❹ Set up the details of the recurrence. The options change depending on your choice in step 3.

❺ If the recurrence should end on a certain date or after a certain number of times, set that up.

❻ Click OK.

❼ In the task window, click Save & Close.

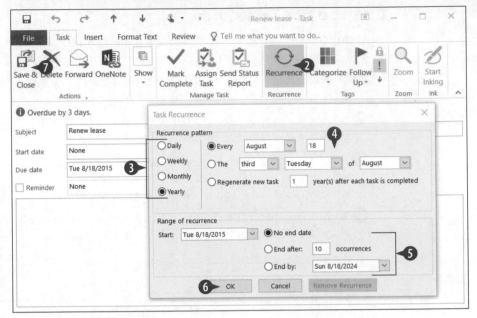

Figure 13-19: Set up task recurrence.

If you want to remove the recurrence on a task, repeat steps 1–2 and then click Remove Recurrence.

Send a status report

Your manager or supervisor will want to know how you are progressing on any work-related tasks. You can quickly send someone a status report on a task by doing the following:

1. From the Tasks area, double-click the task to open it.

2 On the Task tab, click Send Status Report. A new email window opens.

The Subject line shows *Task Status Report* plus the name of the task. (See **A** in Figure 13-20.)

The status report appears in the message body. (See **B** in Figure 13-20.)

3 Compose and send the email as you would any other message.

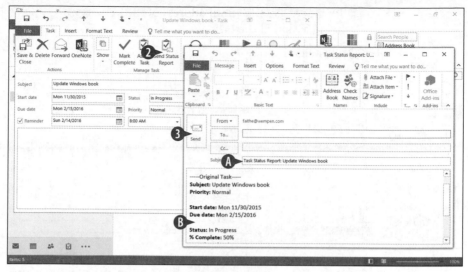

Figure 13-20: Email a status report for a task.

Assign the task to someone else

Assigning a task to someone else in Outlook accomplishes several things at once:

- It sends an email containing the task details to the person to whom you assign it.
- It gives them the choice of accepting or declining the task and sends their reply back to you.
- If they accept the task, it places it on their Tasks list in Outlook (if they use Outlook).

To assign a task, follow these steps:

1. Double-click the task to open it.

2. On the Task tab, click Assign Task. An email composition screen appears within the task window.

Figure 13-21: Click the Assign Task button in the open task window.

3 Type or select the email address of the person who is being assigned the task.

4 Click Send.

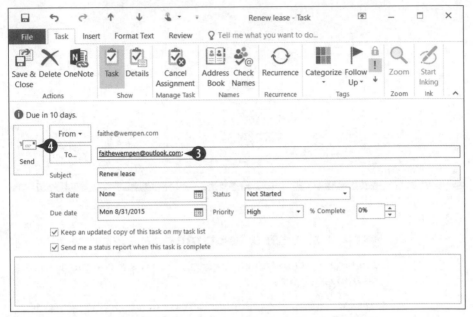

Figure 13-22: Email the task to the person to whom you want to assign it.

After you have sent the assignment, the task's icon changes in the task list. (See **A** in Figure 13-23.)

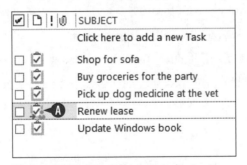

Figure 13-23: The task's icon indicates it has been assigned to someone.

Receive an assigned task

When you receive an email-based task assignment from some other user, it comes to your Inbox along with the rest of your email. When you open it, you see the task information.

1. Accept or decline the task:

Ⓐ To accept the task, click Accept.

OR

Ⓑ To decline the task, click Decline.

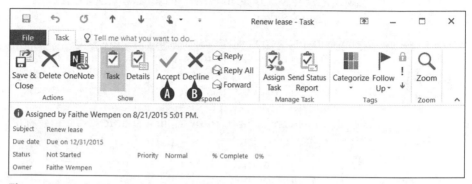

Figure 13-24: Receive and accept a task.

❷ The sender will receive an email with your response. If you want to edit that email, click Edit the response before sending. If not, leave Send the response now selected.

3. Click OK.

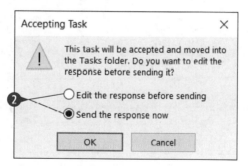

Figure 13-25: Send your response to the requester.

4. If you chose to edit the response in step 2, make any changes or comments on the email, and then click Send.

Change a task status

As you make progress on a task, you will want to update its status in Outlook. Here's how:

1. Double-click the task to open its window.

2 Open the Status drop-down list and choose a different status if needed.

Completing the task doesn't delete it, although a completed task may vanish from your list. When you set a task to a status of Completed, it changes which views it appears in. For example, if you are using Active view, a completed task will appear to vanish. Switch to a view that includes completed tasks, like Simple List, and you'll see it again.

3 Set the % Complete value to the approximate percent of completion for the task.

If you set the % Complete to 100%, the Status field changes to Completed automatically.

4 Click Save & Close.

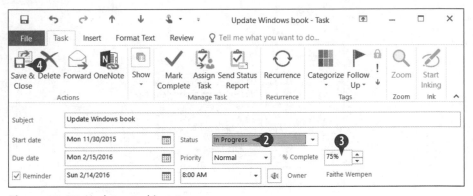

Figure 13-26: Update a task's status.

You can also update a task's status from certain views without opening the task's window. For example, Active view contains a % Complete column, and you can click there and type a different number. (See **A** in Figure 13-27.)

Figure 13-27: You can also update a status from certain views.

Delete a task

As I mention earlier, completing a task doesn't delete it. You might want to keep completed tasks around for later reference. If you don't want to see them, switch to a view that doesn't include completed tasks, such as the Active view. If you're sure you want to delete a task, though, it's easy enough to delete it.

To delete a task, do any of the following:

(A) Right-click the task and click Delete.

(B) Select the task and click Delete on the Home tab.

(C) Select the task and press Delete on the keyboard.

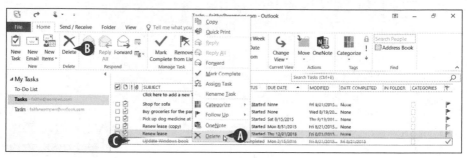

Figure 13-28: Delete a task.

CHAPTER FOURTEEN

Getting Started with PowerPoint

PowerPoint is the most popular presentation software in the world. Presentation software creates support materials for people who give speeches. You can project PowerPoint slides on a big screen behind you as you speak, create handouts to distribute to the audience, and print note pages for your own reference. PowerPoint can also create self-running presentations for distribution via CD or online.

This chapter offers you some basics for working with PowerPoint. You learn how to start a new presentation, add slides and text to it, and move and resize the content on a slide. In later lessons, you learn how to add other types of content and special effects to a show.

Start a new presentation

When you start PowerPoint, as with the other Office applications, a Start screen appears. From here, you can:

Ⓐ Click Blank Presentation, or press Esc, to start a new blank presentation.

In This Chapter

- ⇒ Moving around in a presentation
- ⇒ Choosing the right view
- ⇒ Creating a new presentation with a template
- ⇒ Adding and removing slides
- ⇒ Using content placeholders
- ⇒ Manually placing text on a slide
- ⇒ Moving and resizing slide objects
- ⇒ Deleting slide objects

(B) Click one of the other templates to start a new presentation based on it

(C) Open an existing presentation.

Figure 14-1: The Start screen in PowerPoint.

To start a new presentation at any other time than startup, press Ctrl+N for a blank one, or click File ➪ New and choose a template.

Move around in a presentation

A *slide* is an individual page of the presentation. The term *page* isn't a perfect descriptor, though, because PowerPoint slides are designed to be displayed on a computer screen or with a projector rather than printed. A *presentation* is a collection of one or more slides saved in a single data file.

At a big-picture level, the PowerPoint interface is very similar to that in Word and Excel: It has a Ribbon, a File tab, and a status bar. The default view of the presentation, called *Normal view*, consists of three panes, as shown in Figure 14-2.

The presentation shown in Figure 14-2 was created with the Welcome to PowerPoint template. Here are some things to note:

A The Slides pane is the bar along the left side. Thumbnail images of the slides appear here. It is sometimes called the *thumbnails pane* or the *slides pane*.

B The Slide pane (that's singular, not plural) in the middle shows the active slide in a large, editable pane. Here's where you do most of your work on each slide. It is sometimes called the *editing pane*.

C The Notes pane runs along the bottom of the screen. Here you can type any notes to yourself about the active slide. These notes don't show onscreen when you display the presentation, and they don't print (unless you explicitly choose to print them).

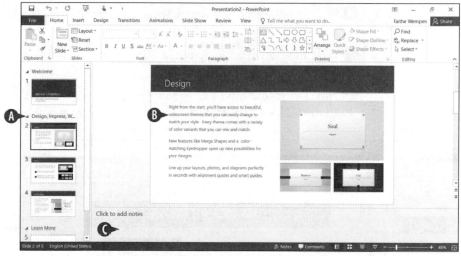

Figure 14-2: Normal view consists of three panes.

D The Notes pane is minimized in a new blank presentation. To see it, position the mouse pointer just above the status bar (orange bar) at the bottom of the screen and drag upward. Drag the top border of the Notes pane down again to hide it.

E Another way to display or hide the Notes pane is to click the Notes indicator on the status bar.

Figure 14-3: Drag upward from the status bar to display the Notes pane.

You can navigate a presentation in many of the same ways you moved through other applications' content.

F Click above or below the vertical scroll bar in the Slide pane, or press Page Up or Page Down, to move one slide at a time.

G You can also drag the scroll box to move more quickly as well.

H You can click an up or down arrow on a scroll bar to scroll a small amount at a time.

I You can also click a slide in the Slides pane to jump directly to that slide.

J The Slides pane has its own scroll bar, in case you can't see all the slides there at once.

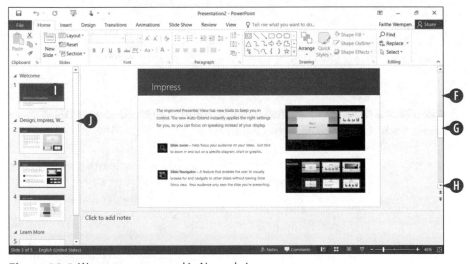

Figure 14-4: Ways to move around in Normal view.

Choose the right view

PowerPoint provides several views for you to work with. Each view is useful for a different set of activities. Here are some things to remember about views:

Ⓐ To switch views, on the View tab, click a button for the view you want.

Ⓑ The Master views are not regular PowerPoint views; they enable you to edit the underlying designs and layouts on which individual slides are based. You will learn about them in Chapter 15.

Ⓒ Slide Show view is not represented on the View tab. To switch to Slide Show view, use the From Beginning or From Current Slide button on the Slide Show tab instead.

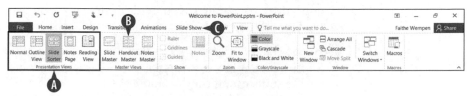

Figure 14-5: View buttons on the View tab of the Ribbon.

You can also click one of the View buttons in the bottom-right corner of the PowerPoint window:

Ⓓ Normal

Ⓔ Slide Sorter

Ⓕ Reading View

Ⓖ Slide Show

Figure 14-6: View buttons on the status bar.

Here's a quick overview of the available views:

- **Normal:** You've already seen this one in Figure 14-4; it's the default. It consists of a Slides pane, a Slide pane in which you can edit the slide, and a Notes pane in which you can record private notes and comments.

- **Outline:** This view is identical to Normal view except instead of the Slides pane there is an Outline pane that shows a text outline for each slide.

In Outline view, only text from the slide's text placeholders appears in the Outline pane. If you have any manually created text boxes (such as those you create with Insert ⇨ Text Box), their text doesn't appear there.

- **Slide Sorter:** This view shows thumbnail images of each slide, like the Slides pane does in Normal view, but it takes up the entire window. You can't edit slide content in this view, although you can rearrange and delete slides. See Figure 14-7:

    H If your presentation has sections, as the Welcome to PowerPoint template's presentation does, each section appears on a separate row in Slide Sorter view. You can manage sections with the Home ⇨ Section command.

    I To zoom in or out on the thumbnail view, drag the Zoom slider. A lower zoom means more slides are visible at once, and they're smaller. A higher zoom means fewer slides are visible, but you can see each one more easily.

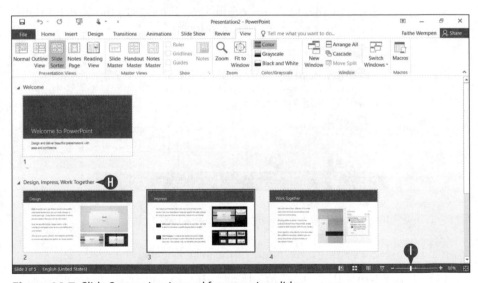

Figure 14-7: Slide Sorter view is good for arranging slides.

- **Notes Page:** This view shows a vertically oriented page for each slide, as shown in Figure 14-8:

    J The top half of the page shows the slide.

    K The bottom half of the page provides a large text box into which you can enter and edit note text.

    L Use the Zoom slider to zoom in to make the note text easier to see as you work with it if desired.

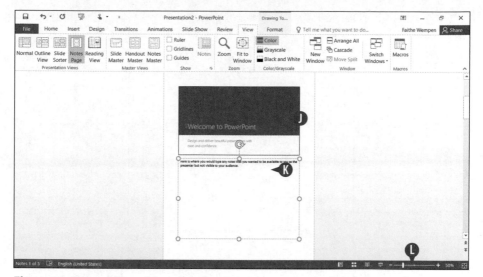

Figure 14-8: Notes Page view makes it easy to compose and edit lengthy speaker notes.

- **Slide Show:** This is the view you would use to show the presentation full-screen on your monitor. It's covered in detail in Chapter 17. Each slide fills the entire screen, one by one, and you click to advance.

- **Reading:** Reading view is like Slide Show view except the presentation runs in a window rather than full-screen. That's useful because you can do other things, like work with other programs or windows, while the presentation is running.

Most people prefer to work in Normal view most of the time when creating a presentation, so switch back to Normal view before you go any further, after experimenting with the other views.

Add and remove slides

Each new blank presentation begins with one slide in it: a title slide. (Presentations based on other templates may have more.) You can easily add more slides to the presentation by using the default layout (Title and Content) or any other layout you prefer.

Several methods are available for creating new slides, and each one is best suited for a particular situation. In the following sections, you learn each of the methods.

Create a new slide in the Slides pane

In the Slides pane in Normal view, you can click to place a horizontal insertion point between two existing slides or at the bottom of the list of slides and then press Enter to create a new slide. (See Figure 14-9.)

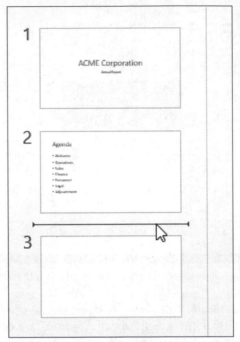

Figure 14-9: Create a new slide from the Slides pane (Normal view).

The layout of the new slide depends on the layout of the slide immediately before (above) it. If that slide uses the Slide Title layout, the new slide uses the Title and Content layout. Otherwise the new slide uses the same layout as the preceding slide. You learn more about slide layouts in Chapter 15.

Create a new slide in the Outline pane

In Outline view, you can create a new slide as follows:

1. In the Outline pane, click at the beginning of the title of the slide that the new slide should come *before*.

2. Press Enter. A new paragraph (a slide title) is created, and that causes a whole new slide to be created also.

3. Press the Up arrow key once to move the insertion point up into the new blank slide title, and type the title text.

Figure 14-10: Create a new slide from the Outline pane (Outline view).

Create a new slide from the Ribbon

When you create using the Ribbon, you can select the layout you want for the new slide. Follow these steps:

1 In Normal view, select the slide that the new slide should come *after*.

2A On the Home tab, click New Slide to create a slide with the same layout as the selected one (unless the selected one is a title slide, in which case the layout will be Title and Content).

OR

2B Click the arrow on the New Slide button, and then select the desired layout from the gallery that appears.

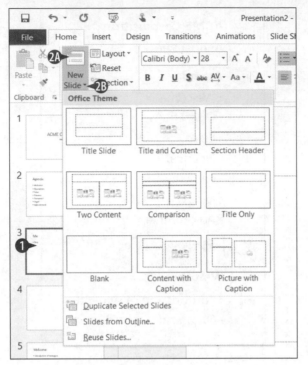

Figure 14-11: Create a slide by selecting a layout from the New Slide button's gallery.

Duplicate a slide

If you need to create a series of very similar slides, you might find it easier to copy or duplicate a slide and then make the small modifications to each copy.

Copying and duplicating are two separate commands in PowerPoint, but they have essentially the same result.

When you copy a slide (or multiple slides), you place a copy of it on the Clipboard, and then you paste it from the Clipboard into the presentation. You can paste anywhere in the presentation or into a different presentation (or, for that matter, a different document altogether).

To copy a slide:

1. Select the slide in the Slides pane.

2. Press Ctrl+C or choose Home ⇨ Copy.

3. Click where you want the copy to go. If you want to place the copy after a certain slide, select that slide.

4. Press Ctrl+V or choose Home ⇨ Paste.

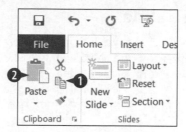

Figure 14-12: Copy a slide using the Clipboard.

When you duplicate a slide (or multiple slides), you don't have to paste, because that command accomplishes both a copy and a paste operation at the same time. However, you also don't get to choose where they're pasted; they're pasted directly below the original selection.

1 Select the slide(s) to be duplicated. To select more than one slide, hold down Ctrl as you click each one in the Slides pane.

2 Click the arrow on the New Slide button to open its menu.

3 Click Duplicate Selected Slides.

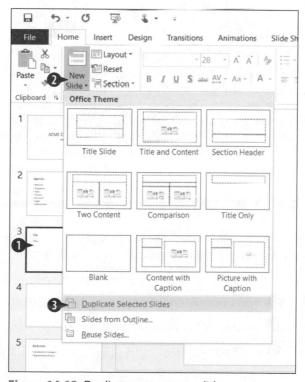

Figure 14-13: Duplicate one or more slides.

Delete a slide

Deleting a slide removes it from the presentation. To delete a slide, right-click it and choose Delete Slide, or select it in the Slides pane and press the Delete key. (See **A** in Figure 14-14.)

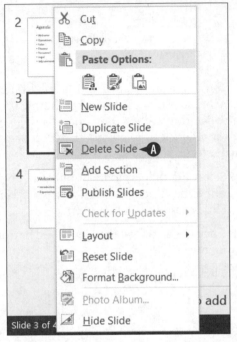

Figure 14-14: Delete a slide.

There's no Recycle Bin for slides; you can't get them back after you delete them. However, you can undo your last action(s) with the Undo button on the Quick Access toolbar, and that includes undoing deletions. If you haven't saved your work since you made the deletion, you can also get a deleted slide back by closing the file without saving changes and then reopening it.

Change the slide layout

A slide's layout determines the placeholders that appear on it and the arrangement and positioning of those placeholders.

To change a slide's layout, follow these steps:

1. Select the slide to change in the Slides pane.

2. On the Home tab, click Layout to open a gallery.

3. Click the desired layout.

The layouts available depend upon several factors, including the template you started with, the theme that is applied (see Chapter 15), and any custom layouts you may have created in Slide Master view. The nine layouts shown in Figure 14-15 are the default ones that come with the Blank template.

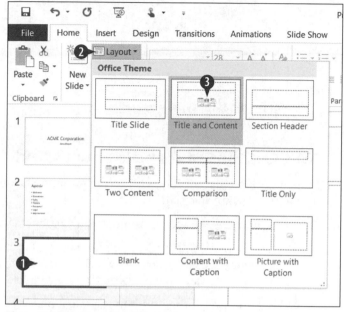

Figure 14-15: Choose a different layout.

Use content placeholders

The most common type of placeholder is a multipurpose Content placeholder. It gives you a choice of filling it either with text or with one of six types of graphical content.

You can fill each placeholder with only one type of content; if you want other content on the slide, you must use a layout with multiple content placeholders or add the extra content manually, as described in the next two sections. The available types of content are:

- Ⓐ Table
- Ⓑ Chart
- Ⓒ SmartArt Graphic
- Ⓓ Picture
- Ⓔ Online Picture
- Ⓕ Video

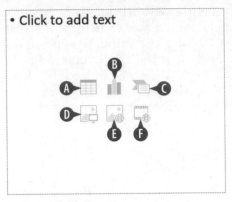

Figure 14-16: The types of graphical content for a Content placeholder.

Fill a Content placeholder with text

To fill a Content placeholder with text, click in the box and start typing. It's as simple as that!

Here are some things to keep in mind about Content placeholders:

(A) Most templates and designs use bulleted lists in the Content placeholder boxes by default, which means any text you type will automatically be formatted as a bulleted list.

(B) You can turn off the bullet for a paragraph by clicking the Bullets button on the Home tab.

(C) Use the Numbering button to convert a bulleted list to a numbered one.

(D) To demote (indent) a paragraph — for example, to create a subordinated bulleted list within a list, click Increase List Level on the Home tab.

(E) To promote a paragraph, click Decrease List Level.

It might seem counterintuitive to increase something you are demoting, but think about the list level as a hierarchy, with 1 as the most superior. If you increase the level, you demote the item to a later, less-important level.

Another way to demote a paragraph is to press Tab when the insertion point is at the beginning of the paragraph. Another way to promote is Shift+Tab.

You can use the commands in the Font and Paragraph groups on the Home tab to format the text in the placeholder, the same as you do in Word. Here are a few minor differences to note:

F Shadow adds a shadow to the text.

G Character Spacing lets you adjust the spacing between letters from the Ribbon. In Word this capability is available in the Paragraph dialog box.

H Clear All Formatting removes all manually applied formatting, reverting back to the formatting specified by the template or the design.

I Columns enables you to set a text placeholder box in multiple columns.

J Align Text enables you to set vertical alignment within the text box of Top, Middle, or Bottom.

K Text Direction changes the orientation of the text to vertical, stacked, or rotated.

L Convert to SmartArt Graphic converts the selected paragraphs to a SmartArt graphic.

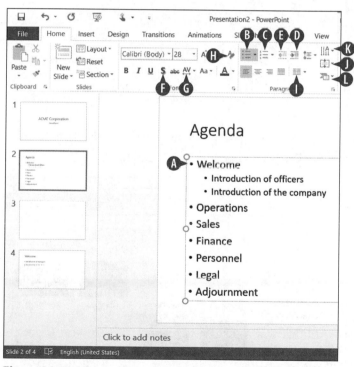

Figure 14-17: Here are some text formatting buttons that are different in PowerPoint than in Word.

Fill a Content placeholder with a graphical element

To use one of the graphical types of content, click the corresponding icon in the Content placeholder. A dialog box appears that guides you in selecting the content to include. The process is a bit different for each of the content types. Most of these content types you have worked with in earlier chapters; the dialog boxes are the same or nearly the same as in other Office applications. The one type you haven't used yet, SmartArt graphics, is covered in Chapter 15.

Just as an example, here's how to use a Content placeholder to insert a picture:

1 Click the Pictures icon in the Content placeholder.

Figure 14-18: Click the placeholder icon you want.

2 In the Insert Pictures dialog box, select the desired picture.

3 Click Insert.

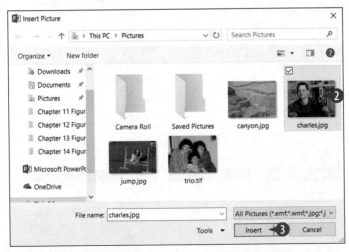

Figure 14-19: In the dialog box that appears, choose the content to place in the placeholder.

Manually place text on a slide

First, a warning. Whenever possible, you should use the place-holders on the slide layouts and *not* create text boxes manually. One reason is that text in manual text boxes doesn't appear in the Outline pane in Outline view. Manually placed text boxes also aren't affected when you change layouts or designs for a slide, so with the new arrangement of placeholders the text box might be obscured, or might obscure other content.

Nevertheless, sometimes you really do need a manual text box. For example, you might want a little informational box to appear floating next to a picture or chart to explain it.

To create a text box on a slide, follow these steps:

1 On the Insert tab, click Text Box.

2 Drag to draw the desired text box on the slide.

3. Release the mouse button, and then type in the text box that appears.

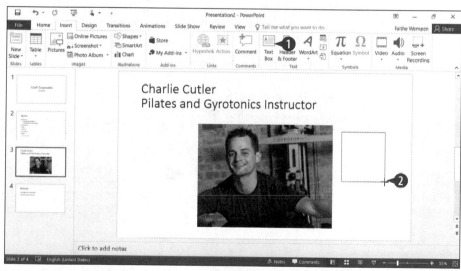

Figure 14-20: In the dialog box that appears, choose the content to place in the placeholder.

Manually place a picture on a slide

Same warning here as in the previous section: Try not to manually place pictures if you can help it. Use placeholders whenever possible. If you make changes to the layouts or change to a different design later, you'll thank me for this advice, because pictures in placeholders resize and move as needed, rolling with the changes. Manually placed pictures don't.

To manually insert a picture, do the following:

1. On the Insert tab, click Pictures.

2. In the Insert Pictures dialog box, select the desired picture. (It's the same dialog box as in Figure 4-19.)

3. Click Insert.

You can also insert various other types of graphics manually using the buttons on the Insert tab, such as Online Pictures, Chart, and SmartArt.

Move and resize slide objects

Objects on a slide are all free-floating frames. You can move and resize them just like in Word and Excel:

Ⓐ Drag an object by any part except the selection handles to move it. If it's a picture, you can drag it by any part, including the middle. If it's a text box, you have to drag it by its border.

Ⓑ Drag a selection handle to resize it. To maintain the aspect ratio, hold down Shift and drag only the corner selection handles.

Ⓒ Drag the rotation handle to rotate it.

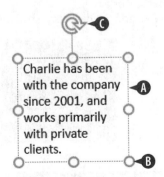

Figure 14-21: Drag the object's border to move it, or drag a selection handle to resize.

You can specify an exact size for an object in the Size group:

Ⓐ The tab on which the Size group appears depends on the object type. For example, for a picture, it's on the Picture Tools Format tab, and for a chart it's on the Chart Tools Format tab.

B Set an exact height in the Height box.

C Set an exact width in the Width box.

Figure 14-22: Control an object's size precisely with the Height and Width settings.

Delete slide objects

To delete an object on a slide, select the object and press Delete on the keyboard. You can get a deleted object back immediately after deleting it by using Undo. Click the Undo button on the Quick Access toolbar or press Ctrl+Z. (See **A** in Figure 14-23.)

Figure 14-23: Undo a deletion with the Undo button or Ctrl+Z.

CHAPTERFIFTEEN

Formatting a Presentation

One reason PowerPoint is so popular is that it's easy for anyone to create great-looking presentations. In this chapter, you learn how simple and even fun it is to create different looks for your presentations, including different themes, colors, and fonts. You also learn how to modify the presentation's overall formatting in Slide Master view, and how to format text boxes and placeholders. Finally, you learn how to create and format SmartArt graphics that can change dull bulleted lists into interesting graphical diagrams.

Understanding templates versus themes

Back in Chapter 14, you learned how to create a presentation based on a template, and the template came with its own theme settings, such as font, color, and background choices. So what's the difference between a template and a theme? Doesn't a theme provide all those things too? Perhaps a quick overview is in order before we launch into themes in this chapter.

In This Chapter

⟶ Changing the theme

⟶ Changing the presentation colors and fonts

⟶ Modifying the theme in Slide Master view

⟶ Enabling footer placeholders

⟶ Formatting text boxes and placeholders

⟶ Creating SmartArt graphics

⟶ Modifying the structure of a SmartArt graphic

⟶ Formatting a SmartArt graphic

A *template* is a file on which you can base new presentations. PowerPoint templates typically have a .potx extension (or a .potm extension if macro-enabled). A template file may contain one or more themes (that is, sets of design choices), plus one or more slides containing sample content.

A *theme* is both simpler and more complex than a template. A theme can exist either inside of a template or as a separate file with a .thmx extension. A theme is simpler in that it cannot hold some of the things that a template can, such as sample content. A theme can provide only variant, font, color, effect, background, and layout settings. On the other hand, a theme can also do *more* than a template, in that you can apply a theme saved as a separate file to other Office applications, so you can share the theme's formatting settings with Word or Excel, for example. You can't do that with a template.

Change the theme

As you learned in Chapter 9, Office applications share a common set of themes. A theme includes color choices, font choices, and effect choices. Chapter 2 and Chapter 9 offer longer explanations of the features if you didn't catch them the first time through.

Themes are especially important in PowerPoint because there's typically more color and flash in a presentation than in a document or a spreadsheet. Accordingly, themes have a few extra features in PowerPoint:

(A) Many themes provide decorative background graphics that repeat on each slide.

(B) Certain slide layouts, such as title slides, may have different background graphics than the other slides.

(C) You can choose *variants* of a theme. Usually a variant is the same theme with a different background color and color scheme, but for some themes the variants have different background graphics as well.

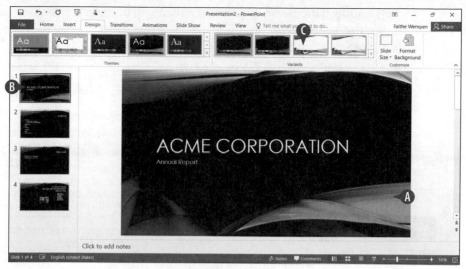

Figure 15-1: Theme features in PowerPoint.

To change the theme, follow these steps:

1 On the Design tab, in the Themes group, choose a theme.

You can click More to see additional themes. (See **D** in Figure 15-2.)

2 In the Variants group, click the desired variant of the chosen theme.

Most themes have only a few variants, but if there are more than can be displayed in the Variants group, you can click the More button in that group to see the additional variants. (See (**E**) in Figure 15-2.)

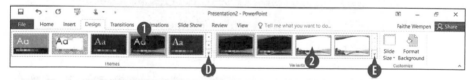

Figure 15-2: Choose a theme and a variant.

You can modify most aspects of the theme, including removing or repositioning the background graphics and the placeholders, in Slide Master view. See "Modify the theme in Slide Master view" later in this chapter for details.

It is generally expected in business presentations that you will use the same theme across all the slides in your presentation, because it makes for a more consistent and professional look. However, you might occasionally have a situation where you need to use a different theme, or perhaps a different variant of the theme, for certain slides

To apply a theme or a variant of a theme to only certain slides, do the following:

1. In the Slides pane in Normal view, or in Slide Sorter view, select the slide(s) to affect.

2. On the Design tab, right-click the desired theme or variant.

3. On the menu that appears, click Apply to Selected Slides.

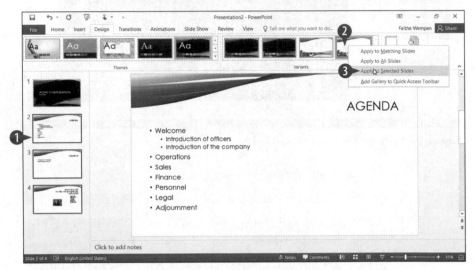

Figure 15-3: Apply a theme or variant to only certain slides.

Change the presentation colors and fonts

Just like in Word and Excel, you can change the color and font schemes separately from the theme itself. The main difference in PowerPoint is in where those commands are located.

Here's how to access the color schemes:

1. On the Design tab, click the More button in the Variants group.

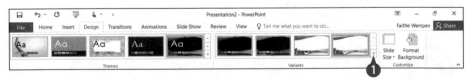

Figure 15-4: Click More in the Variants group.

2. Point to Colors.

3. Click the desired color scheme.

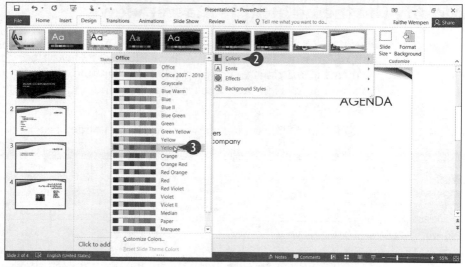

Figure 15-5: Choose a different color scheme.

Yes, you can customize the color schemes, just like in Word and Excel. Just click Customize Colors to get started with that. Check out "Create a custom theme" in Chapter 9 for help.

It's pretty much the same thing for the font schemes:

1. On the Design tab, click the More button in the Variants group.

2 Point to Fonts.

3 Click the desired font scheme.

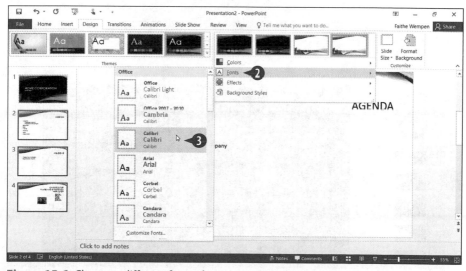

Figure 15-6: Choose a different font scheme.

Modify the theme in Slide Master view

Slide Master view is where you can really get down to the nitty-gritty of formatting a presentation. It enables you to customize the theme formatting by changing colors, backgrounds, layouts, fonts, and more. Here are some things to keep in mind about Slide Master view:

Ⓐ To enter Slide Master view, choose View ⇨ Slide Master.

Figure 15-7: Enter Slide Master view.

In Slide Master view, the navigation pane at the left shows thumbnail images of slides.

Ⓑ The topmost thumbnail is the *theme master,* and it represents the theme as a whole. Any changes you make to this slide affect all slides that use that theme, regardless of their layout.

Ⓒ Each of the thumbnails beneath that topmost one is a *layout master* and represents an individual layout. Any changes you make to one of these affect only slides that use that layout.

Ⓓ If you need to know which layout a particular thumbnail represents, point at it with the mouse and read the name in the ScreenTip. The ScreenTip also tells how many slides in the presentation use that layout.

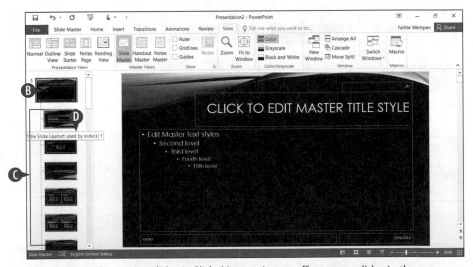

Figure 15-8: Customize slides in Slide Master view to affect many slides in the presentation at once.

E If there is more than one theme applied in the presentation (for example, if you chose to apply an alternate theme or variant to selected slides), there will be multiple theme masters in the navigation pane. Scroll down to find the other(s).

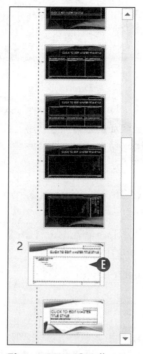

Figure 15-9: Scroll down in the navigation pane to find other themes used in this presentation.

The following sections outline some things you can do in Slide Master view.

Create a new layout

Before you start fiddling with a layout, it's a good idea to make a copy of it. Then you can make your changes to the copy, and the original layout remains safe.

To duplicate a layout, right-click a layout master and choose Duplicate Layout. (See **A** in Figure 15-10.)

Figure 15-10: Duplicate a layout.

You can also create a new layout from scratch. To do so, follow these steps:

1 Select the theme master (the big slide at the top of the navigation pane).

2 Click Insert Layout.

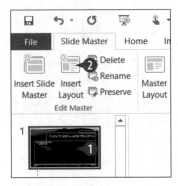

Figure 15-11: Create a new layout.

A new layout appears in the navigation pane, below the other layouts for that theme. (See B in Figure 15-12.)

The new layout contains a title placeholder, but no content placeholders. (See C in Figure 15-12.)

If the theme master contains a slide number, footer, or date placeholder, the new layout inherits them. (See D in Figure 15-12.)

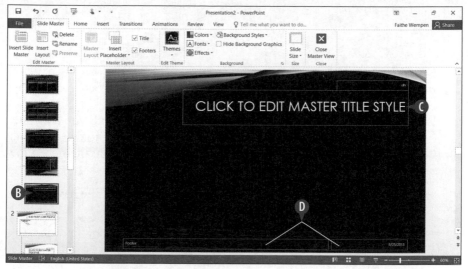

Figure 15-12: The newly created layout.

To add content placeholders to the new layout, see, "Add placeholders" later in this chapter. To reposition any of the placeholders on the layout, see "Reposition and resize a placeholder."

Remove placeholders

To remove a placeholder from a layout, select the placeholder's outer frame and then press Delete on the keyboard.

Make sure you have the correct layout master or theme master selected in the navigation pane before you delete a placeholder. Deleting a placeholder from the theme master also removes it from all layouts; deleting from a layout master affects only that layout.

Certain placeholders can be hidden (that is, toggled off) without deleting them. That's useful in case you might want to toggle them back on again later. Consider Figure 15-13:

(A) To temporarily hide the title placeholder, clear the Title check box on the Slide Master tab.

(B) To temporarily hide the slide number, footer, and date placeholders (all of them as a group), clear the Footers check box there.

Figure 15-13: You can clear check boxes to hide certain placeholders.

When working with the theme master (not an individual layout master), you can toggle each of the default placeholder elements on or off; this change affects all layouts under that theme. Follow these steps:

1. Make sure the theme master is selected in the navigation pane.

2. On the Slide Master tab, click Master Layout.

3. In the Master Layout dialog box, clear the check box for any element you don't want to use.

4. Click OK.

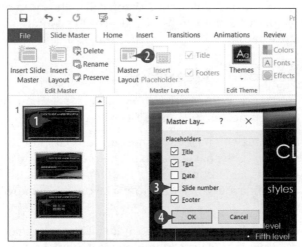

Figure 15-14: The check boxes in the Master Layout dialog box affect all layouts.

Enabling the placeholders for footer, slide number, and date does not make those elements automatically appear on the slides. All it does is define where those items will go if you *choose* to enable them. See "Enable footer placeholders" later in this chapter to learn how.

Add placeholders

To add a placeholder to a slide, follow these steps:

1. Make sure the desired layout is selected in the navigation pane.

2. On the Slide Master tab, click Insert Placeholder.

3. Click the desired content type. Content is the most flexible; the other choices limit users to a specific type of content.

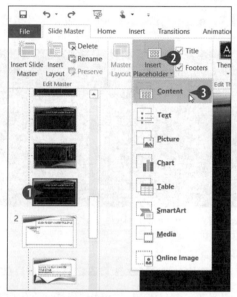

Figure 15-15: Add a placeholder.

4. Drag on the slide to draw a rectangular frame where the placeholder should appear. A colored box appears showing the dimensions of the new placeholder.

Figure 15-16: Draw the placeholder on the layout master.

When you release the mouse button, the new placeholder appears on the slide. See the next section if you need to move or resize it.

Reposition and resize a placeholder

Placeholders are like any other objects on a slide. You can move and resize them freely:

> Ⓐ To move a placeholder, drag its border (but not a selection handle).

> Ⓑ To resize a placeholder, drag a selection handle.

Figure 15-17: Move and resize a placeholder as you would any other object.

Hide or remove a background graphic

First, let's get one thing straight: there's a difference between hiding a background graphic and removing it. Removing a background graphic is done on the theme master, and it applies to all layouts. It is not easily reversible; once you delete the graphic, it's gone — at least until you reapply the default version of the theme, which also erases all your other customizations, too. On the other hand, hiding a background graphic is done on an individual layout and is easily reversible.

To hide a background graphic on an individual layout:

> ❶ Select the desired layout master.

> ❷ On the Slide Master tab, mark the Hide Background Graphics check box.

Figure 15-18: Hide the background graphic on an individual layout.

 The preceding steps hide any background graphics that have been inherited from the theme master. They do not hide any background graphics that are directly located on the layout master. To delete those, select them and press Delete. (But remember, if you delete, rather than hide, they're gone for good.)

To delete a background graphic for the entire theme:

1 Select the theme master.

2 Select the graphic to be deleted.

3. Press the Delete key.

Figure 15-19: Delete a graphic from the theme master.

Change the text size

In most cases, it is best to leave the text in the theme's placeholders set to the default size. Locking in the text to a fixed size can result in some awkward-looking layouts if you later change themes or fonts. You can change the fonts used by choosing a different font scheme, as you learned earlier in the chapter.

However, sometimes you might need to change the text size, either for all layouts (on the theme master) or for an individual layout. For example, if the bulleted text in a Content placeholder is too small for the audience to read comfortably, you might bump it up a few points.

To change the text size for a text placeholder, you can use any of the standard methods of changing font size that you've learned throughout this book. I prefer to use the Shrink Font and Grow Font buttons rather than choosing specific sizes, personally, because that way I can change multiple outline levels at once.

Follow these steps to increase the font sizes for all outline levels on a Content placeholder, for example:

1. Select the theme master or an individual layout master. (It's usually better to change the theme master because then the font size is consistent across all layouts.)

2. Drag to select all the text in the Content placeholder, or click inside the placeholder and press Ctrl+A.

3. On the Home tab, click the Grow Font button until the fonts are sufficiently larger.

   If you wanted the fonts smaller, you could instead click Shrink Font. (See Ⓐ in Figure 15-20.)

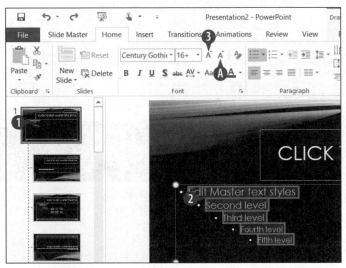

Figure 15-20: Shrink or grow the text in the Content placeholder on the theme master.

Exit from Slide Master view

When you are finished working in Slide Master view, click the Close Master View button on the Slide Master tab. (See Ⓐ in Figure 15-21.)

Figure 15-21: Exit from Slide Master view to return to normal editing of individual slides.

There are also Master views for handouts and notes pages. You can these to customize the layout of your printouts of those items. They aren't covered in this book, but you may want to experiment with the Handout Master and Notes Master buttons on the View tab on your own.

Enable footer placeholders

As I mentioned earlier in this chapter, just having the footer, slide number, and date placeholders on a slide is not enough to make anything appear in them. You have to enable those items.

Those items, by the way, are collectively known as *footer placeholders*, even though only one of them is technically the footer, and even though, depending on the theme and layout, some of them may appear at the top rather than the bottom of each slide.

To enable one or more of them, follow these steps:

1. Exit from Slide Master view if you're still there. See the preceding section.

2. If you want to affect only certain slides, select them in the Slides pane in Normal view, or select them in Slide Sorter view. Normally you will want the setting to be consistent throughout the entire presentation, but there might be special circumstances, such as wanting to place certain items only on the first or last slide.

3. On the Insert tab, click Header & Footer.

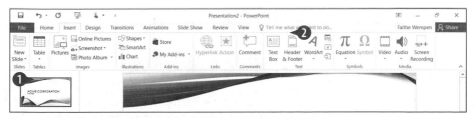

Figure 15-22: Choose Header & Footer to enable footer placeholders.

④ If you want the date or time to appear, mark the Date and Time check box:

   Ⓐ You can choose a date or time format from the Update Automatically drop-down list.

   Ⓑ Click Fixed if you don't want the date to update automatically, and then enter the desired date in the Fixed text box, in the format you prefer.

⑤ If you want the slide number to appear, mark the Slide number check box.

⑥ If you want the footer to appear, mark the Footer check box, and then type the desired text in the footer text box.

If you don't want these elements on the title slide, mark the Don't Show on Title Slide check box. (See Ⓒ in Figure 15-23.)

⑦ Click Apply to apply the setting only to the selected slides, or click Apply to All to apply it to the entire presentation.

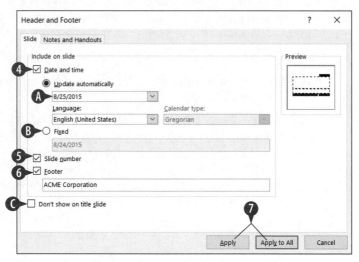

Figure 15-23: Choose what you want to appear as footer information.

Format text boxes and placeholders

Each placeholder box, and each manually placed text box, can be formatted in several ways. Of course, you can format the text itself, like you do with any text, but you can also format its border and its fill:

   Ⓐ *Border* (or *outline*) refers to the line around the outside of the box. A border can have a line style (like dotted or solid), a line weight (thickness), and a line color.

B *Fill* refers to the background inside the box. A fill can be a solid color or can be a pattern, gradient, texture, or photo.

Figure 15-24: A text box has a border and a fill.

If you have a manually created text box where the text overflows the box, no matter how you try to resize the box, do this: Right-click the text box and choose Format Shape. In the Format Shape task pane, click Text Options and then click the Textbox icon. Change the AutoFit setting to either Do not Autofit or Shrink text on overflow.

Apply a shape style

Shape styles provide a simple way of formatting a text box using one of the theme's colors. Each shape style includes a fill setting, a border setting (even if that setting is "no border"), and in some cases effect settings such as a beveled edge.

To apply a shape style:

1 Select the text box.

2 On the Drawing Tools Format tab, click the More button to open a gallery.

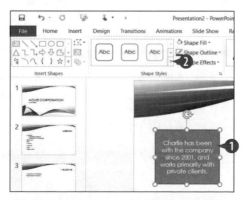

Figure 15-25: Select the text box and then open the Shape Styles gallery.

③ Click one of the shape styles.

Each row contains the same style implemented in a different one of the theme's colors.

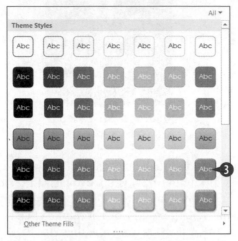

Figure 15-26: Select the desired shape style.

Format a text box border

Don't like the default outline, or the one that the shape style provided? Set a text box's outline manually as follows:

1. Select the text box.

② On the Drawing Tools Format tab, click Shape Outline.

3. Click the desired outline color.

Ⓐ Choose a theme color to allow the color to change if you change themes or color schemes later.

Ⓑ Choose a standard color to assign a fixed color.

Ⓒ Click More Outline Colors to choose a fixed color from a dialog box.

Ⓓ Click Eyedropper and then click a color somewhere else in the presentation to pick up that color for use as the text box's border color.

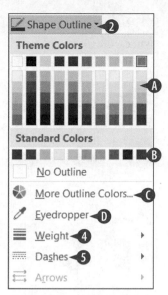

Figure 15-27: Choose the outline color.

④ If you want to change the outline weight, click Shape Outline again to reopen the menu. Then click Weight and then click the desired weight.

⑤ If you want to change the outline style, click Shape Outline again to reopen the menu. Then click Dashes and then click the desired line style.

Format a text box fill

Text box fill options are similar to those for the outline, as detailed in the previous section. You can choose a theme color or standard color, or you can pick up a color with the Eyedropper.

In addition to those choices, though, you can also do any of the following for the text box's fill:

Ⓐ Click Picture and then select a picture to use for the text box background.

Ⓑ Point to Gradient and then click the desired gradient option, or click More Gradients to configure a custom gradient.

Ⓒ Point to Texture and then click the desired texture. A texture is a small image that is tiled (repeated) to make it look like one unified surface.

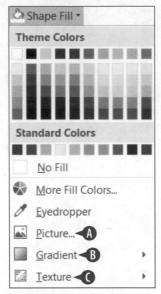

Figure 15-28: Fill options for a text box.

Apply text box effects

The same effects apply in PowerPoint as with objects in the other Office applications, but in PowerPoint these effects are perhaps more useful and relevant because of the graphical nature of a presentation as compared to a spreadsheet or letter.

To apply text box effects, follow these steps:

1. Select the text box.

2 On the Drawing Tools Format tab, click Shape Effects.

3 Point to one of the menu options to display its submenu.

Preset offers a variety of presets that span more than one of the effect categories, such as beveling plus 3-D rotation or a shadow. (See **A** in Figure 15-29.)

4 Click the desired setting on the submenu.

You can click the Options command at the bottom of a submenu to open a task pane containing more options for that effect. (See **B** in Figure 15-29.)

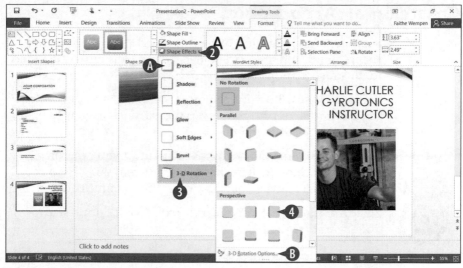

Figure 15-29: Choose an effect.

So what are these text effects? Table 15-1 has a quick summary.

Table 15-1	Text Effects Applied to a Text Box	
Effect	**Description**	**Example**
Shadow	Places a shadow behind the box, as if a light were shining on its face.	ACME
Reflection	Shows a faint reflection of the box, as if it were sitting on a shiny surface.	ACME
Glow	Adds a colored glow around the outside of the box.	ACME
Soft Edges	Makes the edges of the box somewhat fuzzy.	ACME
Bevel	Makes the edges of the box look like they are raised and beveled.	ACME
3-D Rotation	Tilts the box using 3-D perspective.	ACME

Create SmartArt graphics

SmartArt is a special class of graphic object that combines shapes, lines, and text placeholders. SmartArt is most often used to illustrate relationships between bits of text.

You can create a SmartArt graphic from scratch and then enter the text into it, or you can convert the existing paragraphs on a slide into a SmartArt graphic.

Table 15-2 summarizes the types of SmartArt you can create. Note that each of the types has many different designs, so you aren't limited to the graphic shown in the Example column.

SmartArt is available in Word and Excel too; it's not just a PowerPoint feature.

Table 15-2	SmartArt Graphics	
Type	*Description*	*Example*
List	Presents information in a straightforward, text-based way, somewhat like a fancy outline. Useful when the information is not in any particular order, or when the process or progression is not important.	
Process	Similar to a list, but with directional arrows or connectors that show the flow of one item to another.	
Cycle	Illustrates a repeating or recursive process in which there is no fixed end point.	
Hierarchy	An organization chart, showing structure and relationships between people or things in standardized levels.	

Type	Description	Example
Relationship	Illustrates how parts relate to a whole. One common type is a Venn diagram, shown here.	Corporate Trainers / Academic Instructors / Content Developers
Matrix	Also shows relationships of parts to a whole, but it does so with the parts in orderly looking quadrants and does not reflect a relationship between the items.	Sales / Marketing / Operations / Accounting
Pyramid	A striated triangle with text at various levels, representing the relationship between the items and also implying that some items are more important or less numerous.	Executives / Managers / Workers
Picture	Any of the above types of diagrams that contain placeholders for pictures.	

Create a new SmartArt graphic

Here's how to create a new SmartArt graphic:

1 Click the SmartArt icon in an empty Content placeholder on the slide.

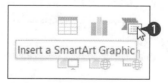

Insert a SmartArt Graphic

Figure 15-30: Select the SmartArt icon.

You can also choose Insert ⇨ SmartArt, but doing so creates a free-floating SmartArt, rather than it being attached to a placeholder. When possible, it's better for objects to be associated with placeholders, because it makes the transition smoother if you switch designs or layouts.

2 Click the desired category.

③ Click one of the designs.

A preview of the selected design appears, along with its description. (See Ⓐ in Figure 15-31.)

④ Click OK.

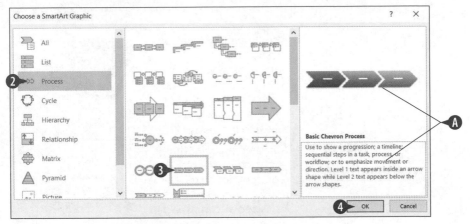

Figure 15-31: Select the SmartArt icon.

⑤ Type the text that should appear into each box, clicking a box to move to it as needed. Text automatically resizes as needed to fit in the available space in the shape:

Ⓑ You can also type text in the Text pane.

Ⓒ If the Text pane doesn't appear, click Text Pane on the SmartArt Tools Design tab.

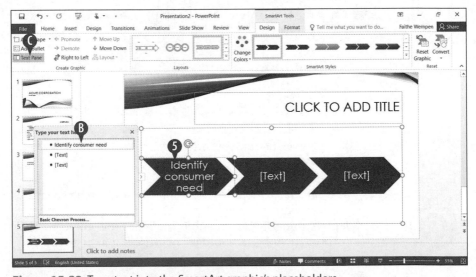

Figure 15-32: Type text into the SmartArt graphic's placeholders.

Convert existing text to SmartArt

An existing bulleted list (or other set of paragraphs with or without bullets) can easily be converted to a SmartArt graphic. Here's how:

1 Select the paragraphs.

2 On the Home tab, click Convert to SmartArt Graphic.

3 Click More SmartArt Graphics.

If you happen to see the layout you want, you can click it in step 3 and then skip the rest of the steps. (See **A** in Figure 15-33.)

4 Click the desired category.

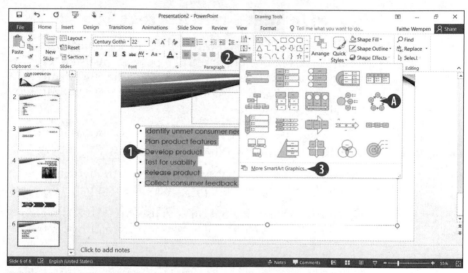

Figure 15-33: Click Convert to SmartArt Graphic on the Home tab.

5 Click one of the designs.

A preview of the selected design appears, along with its description. (See **B** in Figure 15-34.)

6 Click OK. The text is replaced by a SmartArt graphic that uses that same text.

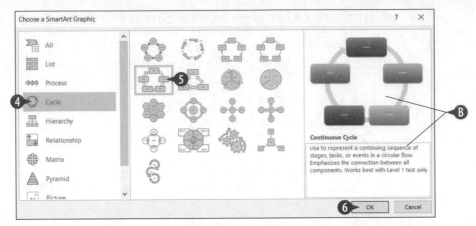

Figure 15-34: Select the design to use.

Edit and format SmartArt text

All SmartArt has text placeholders, which are basically text boxes. You simply click in one of them and type. Use the usual text-formatting controls (Font, Font Size, Bold, Italic, and so on) on the Home tab to change the appearance of the text. Some things to note about SmartArt text:

Ⓐ You can also select the text and then use the formatting tools on the mini toolbar.

Ⓑ You can also type, edit, and format text in the Text pane. The formatting will not preview in the Text pane, however.

Ⓒ Another formatting option is to use WordArt Styles group on the Format tab to apply WordArt formatting.

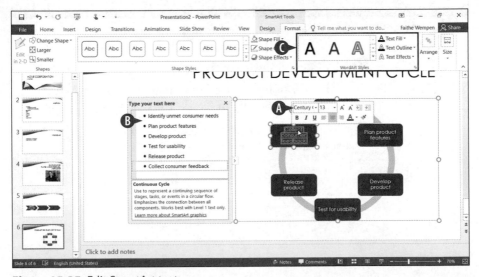

Figure 15-35: Edit SmartArt text.

The text in the outline pane is not always in the order you would expect it to be for the graphic because it forces text to appear in linear form from a graphic that is not necessarily linear. It does not matter how the text appears in the Text pane because only you see that. What matters is how it looks in the actual graphic.

Here are some tips for working with SmartArt text:

- To leave a text box empty, just don't type anything in it. The [Text] placeholders do not show up in a printout or in Slide Show view.

- To promote a line of text, press Shift+Tab; to demote it, press Tab in the Text pane.

- Text wraps automatically, but you can press Shift+Enter to insert a line break if necessary.

- In most cases, the text size shrinks to fit the graphic in which it is located. There are some exceptions to that, though; for example, at the top of a pyramid, the text can overflow the tip of the pyramid.

- If you resize the SmartArt graphic, its text resizes automatically.

- All of the text in a SmartArt graphic is the same size, so if you enter a really long string of text in one box, the text size in all of the related boxes shrinks too. You can manually format parts of the SmartArt graphic to change this behavior. For example, you can select one shape and choose a different font size for the text in it.

Modify the structure of a SmartArt graphic

The structure of the SmartArt graphic includes how many boxes it has and where they are placed. Even though the graphic types are all very different, the way you add, remove, and reposition shapes in them is surprisingly similar across all types.

Not all SmartArt graphic types can accept different numbers of shapes. For example the four-square matrix graphic is fixed at four squares, and you can't add or remove shapes.

Insert a shape

To insert a shape:

1. Click a shape that is adjacent to where you want the new shape to appear.

2 On the SmartArt Tools Design tab, click the arrow on the Add Shape button to open a menu.

③ Click the desired shape to add. The choices on the menu depend on the graphic type and the type of shape selected.

If you click the face of the Add Shape button instead of the arrow, you add a shape of the same level and type as the selected one, and the menu does not appear. (See Ⓐ in Figure 15-36.)

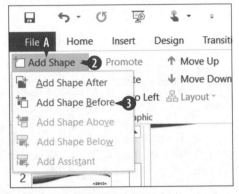

Figure 15-36: Add a shape.

Delete a shape

To delete a shape, click it to select it in the SmartArt graphic, and then press the Delete key on the keyboard. You might need to delete subordinate shapes before you can delete the main shape.

Promote and demote text

The difference between a shape and a bullet is primarily a matter of promotion and demotion in the Text pane's outline. The Text pane works just as the regular Outline pane does in this regard; you can promote with Shift+Tab or demote with Tab. You can also use the Promote and Demote buttons on the SmartArt Tools Design tab.

Reorder shapes or change the flow direction

You can easily reorder individual shapes. For example, suppose you have a graphic that illustrates five steps in a process and you realize that steps 3 and 4 are out of order. You can move one of them without having to retype all of the labels:

Ⓐ Select a shape and then on the SmartArt Tools Design tab, click Move Up or Move Down.

Each SmartArt graphic flows in a certain direction. A cycle graphic flows either clockwise or counterclockwise. A pyramid flows either up or down. If you realize after typing all of the text that you should have made the SmartArt graphic flow in the other direction, you can change it.

B Click the Right to Left button on the SmartArt Tools Design tab. It is a toggle; you can switch back and forth freely.

Figure 15-37: Use the buttons on the Design tab to reorder the shapes.

Reposition shapes

You can individually select and drag each shape to reposition it on the SmartArt graphic. Any connectors between it and the other shapes are automatically resized and extended as needed.

Reset a SmartArt graphic

After making changes to a SmartArt graphic, you can return it to its default settings.

On the SmartArt Tools Design tab, click Reset Graphic. This strips off everything, including any SmartArt styles and manual positioning, and makes it exactly as it was when you inserted it, except it keeps the text that you've typed. (See **A** in Figure 15-38.)

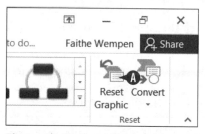

Figure 15-38: Reset the graphic.

Change to a different layout

When you insert a SmartArt graphic you choose a type, and you can change that type at any time later:

A To change the layout type, choose from the Layouts gallery on the SmartArt Tools Design tab.

B If the type you want doesn't appear, click More Layouts at the bottom of its menu to redisplay the same dialog box as in Figure 15-34, from which you can choose any layout.

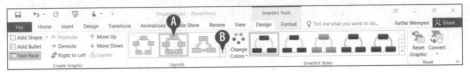

Figure 15-39: Choose a different layout.

Format a SmartArt graphic

Next let's look at some ways to improve the appearance of a SmartArt graphic. You can format a SmartArt graphic either automatically or manually. Automatic formatting is the default, and many PowerPoint users don't even realize that manual formatting is a possibility. The following sections cover both.

Apply a SmartArt style

SmartArt Styles are preset formatting specs (border, fill, effects, shadows, and so on) that you can apply to an entire SmartArt graphic. They make it easy to apply surface texture effects that make the shapes look reflective or appear to have 3-D depth or perspective.

To apply a SmartArt style:

1. Select the SmartArt graphic.

   2A On the SmartArt Tools Design tab, click one of the samples in the SmartArt Styles group.

   OR

   2B Click the More button and then select from a larger list.

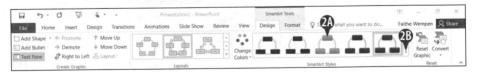

Figure 15-40: Apply a SmartArt style.

Change SmartArt colors

After you apply a SmartArt style, as in the preceding section, you might want to change the colors used in the graphic. You can choose a Colorful scheme (one in which each shape, or the shapes at each level, have their own colors), or you can choose a monochrome color scheme based on any of the current presentation color theme's color swatches.

To change the colors:

1. Select the SmartArt graphic.

2 On the SmartArt Tools Design tab, click Change Colors.

3 Click the desired color combination.

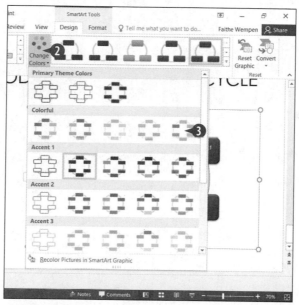

Figure 15-41: Change SmartArt colors.

Manually apply colors and effects to individual shapes

In addition to formatting the entire graphic with a SmartArt Style, you can also format individual shapes using Shape Styles. This is pretty much like formatting text boxes, as you learned earlier in this chapter. Here's a quick review.

1. Select a shape in a SmartArt graphic.

2 On the SmartArt Tools Format tab, select a shape style from the Shape Styles gallery.

3 (Optional) Fine-tune the style by using the Shape Fill, Shape Outline, and/or Shape Effects buttons, and their associated menus.

Figure 15-42: Format an individual shape manually.

CHAPTER SIXTEEN

Adding Movement and Sound to a Presentation

Have you ever heard the phrase "Death by PowerPoint"? It means being bored to death by a dull, long, lifeless presentation, usually with someone droning on about the slide's text-heavy content in too much detail.

To avoid causing this kind of agony for your audience, you can enliven your slides by adding movement and sound to them. You can set up different transition effects for moving from one slide to another, and you can animate the individual objects on a slide so that they enter or exit the slide or emphasize a certain point. (Don't go overboard in the other direction, though; too much bling can be worse than none at all.)

You can also add sound and video clips to a presentation. In earlier versions of PowerPoint, some types of video were difficult to integrate, but today's PowerPoint is greatly improved in this area, and you can integrate many sound and video types seamlessly into your show.

In This Chapter

➡ Adding slide transition effects

➡ Setting slides to advance manually or automatically

➡ Animating objects

➡ Inserting a sound clip on a slide

➡ Associating a sound with an event

➡ Inserting a video clip on a slide

Add slide transition effects

Transitions are movements from one slide to another. The default transition effect is None, which means the slide simply goes away and the next one appears. Some of the alternatives include Fade, Push, Wipe, Split, and Cut, to name only a few. Some things to note about transitions:

A You can apply transitions from the Transitions tab.

B Click More in the Transitions to this Slide group to see more choices.

Some of the transition effects have options that determine the direction of the action. For example, a Wipe transition might wipe from the left, right, top, or bottom, or from one of the corners. Other effects have no such options because they can happen only one way.

C If options are available, you can click the Transitions tab and choose them from the Effect Options button.

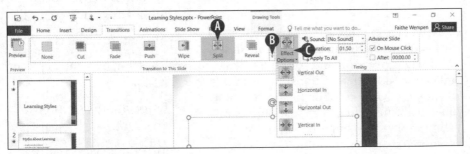

Figure 16-1: Apply transitions from the Transitions tab.

D You can also set several other properties for a transition. You can assign a sound to it, for example. To do so, open the Sound drop-down list and select a sound.

E At the bottom of the Sound list you can click Other Sound to use a sound file of your own.

F To control the speed of the transition, change the Duration setting (measured in seconds). A longer duration will make the transition occur more slowly.

G In most cases, you should make all the slides in your presentation have the same transition, sound (if any), and duration. To quickly do so, click Apply to All after making your choices.

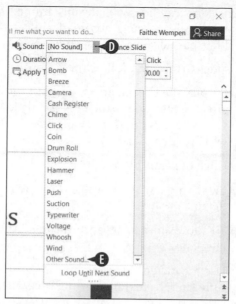

Figure 16-2: Apply transitions from the Transitions tab.

Figure 16-3: Set the transition's duration, and optionally apply the same transition to all slides.

Set slides to advance manually or automatically

You can choose on the Transitions tab how slides advance even if you do not use any transition effect (that is, transition setting is None).

By default, slides advance only on mouse click. That means that no matter how long you leave a slide onscreen, PowerPoint doesn't try to advance to the next slide until you give the signal. (That signal can be an actual mouse click or the press of a key, such as Enter, spacebar, or the right-arrow key.)

If you want some (or all) slides to advance automatically after a certain amount of time, you can specify this advancement on the Transitions tab. You can specify an automatic transition instead of or in addition to the default On Click behavior. If you mark both check boxes, slides will advance immediately on mouse click, but will also advance automatically after the specified time interval has passed since the last slide.

To set slides to advance, follow these steps:

1. Display the slide to affect, or select multiple slides to affect in the Slides pane in Normal view, or in Slide Sorter view. If you want to affect all slides, it does not matter which slide you select.

2. Click the Transitions tab.

3. Make sure On Mouse Click is marked. (It is marked by default.)

4. To allow slides to advance automatically, mark the After check box.

5. Use the increment arrow buttons to specify an amount of time (in seconds) in the After box.

6. To apply this setting across all slides, click Apply to All.

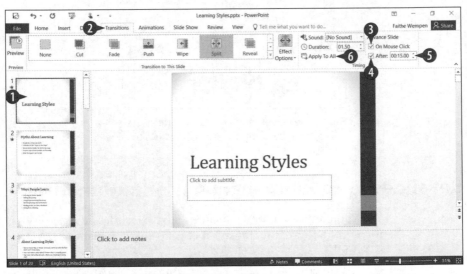

Figure 16-4: Choose how slides will advance.

Animate objects

Animations are movements that are somewhat like transitions except they apply to individual objects on a slide rather than the entire slide. For example, you can animate a picture so that it appears after everything else on the slide has already appeared, or you can make the bullet points on a slide appear one by one rather than all at once.

You can create four types of animations in PowerPoint:

- An **entrance animation** governs how an object appears on the slide.

- An **exit animation** governs how an object leaves the slide.

- An **emphasis animation** makes the object do something to call attention to itself when it is neither entering nor exiting; this might include changing color, moving around, or making a sound.

- A **motion path animation** (not covered in this chapter) moves an object on the slide following a predefined path you specify. It's kind of like setting down model railroad tracks and letting the object be the train moving on the track.

Create an entrance animation

Use an entrance animation whenever you want certain content on a slide to appear after the slide background has already appeared (and possibly other content on the slide, too). Any objects that you don't animate will appear at the same time the slide background does; any objects you animate will appear after that in a sequence you specify.

To create an entrance animation, follow these steps:

1 Select the object to animate. If you want to animate text, select the paragraph(s) to animate, or select the outer border of a text box to animate all text inside it.

Keep in mind that during a presentation, anything that *doesn't* have an entrance animation appears when the slide itself appears, and animations happen after that. So, for example, if you animate the first paragraph of a bulleted list but not the other paragraphs, when the slide displays you'll initially see all the other paragraphs, but not the first one.

2 On the Animations tab, click Add Animation.

A You can also click the More button in the Animation group to choose an animation; the menu that appears is the same as the menu for the Add Animation button.

When animating an object or text that currently has no animation, the menus on the More button and on the Add Animation button work the same. The difference comes in later. If you want to change to a different animation later (of the same type: entrance, emphasis, exit, or motion path), use the menu on the More button. If you want to set up multiple animations for the same object, add each new one with the Add Animation button.

Ⓑ If the animation you want happens to appear in the Entrance section of the menu, you can click it and then skip the rest of the steps.

③ Click More Entrance Effects.

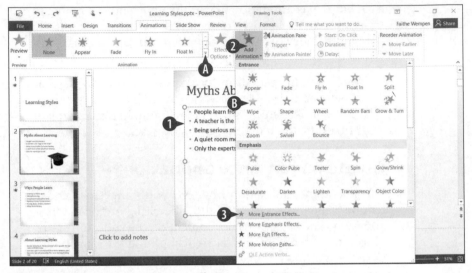

Figure 16-5: Create a new entrance effect.

④ Click an entrance effect, and watch the preview of it on the slide, behind the dialog box. Drag the dialog box to the side if needed.

Effects in the dialog box are ordered by category: Basic, Subtle, Moderate, and Exciting. Your opinion may be different, of course, but these categories provide a starting point for making your choice.

⑤ After you have selected the desired effect, click OK.

After you apply an animation to a text box that contains multiple paragraphs, each paragraph has a number next to it, indicating the order in which the paragraphs will be animated. (See Ⓒ in Figure 16-7.)

To adjust an animation's options, see the section "Change an animation's options" later in this chapter. To resequence the order of the animations on a slide, see the section "Change animation sequence."

Figure 16-6: Select the desired effect and click OK.

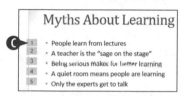

Figure 16-7: Numbers represent the animation sequence.

Create an emphasis animation

An emphasis animation calls attention to an object on a slide when it is neither entering nor exiting. PowerPoint offers many types of emphasis animations, including Grow/Shrink, Spin, and various color changes.

The following process is very similar to that of adding an entrance animation, so glance back at the preceding section for some additional tips and details:

1. Select the object to animate. If you want to animate text, select the paragraph(s) to animate, or select the outer border of a text box to animate all text inside it.

2. On the Animations tab, click Add Animation.

3. Click More Emphasis Effects.

4. Click an emphasis effect, and watch the preview of it on the slide, behind the dialog box. Drag the dialog box to the side if needed.

Some animation effects may be unavailable for the type of object you are animating. For example, Font Color is not available for a graphic. (See Ⓐ in Figure 16-8.)

⑤ After you have selected the desired effect, click OK.

Figure 16-8: Choose an emphasis effect.

Create an exit animation

An exit animation causes an object to leave the slide before the next slide appears. Without an exit animation applied, an object stays onscreen until the next slide appears. Exit animations are often used in combination with entrance animations to make an object enter, stay for a specified time, and then exit.

The following process is very similar to that of adding an entrance animation, so look back at that section for some additional tips and details:

1. Select the object to animate. If you want to animate text, select the paragraph(s) to animate, or select the outer border of a text box to animate all text inside it.

2. On the Animations tab, click Add Animation.

3. Click More Exit Effects.

④ Click an exit effect, and watch the preview of it on the slide, behind the dialog box. Drag the dialog box to the side if needed.

⑤ After you have selected the desired effect, click OK.

Figure 16-9: Choose an exit effect.

Choose a different animation

To choose a different animation for an object, do the following:

1 Select the object.

2 On the Animations tab, click the More button in the Animations group.

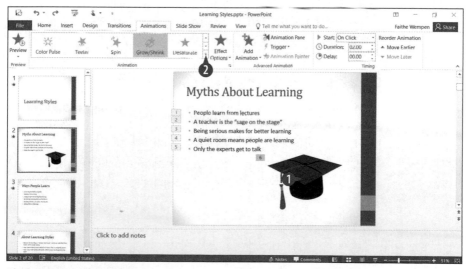

Figure 16-10: Click More.

③ Click the command that corresponds to the type of animation you want to change to.

You can also choose one of the options from the menu and skip the rest of the steps. (See Ⓐ in Figure 16-11.)

In step 3, it does not have to be the same type as was previously applied. For example, you can replace an entrance effect with an emphasis effect.

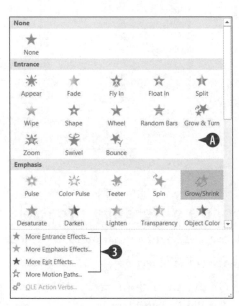

Figure 16-11: Choose a different animation.

4. Click the desired animation.

5. Click OK.

Change an animation's options

Animation options include the duration, the delay, and the sound effects assigned to an animation. You can set all these from the Animations tab. Consider Figure 16-12:

Ⓐ Set an animation's start trigger using the Start drop-down list on the Animations tab.

Figure 16-12: Choose what will cause the animation to start.

An animation event can be set to start in any of these ways:

- *On mouse click:* The event occurs when you click the mouse (or do some other equivalent action to advance the presentation, such as press Enter).

- *With previous:* The event occurs simultaneously with the previous animation event. If there is no previous animation event for this slide, it occurs simultaneously with the slide itself displaying.

- *After previous:* The event occurs after the previous animation event has completed. If there is no previous animation event for this slide, it occurs after the slide itself displays.

The animation's Duration determines how quickly it executes. A longer duration means a slower execution.

The Delay setting determines the length of the pause between the previous event and this one.

Figure 16-13: Set the animation duration and delay.

You can also choose effect options from a dialog box for more choices. Display the animation pane (covered next), and then right-click the animation effect in the Animation pane and choose Effect Options.

Display the Animation Pane

If you have more than one animated object on a slide, you may find it useful to see all the animations in a list form. The Animation pane provides such a list:

(A) To display the Animation pane, click the Animation Pane button on the Animations tab.

(B) When the paragraphs in a text box are individually animated, they show by default as a collapsed group in the Animation pane.

(C) You can click the gray bar below the group to expand it to see each paragraph's animation individually listed.

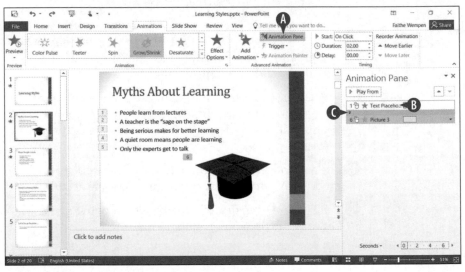

Figure 16-14: Display the Animation pane.

(D) You can tell the animation type by the color of the bar on it. Entrance is green; emphasis is yellow; exit is red; and motion path is gray.

(E) You can tell the duration of an animation by the length of the colored bar.

(F) The seconds scale gives you a visual benchmark for the number of seconds a colored bar represents.

(G) A mouse icon next to an animation means it is triggered on mouse click.

(H) A clock icon means the animation is triggered automatically after the previous animation event.

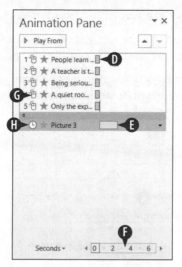

Figure 16-15: Use the Animation pane to get information about the animations.

Set text animation options

You can animate graphic objects or text. If you animate text (for example, a bulleted list), you can control whether the text animates as a whole or paragraph-by-paragraph.

To change the way text is animated, follow these steps:

1 In the Animation pane, right-click the animation to change. If there are multiple paragraphs, each listed as separate animations, you can right-click any of them in the set.

2 Click Timing.

Figure 16-16: Choose Timing to access text animation options.

③ Click the Text Animation tab.

④ Open the Group Text drop-down list and choose how to separate the text for individual animations.

⑤ (Optional) To animate text from bottom to top (rather than top to bottom, the default), mark the In reverse order check box.

⑥ Click OK.

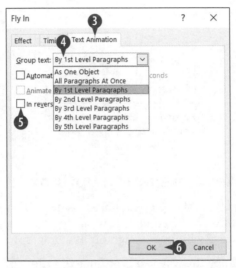

Figure 16-17: Set text animation options.

Copy animation effects between objects

You can quickly copy animations from one object to another with the Animation Painter command. This command is handy when several objects on a slide should be animated identically.

To copy an animation effect:

1. Select the object that contains the effect already.

② On the Animations tab, click Animation Painter.

3. Click the object that should receive the animation.

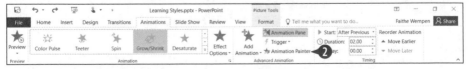

Figure 16-18: Use Animation Painter to copy animation.

Change animation sequence

Here are some tips for changing the order in which animations are sequenced on a slide.

Ⓐ Animations are sequenced in the order in which they are created, and they appear in that order in the Animation pane.

Ⓑ The numbers assigned to each animation effect also reflect the order.

To move an animation up or down in the sequence:

① Select the effect in the Animation pane.

② Click The Up or Down arrow to move the animation.

Ⓒ You can also use the Move Earlier or Move Later command on the Animations tab. These are useful if the Animation pane is not open, for example.

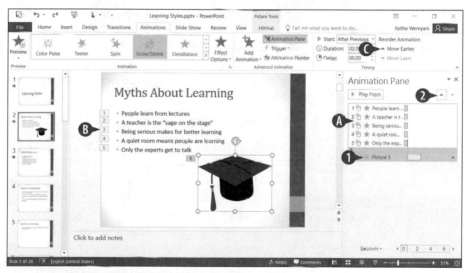

Figure 16-19: Use Animation Painter to copy animation.

You can also drag an animation up or down on the list to change its sequence.

Insert a sound clip

When you place a sound clip (sometimes called an audio clip) on a slide, a speaker icon appears to represent it. Playback controls appear beneath the icon, so you can control the clip during the show. You can also assign a sound to an object, so that clicking the object plays the sound.

Insert a sound clip icon on a slide

With this method, an actual sound object is placed on the slide, represented by a speaker icon. You can set up the sound to play automatically or to wait until someone clicks the speaker icon.

To insert a sound clip icon:

1 Display the slide on which the sound clip icon should be placed.

2 On the Insert tab, click Audio.

3 Click Audio on My PC.

Figure 16-20: Choose Audio on My PC to insert an existing sound clip.

4 Browse to and select the audio clip. PowerPoint supports a variety of formats.

5 Click Insert. The sound clip icon is placed in the center of the slide.

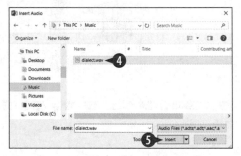

Figure 16-21: Select the sound clip.

6. (Optional) Drag the speaker icon to move it if desired.

After inserting the sound clip, you can adjust it using the options in the Audio Options section of the Audio Tools Playback toolbar, as follows:

A Choose how the sound should be triggered. The default is On Click, but you can also choose Automatically so that the sound plays as soon as the speaker icon appears.

(It appears when the slide itself appears unless you set an entrance animation for it.)

B If the sound clip is long, and you want it to continue playing if it isn't finished when the next slide appears, mark the Play Across Slides check box.

C If you want the sound to repeat, mark Loop until Stopped.

D To hide the speaker icon, mark Hide During Show. Don't do this if you have the Start setting set to On Click, though, because it'll make it impossible for the sound to ever be triggered.

E The Play in Background button automatically sets up a sound clip to serve as a soundtrack for the presentation by making the following setting adjustments: Start automatically, Play Across Slides, Loop Until Stopped, and Hide During Show all selected.

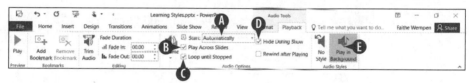

Figure 16-22: Adjust sound playback options.

Attach a sound to a picture on a slide

If you plan on keeping the speaker icon on the slide, why not replace that boring speaker with a more interesting piece of artwork? This is also a good way to camouflage the sound icon if you need to keep an icon somewhere on the slide for the sound but you don't want the audience to notice. The drawback of this method is its lack of flexibility; you don't get playback tools with this method like you do with the speaker icon, and you can't make the sound play automatically.

To associate a sound with an object, follow these steps:

1 Select the picture.

2 On the Insert tab, click Action.

3 On the Mouse Click tab, mark the Play Sound check box.

4 Open the Play Sound drop-down list and choose Other Sound. The Add Audio dialog box opens.

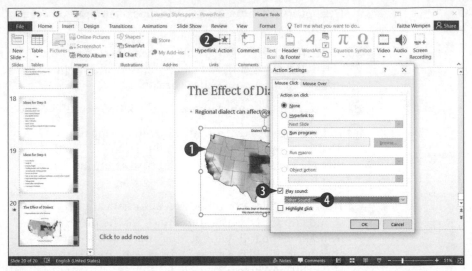

Figure 16-23: Choose a sound as the action associated with the picture.

⑤ Navigate to and select the audio clip.

⑥ Click OK.

Figure 16-24: Choose the audio clip.

Here's an alternate method of making a sound play on click of a particular object:

1. Insert the sound icon on the slide, as you learned in "Insert a sound clip icon on a slide" earlier in this chapter.

② If needed, insert the object on the slide that should be clicked to play the sound. If you don't already have one in mind, you might draw a simple circle or square with the Drawing tools, for example.

③ Select the sound icon.

④ On the Audio Tools Playback tab, click No Style to clear previous settings.

⑤ Mark the Hide During Show check box.

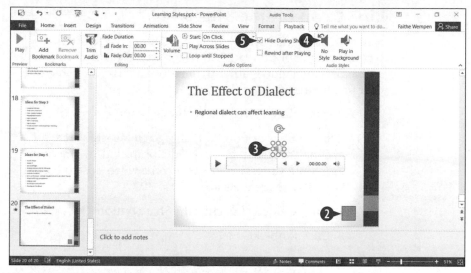

Figure 16-25: Make sure the sound icon is set to not appear during the show.

⑥ On the Animations tab, click Trigger.

⑦ Point to On Click Of.

⑧ Click the desired object that should trigger the sound.

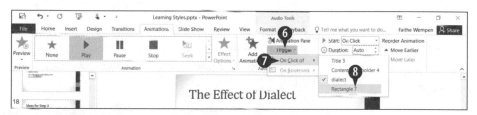

Figure 16-26: Select the object that will trigger the sound.

After creating a trigger-based animation, you will probably want to test it in Slide Show view. From the Slide Show tab, click From Current Slide. Then click the trigger object to see if the sound plays.

Insert a video clip on a slide

PowerPoint 2016 accepts video clips in a variety of formats, including Windows Media, Windows Video, QuickTime, MP4, and Flash. You can place a video clip on a slide either within a content placeholder or as a standalone item. You can also apply formatting to a video clip, such as a video style that governs the shape and appearance of the clip's frame.

You have a choice of video sources. You can insert a video stored on your own PC, or you can link to an online video.

Link to an online video

Many web sites host online videos. If you will have Internet access during your presentation, you might choose to link to an online copy of a video rather than embed a large video file in your presentation.

To link to an online video, follow these steps:

1. If the video is not on YouTube, go to the site where it is hosting and get an embed code for the video. The exact procedure varies. For example, on a video hosted by Vimeo, here are the steps:

   a. On the video clip, click the Share button.

   b. Click Embed Code.

   c. Select the code and then click Copy or press Ctrl+C to copy the code to the Windows Clipboard.

2. Display the slide on which you want to place the video.

3A On the Insert tab, click Video, and then click Online Video.

OR

3B In an empty content placeholder, click the Insert Video icon.

If you use a content placeholder, the video will be placed in the placeholder. If you use the Video command on the Insert tab, the video will be placed as a free-floating object on the slide.

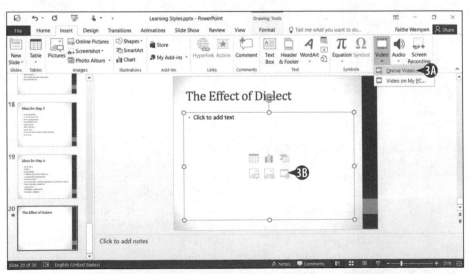

Figure 16-27: Use a content placeholder or choose Video from the Insert tab.

4A If you copied a code in step 1, click in the From a Video Embed Code text box and then press Ctrl+V to paste the code. Then skip to step 6.

OR

4B Click in the Search YouTube box and type keywords representing the video you want to find and insert. Then press Enter.

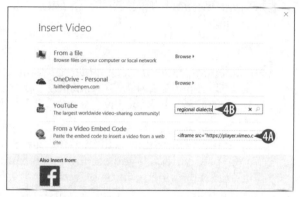

Figure 16-28: Paste an embed code or search YouTube.

5 Select the desired video in the search results.

6 Click Insert.

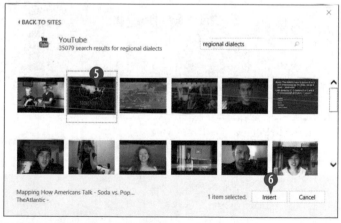

Figure 16-29: Select a video to insert.

Most of the commands on the Video Tools Playback tab on the Ribbon are unavailable for web-hosted video clips.

Insert a video from your PC

When the video is from your own PC, you can insert it into the presentation so that it will be available all the time, even when there is no Internet connection available. The downside is that the video embedded in the presentation file increases the file's size.

1 Display the slide on which you want to place the video.

2A On the Insert tab, click Video, and then click Video on My PC.

OR

2B In an empty content placeholder, click the Insert Video icon. Then in the Insert Video dialog box (refer back to Figure 16-28), click the Browse hyperlink next to From a File.

If you use a content placeholder, the video will be placed in the placeholder. If you use the Video command on the Insert tab, the video will be placed as a free-floating object on the slide.

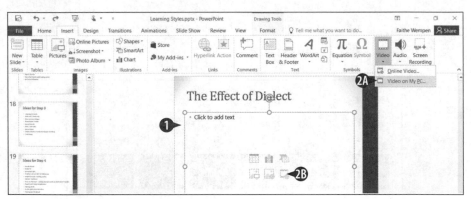

Figure 16-30: Choose to insert a video from a file.

3. In the Insert Video dialog box, navigate to and select the video clip.

4. Click Insert.

You can control the video's playback with the Video Tools Playback tab. While video editing in PowerPoint is beyond the scope of this book, here are a few interesting features to experiment with on your own:

- You can trim a video clip to remove unneeded portions at the beginning or end.

- You can make the video fade in or out.

- You can set a volume for the video clip that's separate from the overall volume.

- You can add a bookmark at a certain point in the video, and then hyperlink to that bookmark elsewhere in the presentation, so that you can jump to a particular spot in the clip easily.

CHAPTER SEVENTEEN

Presenting a Slide Show

PowerPoint gives you various methods for delivering your presentation: You can deliver a presentation live in a meeting room, broadcast it on the Internet, package it on a writeable CD, or send it out via email, just to name a few.

This chapter focuses on the most popular delivery method: delivering a live show to an audience in person. You learn how to display a PowerPoint presentation onscreen, including how to move between slides and how to annotate slides with the Pen tools. You also learn how to print handouts, either in PowerPoint or in Microsoft Word.

 For information about some of the other delivery methods, such as creating a CD or broadcasting and presentation, visit the Help system in PowerPoint or check out my book *PowerPoint 2013 Bible*, also published by John Wiley & Sons. Even though it is about the 2013 version, the two versions are so similar that 99 percent of the instructions still apply.

In This Chapter

➠ Displaying a slide show onscreen

➠ Annotating slides with the Pen tool

➠ Using Presenter view

➠ Printing handouts

➠ Exporting handouts to Word

Display a slide show onscreen

To give an onscreen show, use Slide Show view. It displays each slide full-screen, one at a time. For larger audiences, you may want to hook up a projector to your computer so the audience can see the slides more easily.

Pressing the Windows key and P connects a notebook PC to a projector or a second screen.

Slide Show view is unlike other views in that you don't access it from the View tab. On the Slide Show tab of the Ribbon:

(A) Click From Beginning to start Slide Show view with the first slide in the presentation. Keyboard shortcut: F5.

(B) Click From Current Slide to start Slide Show view from the current slide. Keyboard shortcut: Shift+F5.

Figure 17-1: Enter Slide Show view from the Slide Show tab.

(C) You can also enter Slide Show view at the current slide by clicking the Slide Show icon in the status bar.

Figure 17-2: Enter Slide Show view from the status bar.

If you want to show your presentation one slide at a time but prefer to do so in a resizable window rather than full-screen, use Reading view (accessible both from the View tab and the status bar).

Move between slides in Slide Show view

To move from one slide to the next or to trigger the next on-click animation on a slide, click the left mouse button, or press any key on the keyboard (except Backspace or the left arrow). To move backwards to the previous slide, press Backspace or the left arrow. That's all you need to know at the most basic level.

Right-click and choose Help in Slide Show view to get a list of the shortcut keys available.

To jump to a specific slide, do the following:

1 Right-click to display the shortcut menu, as in Figure 17-3.

You can also use this shortcut menu to go forward (Next) or back (Previous). (See Ⓐ in Figure 17-3.)

② Click See All Slides.

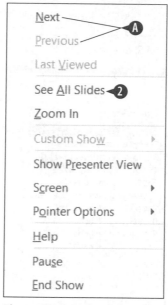

Next ──── Ⓐ
Previous ──
Last Viewed
See All Slides ── ②
Zoom In
Custom Show ▸
Show Presenter View
Screen ▸
Pointer Options ▸
Help
Pause
End Show

Figure 17-3: Right-click in Slide Show view for a shortcut menu.

The current slide has a red border around it. (See Ⓑ in Figure 17-4.)

③ Click the slide you want to display.

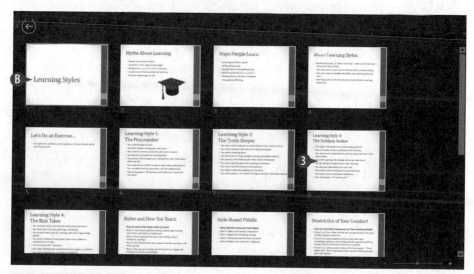

Figure 17-4. From the See All Slides pane, click the desired slide.

Here's an alternate way to jump to a specific slide:

1. Press Ctrl+S for the All Slides dialog box.

2 Click the desired slide.

3 Click Go To.

Figure 17-5: Jump to a specific slide with the All Slides dialog box.

If you happen to know a slide's number, you can type the number and press Enter to jump to it.

End the slide show

A slide show ends automatically when you reach the last slide. A black screen appears, along with a message *End of slide show, click to exit.* When you click, you are returned to whatever view you were working with before entering Slide Show view.

You can also end a slide show early by pressing the Esc key, or by right-clicking to display the shortcut menu (refer to Figure 17-3) and then clicking End Show.

Use the slide show tools

You can also use the buttons in the lower left corner of the screen in Slide Show view. They're very faint at first, but if you move the mouse pointer over one, it becomes solid. Click a button to open a menu or click the right- or left-arrow buttons there to move forward and back in the presentation.

I enhanced Figure 17-6 to show all the buttons in their "bright" mode at once, so you can see them better. In reality, a button lights up only when you point at it, and you can point at only one at a time.

The buttons are:

(A) **Previous:** A left-pointing arrow. Use this to go to the previous slide.

(B) **Next:** A right-pointing arrow. Use this to go to the next slide.

(C) **Pen:** Opens the Pen menu, which you can use to control a mouse-controlled "pen" that draws on the slides. (A closer look at that menu is coming up in the next section.)

(D) **Show All Slides:** Opens the same pane as in Figure 17-4, showing thumbnails of all slides. Click a slide to jump to it.

(E) **Zoom:** Changes the mouse pointer to a large rectangular magnifier. Drag it around onscreen to the area you want to magnify and then click. Press Esc to return to regular viewing.

(F) **Options:** Opens a menu containing several miscellaneous commands for working in Slide Show view.

Figure 17-6: The tools in the lower left corner in Slide Show view.

You might wonder why there are so many different methods of doing the same things. For example, why is there a navigation button that does nothing but duplicate the functionality of a right-click menu? And why are there Previous and Next buttons in Figure 17-5 for moving between slides when there are at least three other methods of doing the exact same thing?

Here's the reason: PowerPoint allows you to lock down or disable certain navigation methods in Slide Show view so that people interacting with your presentation at an unattended computer won't inadvertently (or purposely) disable or damage the presentation. When one method is disabled, you might need to rely on another method to do what needs to be done.

Temporarily blank the screen

If you need to temporarily suspend the presentation, such as for a break or an impromptu discussion, you may want to blank the screen during the break.

To do so, press the B or . (period) key for a black screen or the W or , (comma) key for a white screen. Press the same key again to toggle back to the presentation.

You can also right-click, point to Screen, and then click either Black Screen or White Screen. (See Ⓐ in Figure 17-7.)

Figure 17-7: Blank the screen (either black or white).

The pen tools work when the screen is blank, so you can blank the screen to give yourself an open area in which to draw a quick diagram.

Pause the presentation

If the slides are set up to automatically advance, you might need to pause the show if there's a delay, such as an audience member asking a question. To pause an automatically advancing presentation (without blanking the screen), press the S key, or right-click and then click Pause.

Get help

There are a lot of keyboard shortcuts to remember in Slide Show view. To see a list of them, do the following:

1. Right-click in Slide Show view and choose Help.

2. Review the information provided.

③ Click a tab to see keyboard shortcuts pertaining to a specific activity.

④ When you are done getting help, click OK.

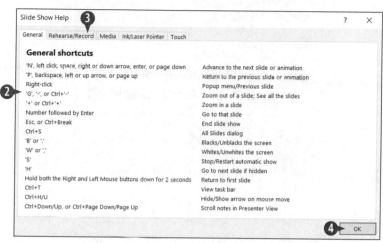

Figure 17-8: Review keyboard shortcut help during a presentation.

Annotate slides with the pen tools

As you're giving a presentation, you may want to make some notes on the slides, such as circling a word, underlining a phrase, or highlighting a key concept. The Pen tools enable you to do all those things. Making these changes is called *annotating*.

Here's a closer look at the Pen menu (from the Pen button in Figure 17-6):

Ⓐ **Laser Pointer:** This tool does not leave marks on the slide.

Ⓑ **Pen:** The Pen leaves a thin line.

Ⓒ **Highlighter:** The Highlighter leaves a thick, semi-transparent line.

Ⓓ **Eraser:** This removes other annotations selectively.

Ⓔ **Erase All Ink on Slide:** This removes all annotations from the current slide.

Ⓕ **Ink color:** This changes the ink color used by the Pen and the Highlighter.

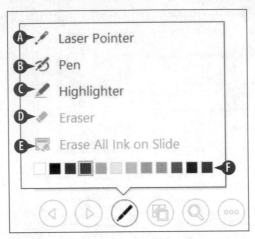

Figure 17-9: The Pen tools enable you to annotate slides.

When you leave Slide Show view after using one of the pen tools, a dialog box pops up, asking whether you want to keep your ink annotations. If you choose to keep them, they appear on the slides as ink annotation objects, which are very much like line drawings that you might create by going to the Insert tab and clicking the Shapes button.

Use Presenter view

Presenter view is like a control panel for a running presentation. With Presenter view running on a separate monitor, you can see any speaker notes for each slide, see what's coming up next, jump around between slides, and more, all without disturbing what the audience sees.

It's possible to enter Presenter view on a single-monitor system, but there's not much point in it, because it interrupts what the audience sees on that single monitor.

From Slide Show view, right-click for the shortcut menu, and then click Show Presenter View.

If the right-click shortcut menu has been disabled for security reasons, here's an alternate method: Click the Options button in the slide show tools (refer to Figure 17-6) and then click Show Presenter View.

Here are the tools and features available in Presenter View:

Ⓐ **Previous:** This button displays the previous slide.

Ⓑ **Next:** This button displays the next slide.

C **Pen and Laser Pointer Tools:** This is the same menu as in Figure 17-9 for the most part.

D **Show All Slides:** This opens the Show All Slides pane (Figure 17-4).

E **Zoom In to the Slide:** Enables you to zoom in to show a close-up of part of a slide.

F **Black or Unblack Slide Show:** This temporarily hides the presentation, replacing it with an all-black screen.

If you want a white screen rather than black, click more slide show options, point to Screen, and then click White Screen.

G **More Slide Show Options:** This button opens a menu of additional options, such as Pause, Help, Screen, and Hide Presenter View.

H **Make the Text Larger and Make the Text Smaller:** These buttons control the font size of any speaker notes for the active slide.

I **End Slide Show:** This ends the slide show (both monitors).

J **Display Settings:** This opens a menu from which you can choose to swap which monitor is showing which image, or make the slide show appear on both monitors (effectively closing Presenter view).

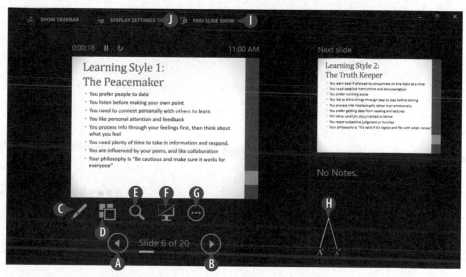

Figure 17-10: Presenter view provides tools for managing a running presentation.

Print handouts

Handouts are paper copies of your presentation that you give to the audience. They give your audience something tangible to refer to and to take home. They can also write on the handouts to make their own notes. (Some handout layouts even include lines for writing.)

When you print in PowerPoint, you have a choice of the type of printout you want. (Technically you can use any of these printout types as handouts, although the Handouts type is obviously custom-made for that purpose.) Here are the choices available:

- **Full Page Slides:** A full-page copy of one slide per sheet.

- **Notes Pages:** One slide per page, but with the slide occupying only the top half of the page. The bottom half is devoted to any speaker notes you typed into PowerPoint.

- **Outline View:** A text-only version of the presentation, structured as an outline, with the slide titles as the top-level outline items.

- **Handouts:** Multiple slides per page (two to nine, depending on your choice of settings), suitable for giving to the audience to take home.

Different numbers of slides per page have different layouts. For example, if you choose three slides per page, the layout has lines next to each slide so the audience can take notes.

To print handouts, follow these steps:

1. Click the File tab, and click Print.

2. Enter the desired number of copies.

3. Choose a different printer if needed from the Printer drop-down list.

4. Click Full Page Slides to open a menu.

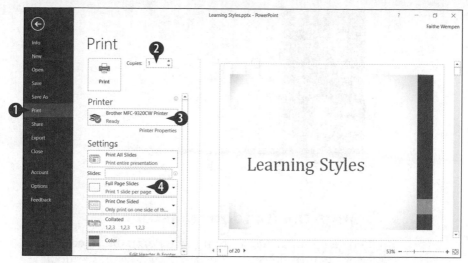

Figure 17-11: From the Print page in Backstage view, set print options for the handouts.

⑤ Click one of the layouts in the Handouts section of the menu.

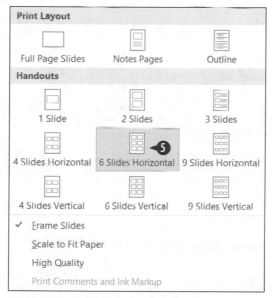

Figure 17-12: Presenter view provides tools for managing a running presentation.

6. Adjust any other print settings as needed.

⑦ Click Print to print the handouts.

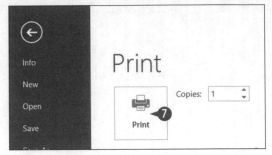

Figure 17-13: Click Print to submit the print job to your printer.

Change the handout masters

When you print handouts from PowerPoint, the Handout Master's settings determine the details of how the handouts appear. You may want to customize the Handout Master before you print. The Handout Master settings apply only when you're printing the Handouts layouts, not when printing full-page slides, notes pages, or outline view.

To customize a handout master:

① On the View tab, click Handout Master.

Figure 17-14: Choose Handout Master.

2. If you see a message about edits being lost when saved to the server, click Check Out.

③ Open the Slides Per Page drop-down list and select the layout you want to modify.

④ To change the orientation, click Handout Orientation and then click Portrait or Landscape.

⑤ To change the slide size, click Slide Size and then click Standard or Widescreen.

⑥ To remove any of the placeholders (in the four corners of the page), clear its check box on the Handout Master tab.

⑦ To change the theme, select a different one from the Themes button's menu.

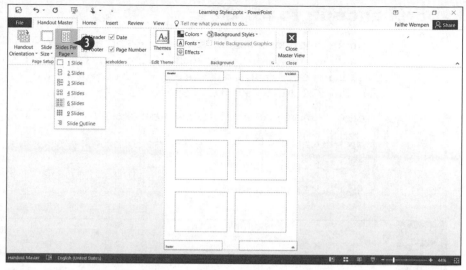

Figure 17-15: Choose which handout master layout to modify.

8. To change the Colors, Fonts, or Effects, make a selection from those buttons' menus.

9. To add a background color to the handout, select one from the Background Styles buttons menu.

10. Click Repeat steps 3–9 to modify other layouts if desired.

11. Click Close Master View.

WARNING!

Using a background style for something designed to be printed, like a handout, will use a lot of printer ink, which can be expensive.

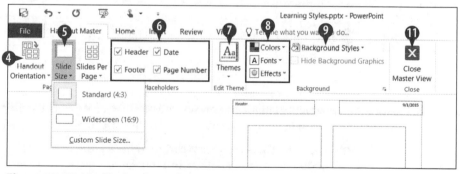

Figure 17-16: Modify the chosen layout.

Export handouts to Word

For more control over handouts, you can export them to Word. When they're in Word, you can make modifications that aren't possible in PowerPoint, such as changing the sizes of the slide graphics or adjusting the page margins.

To export handouts to Word, follow these steps:

1 Click the File tab and click Export.

2 Click Create Handouts.

3 Click Create Handouts.

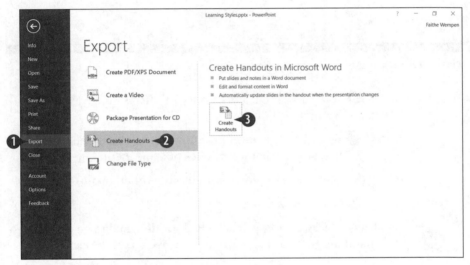

Figure 17-17: Choose to create handouts.

4 Select the layout you want for the handouts.

If you want a link between the presentation and the Word document, so that the Word version is updated if the slides change later, click Paste link. Doing so can create problems later if the presentation file is moved, so use this option only if you really need it. (See **A** in Figure 17-18.)

5 Click OK. Then wait for Word to generate the handout document. It may take a minute or two.

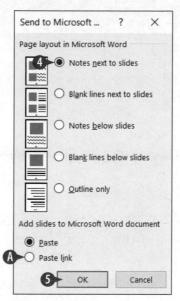

Figure 17-18: Select the handout layout to export.

6. In Word, customize the handout document as desired. You have all of Word's formatting tools at your disposal.

7. Print your handouts from Word, as you would any other Word document.

Index

auto-numbering pictures in Word, 122–124
AVERAGE function (Excel), 187
axis, 268
axis label, 268
axis scale, changing of Excel charts, 263–265

• B •

backgrounds
  applying color to pages in Word, 97–98
  applying to Excel worksheets, 212–214
  hiding graphics in PowerPoint, 370–371
  removing graphics in PowerPoint, 370–371
  shading in Word, 69–70
Backstage view
  Excel, 157
  Office, 11
bar chart, 258, 259
Bcc (blind copy), 293, 294
Bevel effect (PowerPoint), 379
bibliographies, creating in Word, 131–134
Black or Unblack Slide Show (PowerPoint), 423
blanking screen in PowerPoint, 420
blind copy (Bcc), 293, 294
blocked sender list, managing in Outlook, 312–314
blocking senders in Outlook, 311–312
Border Sampler feature, 114
BorderArt, applying in Word, 96–97
borders
  applying to table cells in Word, 112–114
  changing for chart elements in Excel, 274–277
  defined, 112
  page (Word), 95–97

placing around paragraphs in Word, 66–69
PowerPoint, 374
Borders and Shading dialog box, 68
bulleted lists
  creating in Word, 70–72
  PowerPoint, 352
Bullets button (PowerPoint), 352
business card format, 327

• C •

calculating loan terms in Excel, 192–194
Calendar area (Outlook), 283
captioning pictures in Word, 122–124
carbon copy (Cc), 293, 294
cell cursor (Excel), 156
cells
  applying borders to in Excel worksheets, 214–216
  copying data between in Excel, 164–167
  defined, 15
  deleting in Excel, 167–171, 168–171
  editing text in Excel in, 160–162
  entering text in Excel in, 160–162
  formatting in Excel worksheets using cell styles, 217–219
  inserting in Excel, 167–171, 168–171
  moving between in Excel, 157–158
  moving data between in Excel, 164–167
  referencing in formulas in Excel, 179–180
  referencing on worksheets in Excel, 180–182
  referring to with absolute referencing in Excel, 183–184
  referring to with relative referencing in Excel, 182
  selecting in Excel, 158–159

Notes

Notes

Notes

Notes

Notes

Notes

About the Author

Faithe Wempen, MA, is a Microsoft Office Master Instructor and the author of more than 150 books on computer hardware and software, including *PowerPoint 2013 Bible* and *Office 2013 eLearning Kit for Dummies.* She is an adjunct instructor of Computer Information Technology at Purdue University, and her corporate training courses online have reached more than one-quarter of a million students for clients such as Hewlett-Packard, Sony, and CNET.

Dedication

To Margaret

Author's Acknowledgments

Thanks to the wonderful editorial staff at Wiley for another job well done. You guys are top notch!

Publisher's Acknowledgments

Executive Editor: Katie Mohr

Project Editor: Christopher Morris

Copy Editor: Christopher Morris

Editorial Assistant: Claire Brock

Sr. Editorial Assistant: Cherie Case

Production Editor: Suresh Srinivasan

Cover Image: YanLev/Shutterstock

Apple & Mac

iPad For Dummies, 6th Edition
978-1-118-72306-7

iPhone For Dummies, 7th Edition
978-1-118-69083-3

Macs All-in-One For Dummies,
4th Edition
978-1-118-82210-4

OS X Mavericks For Dummies
978-1-118-69188-5

Blogging & Social Media

Facebook For Dummies,
5th Edition
978-1-118-63312-0

Social Media Engagement
For Dummies
978-1-118-53019-1

WordPress For Dummies,
6th Edition
978-1-118-79161-5

Business

Stock Investing For Dummies,
4th Edition
978-1-118-37678-2

Investing For Dummies,
6th Edition
978-0-470-90545-6

Personal Finance For Dummies,
7th Edition
978-1-118-11785-9

QuickBooks 2014 For Dummies
978-1-118-72005-9

Small Business Marketing Kit
For Dummies, 3rd Edition
978-1-118-31183-7

Careers

Job Interviews For Dummies,
4th Edition
978-1-118-11290-8

Job Searching with Social Media
For Dummies, 2nd Edition
978-1-118-67856-5

Personal Branding For Dummies
978-1-118-11792-7

Resumes For Dummies, 6th Edition
978-0-470-87361-8

Starting an Etsy Business
For Dummies, 2nd Edition
978-1-118-59024-9

Diet & Nutrition

Belly Fat Diet For Dummies
978-1-118-34585-6

Mediterranean Diet For Dummies
978-1-118-71525-3

Nutrition For Dummies,
5th Edition
978-0-470-93231-5

Digital Photography

Digital SLR Photography
All-in-One For Dummies,
2nd Edition
978-1-118-59082-9

Digital SLR Video & Filmmaking
For Dummies
978-1-118-36598-4

Photoshop Elements 12
For Dummies
978-1-118-72714-0

Gardening

Herb Gardening For Dummies,
2nd Edition
978-0-470-61778-6

Gardening with Free-Range
Chickens For Dummies
978-1-118-54754-0

Health

Boosting Your Immunity
For Dummies
978-1-118-40200-9

Diabetes For Dummies, 4th Edition
978-1-118-29447-5

Living Paleo For Dummies
978-1-118-29405-5

Big Data

Big Data For Dummies
978-1-118-50422-2

Data Visualization For Dummies
978-1-118-50289-1

Hadoop For Dummies
978-1-118-60755-8

Language & Foreign Language

500 Spanish Verbs For Dummies
978-1-118-02382-2

English Grammar For Dummies,
2nd Edition
978-0-470-54664-2

French All-in-One For Dummies
978-1-118-22815-9

German Essentials For Dummies
978-1-118-18422-6

Italian For Dummies, 2nd Edition
978-1-118-00465-4

 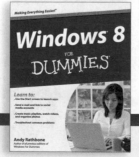  

e **Available in print and e-book formats.**

Available wherever books are sold.

For more information or to order direct visit www.dummies.com

Math & Science

Algebra I For Dummies,
2nd Edition
978-0-470-55964-2

Anatomy and Physiology
For Dummies, 2nd Edition
978-0-470-92326-9

Astronomy For Dummies,
3rd Edition
978-1-118-37697-3

Biology For Dummies, 2nd Edition
978-0-470-59875-7

Chemistry For Dummies,
2nd Edition
978-1-118-00730-3

1001 Algebra II Practice Problems
For Dummies
978-1-118-44662-1

Microsoft Office

Excel 2013 For Dummies
978-1-118-51012-4

Office 2013 All-in-One
For Dummies
978-1-118-51636-2

PowerPoint 2013 For Dummies
978-1-118-50253-2

Word 2013 For Dummies
978-1-118-49123-2

Music

Blues Harmonica For Dummies
978-1-118-25269-7

Guitar For Dummies, 3rd Edition
978-1-118-11554-1

iPod & iTunes For Dummies,
10th Edition
978-1-118-50864-0

Programming

Beginning Programming with C
For Dummies
978-1-118-73763-7

Excel VBA Programming
For Dummies, 3rd Edition
978-1-118-49037-2

Java For Dummies, 6th Edition
978-1-118-40780-6

Religion & Inspiration

The Bible For Dummies
978-0-7645-5296-0

Buddhism For Dummies,
2nd Edition
978-1-118-02379-2

Catholicism For Dummies,
2nd Edition
978-1-118-07778-8

Self-Help & Relationships

Beating Sugar Addiction
For Dummies
978-1-118-54645-1

Meditation For Dummies,
3rd Edition
978-1-118-29144-3

Seniors

Laptops For Seniors For Dummies,
3rd Edition
978-1-118-71105-7

Computers For Seniors
For Dummies, 3rd Edition
978-1-118-11553-4

iPad For Seniors For Dummies,
6th Edition
978-1-118-72826-0

Social Security For Dummies
978-1-118-20573-0

Smartphones & Tablets

Android Phones For Dummies,
2nd Edition
978-1-118-72030-1

Nexus Tablets For Dummies
978-1-118-77243-0

Samsung Galaxy S 4 For Dummies
978-1-118-64222-1

Samsung Galaxy Tabs
For Dummies
978-1-118-77294-2

Test Prep

ACT For Dummies, 5th Edition
978-1-118-01259-8

ASVAB For Dummies, 3rd Edition
978-0-470-63760-9

GRE For Dummies, 7th Edition
978-0-470-88921-3

Officer Candidate Tests
For Dummies
978-0-470-59876-4

Physician's Assistant Exam
For Dummies
978-1-118-11556-5

Series 7 Exam For Dummies
978-0-470-09932-2

Windows 8

Windows 8.1 All-in-One
For Dummies
978-1-118-82087-2

Windows 8.1 For Dummies
978-1-118-82121-3

Windows 8.1 For Dummies, Book +
DVD Bundle
978-1-118-82107-7

Available in print and e-book formats.

Available wherever books are sold.

For more information or to order direct visit www.dummies.com

Take Dummies with you everywhere you go!

Whether you are excited about e-books, want more from the web, must have your mobile apps, or are swept up in social media, Dummies makes everything easier.

Leverage the Power

For Dummies is the global leader in the reference category and one of the most trusted and highly regarded brands in the world. No longer just focused on books, customers now have access to the For Dummies content they need in the format they want. Let us help you develop a solution that will fit your brand and help you connect with your customers.

Advertising & Sponsorships

Connect with an engaged audience on a powerful multimedia site, and position your message alongside expert how-to content.

Targeted ads • Video • Email marketing • Microsites • Sweepstakes sponsorship

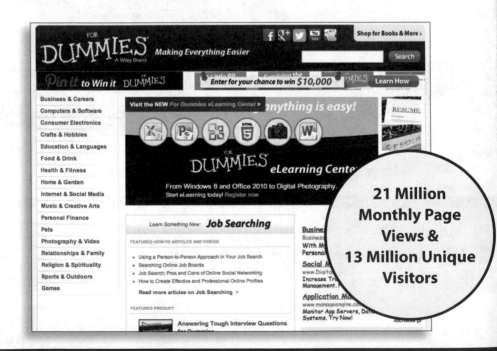

# of For Dummies

Custom Publishing

Reach a global audience in any language by creating a solution that will differentiate you from competitors, amplify your message, and encourage customers to make a buying decision.

Apps • Books • eBooks • Video • Audio • Webinars

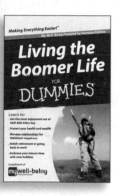

Brand Licensing & Content

Leverage the strength of the world's most popular reference brand to reach new audiences and channels of distribution.

For more information, visit www.Dummies.com/biz

Dummies products make life easier!

- •DIY
- •Consumer Electronics
- •Crafts

- •Software
- •Cookware
- •Hobbies

- •Videos
- •Music
- •Games
- •and More!

For more information, go to **Dummies.com** and search the store by category.